I0815861

TO:

....

FROM:

....

DATE:

....

DAILY WISDOM for Kids

365 ENCOURAGING DEVOTIONS & PRAYERS

BARBOUR kidz
A Division of Barbour Publishing

Print ISBN (Daily Wisdom for Boys) 978-1-63609-905-7

Print ISBN (Daily Wisdom for Girls) 978-1-63609-904-0

Published by Barbour Publishing, Inc., 1810 Barbour Drive, Uhrichsville, Ohio 44683, www.barbourbooks.com

Our mission is to inspire the world with the life-changing message of the Bible.

Printed in China.

002074 0724 HA

INTRODUCTION

My theme song is God's love.
Psalm 101:1 msg

This wonderful wisdom-filled devotional will encourage your heart with regular reminders of God's love. Each refreshing reading touches on life topics that are important to you—such as faith, forgiveness, friendship, and more. Inspiring prayers and easy-to-understand scripture selections will motivate you to grow up God's way.

Read on. . .and experience God's amazing, unending love for you all 365 days of the year!

DAY 1

CATCH SOME ZZZZZZS

When you lie down, you will not be afraid;
when you lie down, your sleep will be sweet.
PROVERBS 3:24 NIV

Do you ever have trouble sleeping? You toss, you turn. You roll around and get tangled up in the covers. You stare at the clock. You stare at the ceiling. You need to sleep, but you just can't. The truth is, you're worried about *so much stuff*. And your mind won't shut off. You worry that you won't pass your math test. You worry that your friend is still mad at you because of the disagreement you had yesterday. Worry, worry, worry!

Well, guess what? You don't have to worry anymore. You have a promise from the Bible that guarantees restful sleep. Proverbs 3:24 says that you will not be afraid and that your sleep will be sweet. Isn't that good news? No more sleepless nights for you!

So the next time you start the whole tossing and turning routine, say out loud, "I will not be afraid, and my sleep will be sweet." "Sweet dreams" is more than just an expression. It's a promise! Quit worrying and start dreaming!

God, I give all of my worries to You.
Thanks for a good night's sleep. Amen.

DAY 2

READY TO CATCH YOU

God is our refuge and strength, an ever-present help in trouble.
PSALM 46:1 NIV

Sometimes life feels mean, like when the kid on the bus teases and pesters you until you feel like you're going to burst. Or the teacher accuses you of cheating on a test when you really didn't. Or your parents have a heated argument, and it leaves you feeling sick all over.

Life can be unfair and painful and scary. Life can feel lonely too, as if you've fallen into a deep black hole. When you worry that your tomorrows will feel the same as today and nothing will *ever* change, what can you do?

Think of God. Reach out to Him. Run to Him like a child who runs to his or her daddy. God's shoulders are big enough to carry you, and His love is bright enough to fill those dark places with a light that is warm and safe and just right.

Jesus, please be near me in my scary times and in lonely times. Let me feel Your presence, know Your love, and feel Your arms around me like a warm and cozy comforter. Amen.

DAY 3

FOLLOW YOUR CREATOR

You created every part of me; you put me together in my mother's womb.
Psalm 139:13 GNT

Did you know that a baby zebra knows its mother by her stripes? When the baby is born, the mother makes sure the baby sees only her stripes first so that the little one will know how to find her if they get separated. The baby identifies with the mother through her stripes and then knows which zebra to follow around.

We have a Creator that we can identify with too. God made each of us unique, but we have the ability to know who He is and to recognize Him if we get lost. We have a special relationship with Him because He made us in His image. He wants us to recognize and follow Him.

Our friends and family know our habits, our likes, and our dislikes. But they can't possibly know the deepest parts of us. Only God knows those things. That's why we can trust Him with everything that concerns us. We can follow Him with confidence because He created us and knows everything we need.

Don't get far away from your Creator. When you get separated from Him by bad choices, all you have to do is look for His stripes! He will be watching for you!

Dear Father, please help me to follow only You. I know You created me and have given me signs that point to You. I will follow You because You know exactly what I need. Amen.

DAY 4

IT'S NOT ABOUT STUFF

"Ask, and it will be given to you; seek, and you will find; knock, and it will be opened to you. For everyone who asks receives, and the one who seeks finds, and to the one who knocks it will be opened."

MATTHEW 7:7–8 ESV

When you first read these verses, it kind of sounds like everything you want is just a prayer away, doesn't it? But here's the deal: this scripture isn't talking about "stuff"—material things that everyone else is getting. Nope. It's definitely not about that. God *does* promise to take care of *all* our needs, but this verse is about seeking after God and wanting what He wants for you.

It's not wrong to wish for a new bike or a new phone. It becomes wrong when you let your desires consume you so much that you become discontent with all the other blessings in your life. God gives you everything you need to live a great life. So count everything you have as a blessing, and keep seeking after Him.

Dear God, thank You for all the blessings in my life. Help me not to be consumed with "stuff." I want to seek after You, and I trust You to take care of all my needs. Amen.

DAY 5

GOD'S WORD IS LIGHT

Your word is a lamp that gives light wherever I walk.
Psalm 119:105 CEV

Have you ever tried to walk through your house when it's dark? You bump into furniture and stumble over toys or shoes, don't you? It's even more difficult to walk through someone else's house in the dark. You haven't had time to memorize where things are before you find yourself stumbling through the darkness!

Just like trying to walk through a dark house, many people are stumbling through life. They have not discovered the truths of God's Word. In the Psalms, we read that the Bible is a lamp to light the way for us. Wherever we go and whatever we do, we can rely on God's Word to guide us. Even in unfamiliar places or at difficult crossroads, you don't have to be afraid or confused.

If you had a flashlight in your hand when you were trying to find your way through a dark home, would you switch it on and use it? Of course! Likewise, allow God's Word to light the paths you travel in life. As you spend time reading the Bible, it will provide light for your journey.

God, thank You for the light You have provided through Your holy Word. Teach me as I read my Bible. Amen.

DAY 6

CLUELESS

"The grass withers, the flower fades,
but the word of our God stands forever."
ISAIAH 40:8 NKJV

Everywhere you go, people are encouraging and instructing you to read the Bible. Don't they realize how much you already have to read for school? You hear God's Word in Sunday school and church. So what's the big deal?

When God inspired the authors of the Bible to write, He knew there were three things every person should understand. First, as our Creator, He wanted us to realize how we were created from His love. Second, He wanted us to have something to turn to when we weren't sure what to do about certain situations in our lives: *How are we supposed to treat others? What is the true meaning of love? How do we know right from wrong?* Finally, He needed to show us Jesus came, He died on the cross, He rose again, and He will come back for us someday.

Without the Bible, we would be clueless. We wouldn't have the confidence to make good decisions. We wouldn't feel God's love and blessings because we wouldn't be able to recognize what they are. We wouldn't pray for help if we couldn't read about the amazing ways He has helped others. The bottom line? . . . God's Word gives us the answers we need.

God, I promise to read Your book as often as I can. Amen.

DAY 7

WHAT GOD WANTS

He has shown you, O man, what is good; and what does the LORD require of you but to do justly, to love mercy, and to walk humbly with your God?

MICAH 6:8 NKJV

It's fun to dream about what God may have in store for us ten years from now. What will we look like? What will we do for a career? Will we get married, and if so, who will we marry?

Even though some of the details may not be clear yet, we already know what God wants us to do every day for the rest of our lives: He wants us to do the right thing.

We may not know what career path to take, but we know God wants us to be kind to others—even when they're not kind to us. We may not know if we'll get married—but we know God wants us to be honest, no matter what. Starting at this very moment, and every moment for the rest of our lives, God wants us to show compassion and mercy. He wants us to stand up for what is right and good. And He wants us to love Him with all our hearts.

Dear Father, thank You for showing me what You want me to do. Help me to always do the right thing. Amen.

DAY 8

JEHOVAH JIREH— YOUR PROVIDER

I was young and now I am old, yet I have never seen the righteous forsaken or their children begging bread.

Psalm 37:25 NIV

The Bible is full of promises. One of them is that if you remain in Jesus and His words remain in you, you can ask whatever you wish, and it will be given to you (John 15:7). You don't have to worry about what you're going to eat or wear because God knows you need these things, and He will provide them (Matthew 6:31–32).

But that doesn't mean God is some kind of magic genie who gives you everything you want. The promise to meet your needs and give you the things you want comes with a condition. The condition is that you seek after God and His righteousness first, and then all these other things will be given to you (Matthew 6:33).

Putting God first will satisfy you in every way. And that's a promise the world can't make or keep.

Dear God, thank You for being my provider. Give me a heart that follows after You so that I won't become focused on the things of this world. Instead, I want to be focused on You. I trust You to provide the things I need. Please let the things I want be the things YOU want for me too. Amen.

DAY 9

QUIET TIME WITH GOD

Be still, and know that I am God; I will be exalted among the nations, I will be exalted in the earth!

PSALM 46:10 NKJV

When you go to God in prayer, do you ever wonder if He hears? Do you wonder exactly what it is He wants *you* to hear *from* Him? Do you sometimes rush through your prayers so you can focus your attention on something else? Try sitting quietly in your room while you pray. Don't answer your cell phone, don't turn on the TV, and stay off the computer. Just concentrate on you and God. Pray; pour your heart out to Him. And when you say "amen," don't rush away. Be still and listen. You just might be surprised at how God makes His presence known to you. The Creator wants you to be still and fully know that He is God, and He will guide you through every step of every day.

Dear God, please help me know that You are always with me, that You have answers for me if I will only listen for them. Please help me to be patient and listen for Your guidance instead of rushing off to do what I want to do. Amen.

DAY 10

I'VE GOT THE JOY!

When anxiety was great within me,
your consolation brought me joy.
Psalm 94:19 NIV

Some days really stink, and you have a hard time finding the joy in them. But our God is so amazing—He's given us His never-ending fountain of joy. It's there, every day, ready for us to dip into. Just like He is always there, ready for us to cast our burdens on Him.

Isn't it awesome to think that the God of the universe loves you? That He knows everything about you? He knows that life here on earth isn't easy. He understands the trials and hardships you go through—even homework! And He's longing for you to reach out and grab onto His joy, which cannot be taken away. *No matter what.*

So next time you find unhappiness knocking at your door and the blues threatening to overtake you—remind yourself that you have access to the heavenly Father's joy, anytime, anywhere. Grab onto it and sing it out, "I've got the joy. . ."

God, thank You for being with me each and every day. Thank You for Your joy. Help me to grab on to it every day and sing praise to You because Your joy is overflowing in my life. And as it overflows out of me, help me to be Your light to those around me. Amen.

DAY 11

JUST WAIT!

Seek good, not evil, that you may live. Then the Lord God Almighty will be with you, just as you say he is.
Amos 5:14 NIV

Before you go too far, listen to this: the Bible tells us that if we seek good and not evil, the Lord God himself will be with us! Don't you want to live each day knowing that God loves you and He is watching over you? Then think twice before you try to bend the rules even just a little.

There will be a lot of temptations around each corner as you get older. It will probably even get more and more difficult to "be good." Just remember to seek good, not evil, and seek the Lord with all of your heart! God promises to always be with you (Hebrews 13:5), He promises to provide a way of escape from temptation (1 Corinthians 10:13), and He promises to protect you from the evil one (2 Thessalonians 3:3). With the promises of God in your heart, He makes it a whole lot easier to "be good."

God, sometimes I get so tired of listening to everyone tell me to behave. . .to be good. Please remind me of the importance to stop and think before I do something I'll regret. Thank You for Your love and guidance. Amen.

DAY 12

WHAT PRAYER SHOULD SOUND LIKE

"But the tax collector stood at a distance. He would not even look up to heaven, but beat his breast and said, 'God, have mercy on me, a sinner.' "

LUKE 18:13 NIV

Does the screeching sound of fingernails on a chalkboard send shivers up your spine? Oddly enough, God is set on edge by something way more serious—a prayer that tells God how much you don't need Him. Then what should a kid's prayer sound like?

One day at the temple, Jesus told the story about the man who tried to impress God with his own good deeds. Jesus explained to the crowd that such a prayer does not make a hit with God. Another man, Jesus said, simply begged God to show kindness to him, a sinner. God gladly listens to that prayer.

As God's child, ask Him to step in and give you His goodness. Now, that's a prayer that'll sound much better than fingernails on the chalkboard.

Lord, thank You for reminders in Your Word on how to pray. Help me to spend daily time in meaningful conversation with You. Help me to speak to You. . .and to listen. Amen.

DAY 13

JUST DO IT!

But don't just listen to God's word. You must do what it says. Otherwise, you are only fooling yourselves.
JAMES 1:22 NLT

The old Nike commercial slogan "Just Do It" is a great reminder for Christians. We read God's Word. . .we hear it at church. . .we sing about the scriptures in songs—but none of it means a thing if we don't do what it says!

"Actions speak louder than words" is a true and common phrase used to help people understand the idea of letting your beliefs or words show through your actions. Founding Father and inventor Benjamin Franklin is credited with the phrase "Well done is better than well said." It's wonderful to hide God's Word in your heart, but if it isn't changing you. . .if you aren't actively doing something about it. . .your faith won't seem very important.

Ask God to use His Word to help you grow and change and take action. *Just do it!*

God, please help me to talk less and do more. I want to hide Your Word in my heart, but I also want to go into the world and use that to make a difference in other people's lives. Amen.

DAY 14

WAITING WITH HOPE

Blessed are all who wait for him!
Isaiah 30:18 NIV

Have you ever had to wait for something that you really wanted? Waiting for God to give you what you want can be really hard. But if you have hope, waiting can feel exciting because you know something great is coming.

It's like a happy-faced dog who knows his master is coming home, so he stays by the door, ready to pounce when he arrives. It's like a freckle-faced boy who waits for Christmas and counts down the days until December 25.

If God has promised you something, and you believe that He keeps His promises, you will have hope. You will have hope because you know that something good is going to happen—in God's time, in God's way. When you trust Him, the tough part of waiting can be easier. Because when you wait with hope, it means you believe that God is working in ways you can't see. And you dream about the great things that will happen when your wait is over.

Lord Jesus, sometimes it's really hard to wait for what I want. But please help me to trust You and wait for Your plans for my life with hope. Help me to believe that You are working in ways that I can't see, and this is why I can be hopeful. I trust You. Amen.

DAY 15

BLESS THE LORD!

Let everything that hath breath praise the Lord.
Psalm 150:6 KJV

If you're breathing, you should be praising! God's in His heaven, and all is right with the world.

Sure, there are problems, sorrows, and big disappointments in life, but everything doesn't have to be perfect for you to praise God. Think of your blessings. Count them, if you can. When the God of the universe is supplying your needs, it's hard to keep track of them all!

Take a deep breath. Feel your chest rise as your lungs expand with air. Then throw your head back and sing to the Lord. Praise Him for life and strength, food and shelter. Praise Him for liberty. For friends and family. Thank God for the birds, trees, sunshine, and clouds. Thank Him for blessing you with talents and for giving you a bright, healthy mind. Thank Him for keeping His promise of providing everything you need. And most of all, thank Him for sending a Savior to die for your sins so that you can have eternal life.

With all that is within you, bless His holy name!

Lord, thank You for loving me and supplying all of my needs. Thank You for showering me with more blessings than I could ever count. You are worthy of all my praise. Amen.

DAY 16

EVERY DAY'S A HOLIDAY

"But seek first the kingdom of God and his righteousness,
and all these things will be added to you."
MATTHEW 6:33 ESV

Did you ever tear open a big Christmas present and then groan inside? Maybe you got a sinking feeling when you saw the gift because it wasn't what you wanted or it was the wrong brand. You had high hopes, but now you'll have to make do with what you received—which, in your opinion, is a not-so-wonderful gift.

The good news is that you're receiving wonderful gifts and blessings from your Father in heaven all the time. Prayers are being answered and mercies given every day. And God knows exactly what to give you because He knows what you need better than anyone else. You won't be forced to just "make do" with an off-brand gift. What God has to give is the best quality, and it won't ever break or go out of style. And His gifts are free and totally undeserved. You can celebrate God's good gifts all year round!

God, thank You for showering me with gifts, even when I don't deserve them. On days when I feel like nothing is going my way, help me to remember all the things You've given me and all the ways You take care of me. Amen.

DAY 17

GOD KNOWS MY THOUGHTS

You know when I am resting or when I am working,
and from heaven you discover my thoughts.
Psalm 139:2 CEV

God knows everything. He sees everything. He even knows your thoughts. God is with you when you're at home or school. He is there when you're playing in the neighborhood or enjoying His creation at the park or lake. If you travel across the world to a foreign land where a different language is spoken, God is right there with you as well!

You have a heavenly Father who knows your name. The Bible says that before you were born, He saw you in your mother's womb. He created you and watched as you developed. He is watching still. He even knows the number of hairs on your head!

Nothing brings God greater joy than when one of His children chooses to spend time with Him. Talk to God throughout your day today. Understand that He is constantly with you. You can whisper a prayer to Him at any time. You can even say a prayer inside your mind. No matter how you pray, He hears!

Thank You, Lord, for always being present. You know me and You love me no matter where I am or what I am doing. Amen.

DAY 18

PLANT SEEDS OF JOY

Clap your hands for joy, all peoples!
Praise God with loud songs!
PSALM 47:1 GNT

Joy is contagious. You feel a certain pleasure when you're around joy-filled people, don't you? It's hard to stay in a bad mood when everyone else is happy.

Praising God is a good way to capture joy in your heart. His Word tells us to clap our hands and sing songs. It's a solid plan to get you going on the path to joy.

The Bible also tells us that joy is a fruit of the Spirit. To get fruit, you must first plant a seed. You can't get a pumpkin from planting an apple seed. And you can't get the fruit of joy from planting seeds of anger or resentment. God wants to give you all the joy you can handle.

God loves to hear our praises, and He sends us joy when we show Him our love and gratitude. When you are filled with this fruit, others will see and want what you have. Think of what a better world it would be if we all shared this kind of joy.

Try praising God today and get a delicious taste of joy!

Heavenly Father, I want to have more joy in my life and be able to share it with others. Thank You for giving me the fruit of joy. I will praise You even when things aren't going well. Amen.

DAY 19

LIVING IN CHRIST

The one who keeps God's commands lives in him, and he in them. And this is how we know that he lives in us: We know it by the Spirit he gave us.
1 John 3:24 NIV

Living in Christ isn't as hard as you might think. All you have to do is believe in Jesus, love others, and obey His commands. When you do that, you will feel Him living inside of you. Wow! What a great feeling!

Some days you may end up doing things *your* way instead of *Jesus'* way, and He knows that. What Christ wants is for you to try every day to do the things He wants you to do. And He will help you. Just ask Him. Before you know it, you'll be growing in Him and finding it easier to do things His way.

You'll know it's working when you feel His Spirit deep inside of you and when you become more like Jesus, your king, each day.

God, thank You for showing me the best plan for my life. . .to live in YOU! Amen.

DAY 20

MY TREASURED DELIGHT, PART ONE

Your word I have treasured in my heart,
that I may not sin against You.
PSALM 119:11 NASB

Psalm 119:9 (NASB) says, "How can a young man keep his way pure? By keeping it according to Your word."

Everything you need—guidance, comfort, character-trait examples, good stories, etc.—are in God's Word, the Holy Bible. By "keeping" your way according to it, you're able to keep your way pure!

"All Scripture is inspired by God and profitable for teaching, for reproof, for correction, for training in righteousness; so that the man of God may be adequate, equipped for every good work" (2 Timothy 3:16–17 NASB). The Bible isn't just a collection of stories, letters, and prophesies. It's God-breathed—God-inspired. It is your guidebook for. . .*everything*!

God has given you His Word to study, delight in, treasure, and apply. His grace is overflowing and abounding. . . . Thank Him today. He's poured out His life, His love, and His Word for *you*.

Father, thank You for Your Word. Thank You that everything I ever need is right there. I know the truth. I know that You love me, died for me, and are preparing a place for me up in heaven. Thank You for Your grace. I love You, Lord. In Jesus' name I pray. Amen.

DAY 21

MY TREASURED DELIGHT, PART TWO

But his delight is in the law of the Lord,
and in His law he meditates day and night.
Psalm 1:2 NASB

God's Word shouldn't be taken for granted. There are many people in restrictive countries who don't have the privilege of sitting down and reading the holy Word of the Most High God.

In our souls, there's a thirst for His Word. . . . We should cherish every tidbit we can get. Why? Because God's Word is everlasting; it will never pass away (Matthew 24:35). It's our guideline, our comfort, the weapon of the armor of God (Ephesians 6:17).

Therefore, memorizing God's Word is one of the best things you can do. That's "accurately handling the word of truth" (2 Timothy 2:15 NASB). Do you think God meant for His Word to be read and then forgotten? Use the magnificent weapon He's supplied by dwelling on it!

"On the glorious splendor of Your majesty, and on Your wonderful works, I will meditate" (Psalm 145:5 NASB).

Lord, thank You for the ability to memorize scripture. I will take up the "sword of the Spirit" and wield it, Lord. Please help me to study and memorize Your Word continually, faithfully, diligently. I love You, Father. In Jesus' name I pray. Amen.

DAY 22

DO YOU KNOW HIS VOICE?

"My sheep listen to my voice; I know them, and they follow me."
JOHN 10:27 NIV

When you're at school and your best friend yells your name from down the hall, don't you immediately hear it? Even though there are many other voices making lots of noise—you still hear one voice over all the others. It's because you've spent so many hours with your best friend; you know that voice.

It should be the same way with God. You should be able to identify His voice in the midst of all the other voices in your life. But you won't be able to know God's voice if you don't spend time with Him. And if you don't know what He says in His Word, then you won't know if it's actually Him speaking to you.

No, He won't talk to you in that big, booming "Darth Vader" kind of way. Instead, you'll have a thought and you'll wonder, *Was that me, or was that God?* If your thought is in line with the Bible, it's probably God. If it doesn't line up with God's Word, then it couldn't have been His voice. Listen carefully. . .He is worth hearing.

God, please help me to know Your voice, and help me to always follow You. Amen.

DAY 23

ROAD MAP

Your word is a lamp for my feet, a light on my path.
Psalm 119:105 NIV

Do you ever feel like you don't know what to do? You want to do the right thing, but you're not sure what that is. And you're not sure how to find out.

God's Word helps us know the right things! When we're not sure which way to go or how to handle a certain situation, the Bible serves as a road map to guide us. The more we read it, the more confident we can be that we're taking the right path.

If you're having a disagreement with a friend, the book of Proverbs is filled with wisdom for relationships. If you're mad at your parents, Ephesians says to honor them and treat them with respect anyway. If you're tempted to make fun of someone, or lie, or cheat on a test, God's Word teaches that we should avoid those behaviors.

Reading the Bible helps us to see more clearly so we don't mess up. And when we do make mistakes, God's Word helps us to pick ourselves up and get back on the right track—every time.

Dear Father, thank You for Your Word.
Help me to read it and understand it. Amen.

DAY 24

AN ANSWER THAT IS ALWAYS "YES!"

If we [freely] admit that we have sinned and confess our sins, He is faithful and just (true to His own nature and promises) and will forgive our sins [dismiss our lawlessness] and [continuously] cleanse us from all unrighteousness [everything not in conformity to His will in purpose, thought, and action].

1 John 1:9 AMPC

A lot of times it's easier to think about the wrong things other people do to us rather than the sins we commit. But *everyone* misses God's mark of perfection. No one can live their life without sinning.

God made a way to fix the broken relationship with Him that sin causes. He sent His Son, Jesus, to take the punishment we deserve.

But the forgiveness isn't automatic. We need to remember to confess our wrongs to God—and the sooner, the better! With as busy as life can get, it's easy to forget to ask for His forgiveness.

Because Jesus died for all of us, His answer to our request is always yes! He is faithful to forgive our sins.

Dear Father, I'm sorry for the sins I've committed today. Thank You for forgiving me and for not having a limit on how many times You'll do that. Please help me to remember to say I'm sorry each time I sin. Amen.

DAY 25

SEEK, AND YOU WILL FIND

But if from thence thou shalt seek the Lord thy God, thou shalt find him, if thou seek him with all thy heart and with all thy soul.

Deuteronomy 4:29 kjv

God loves you. He truly wants a special relationship with you, but He will never force Himself upon you. He wants you to desire His presence in your life too. He has promised that if you seek Him with your whole heart, you will find Him. He won't hide in hard places; you just need to go to the right place to discover Him.

Spend some time with God today. Talk to Him in prayer. Talk to Him just like you would your best friend—that *is* what He wants to be after all. Share your joys with Him. Share your troubles. Let Him experience everything with you. Then choose a passage from the Bible to read, and let God speak to your heart.

Seek Him—you *will* find Him!

God, thank You for always being there just when I need You. I know You'll never hide from me and that You truly want to be with me. . .always. Amen.

DAY 26

FREEDOM

It was for freedom that Christ set us free; therefore keep standing firm and do not be subject again to a yoke of slavery.
GALATIANS 5:1 NASB

Christ set you free so that you would live in *His everlasting freedom*. He doesn't want you to turn back to the worthless and sinful things of this world. He wants you to live in His pure and gracious freedom!

What *is* freedom? Freedom is:

- Being released from the "certificate of debt consisting of decrees against us" which Jesus has nailed to the cross (Colossians 2:14 NASB).
- Being freed from the sins that so easily and strongly hold you down (see John 1:29; Romans 6:6–7, 11, 14; 1 John 1:7).
- Walking away forever from the worldly life and living the never-ending, pure life Jesus has given (see John 3:16; Titus 2:11–14; 1 John 2:15–17).

God is so good! As David put it, "He restores my soul. . . . I will dwell in the house of the LORD forever" (Psalm 23:3, 6 NASB). He has given you freedom and assurance of eternal life with Him!

Lord, thank You for freedom. Thank You for saving me from eternal suffering and punishment. I love You, Lord. Please help me to live freely and not be under "a yoke of slavery." In Jesus' name I pray. Amen.

DAY 27

THE BIBLE WILL GUIDE ME

Jesus commented, "Even more blessed are those who hear God's Word and guard it with their lives!"
LUKE 11:28 MSG

When you feel confused and aren't sure what to do. . .when you feel pressured to do things you just don't feel quite right about. . .remember that you have a fantastic guide to help you with any decisions you must make in this life. You have the Bible, God's Word! There is no other book that can help you live the life God has called you to live. Its pages hold everything you will ever need to know in this life. God has a plan for us, and if we stay in His Word and read it often, He will speak to us through it and show us the way to go. Guard it. Appreciate it. Love it.

Dear God, thank You for Your Word. Thank You for providing guidance through the scriptures. Please help me to read the Bible and understand what it is You would have me to do. Please help me to keep reading so that I may always be able to know Your will and be open to receive Your guidance. Amen.

DAY 28

YOU ARE GOD'S BEST WORK

For you created my inmost being; you knit me together in my mother's womb. I praise you because I am fearfully and wonderfully made; your works are wonderful, I know that full well.

PSALM 139:13–14 NIV

Of all God's creation, man is the only one created in God's image for the purpose of being His friend. Man was God's final creation, a combination of His best designs. . .His masterpiece.

And before Adam ever took his first breath, God had already planned you too. Your days were already written in His book before you were born (Psalm 139:16). God planned you before the world began and then waited with eager anticipation for the day when you made your grand entrance.

You are exactly the person God planned you to be. You are His workmanship. On the day you chose Him as your Lord, you melted His heart. There is nothing He wouldn't do for you, because He's crazy about you!

Dear God, it's amazing to me to think that You knew me before the world even began. Even though there are times when I feel like I've messed things up, help me remember I am exactly who You planned for me to be. I'm Your child. Thank You for making me who I am and loving me no matter what. Amen.

DAY 29

YOUR BEST

Don't you realize that in a race everyone runs, but only one person gets the prize? So run to win!
1 Corinthians 9:24 NLT

Slackers. You know who they are. . . . Whether it's phys ed class, home economics, art, or math, slackers do the bare minimum—they scrape by just enough to get a passing grade. But any extra effort on their part, *no way*!

While God has given each of us special gifts and talents, that doesn't mean we should ditch everything else, not bothering to try those things outside our comfort zones and interests. Just because science isn't your thing doesn't mean you shouldn't put energy into learning it. And just because you're not into running doesn't mean you should walk the entire mile in gym class.

Every opportunity we have is from God. And He expects us to give our all in everything we do. Think about those areas in which you're tempted to slack off, and ask God for His help in keeping you motivated to give 100 percent. He won't let you down!

God, please help me run the race to win. I want to give You my all in everything I do. Amen.

DAY 30

THE MASTER OF YOU-OLOGY

But the very hairs of your head are all numbered.
MATTHEW 10:30 KJV

Think you're an expert when it comes to Y-O-U? There's one who knows better.

As your Creator, God is familiar with every part of you. He knows whether you prefer plain vanilla or triple chocolate with sprinkles, and whether your brain is geared more for reading or math. He can tell how many hairs are on your head and how many got stuck in your hairbrush! He also sees the part that no one else does—the inside.

Why do you react to certain things the way you do? What is it about that particular person that gets on your nerves? The answer is clear to God. Best of all, He knows how to change you. If you have attitudes that need adjusting (and who doesn't?), God has all the right tools for tweaking.

The next time you're troubled over a personality quirk, talk to your Maker. Ask Him to perfect your flaws. You'll never go wrong by putting yourself into the hands of the one who knows—and loves—you best.

Lord, You understand everything about me,
including the things that still need work.
Give me the desire to change when I need to so
that I become more and more like You. Amen.

DAY 31

DO YOU KNOW GOD'S WILL?

Each of you should use whatever gift you have received to serve others, as faithful stewards of God's grace in its various forms.
1 PETER 4:10 NIV

Do you ever hear this statement and feel a bit overwhelmed?

"God has a plan for your life."

Do you ever fear you just might miss it?

Consider this: God has given *everyone* unique strengths. While your friend may be a talented musician, you may not be able to play a note on the piano or sing in the right key. At the same time, perhaps your talents lie in writing or working with young children. Are you organized or mathematically gifted? Do you have an outgoing personality? Do you work with your hands well? Maybe it is none of these things. There are thousands of possibilities.

As a Christian, in addition to talents, you also have spiritual gifts. God wants you to use your gifts and abilities for His glory. When you do, you are fulfilling His will for your life. His plan for you will always match up with the things you do well! Your Creator knew His purposes for you even before you were born.

God, please reveal to me my unique gifts and abilities. May I always use them for Your glory. Amen.

DAY 32

NEED WISDOM?

If you need wisdom, ask our generous God,
and he will give it to you.
JAMES 1:5 NLT

The Bible says that wisdom is worth more than jewels, and nothing else you desire can compare with it (Proverbs 8:11)! Having wisdom means that you know right from wrong, and then you choose to do the right thing. The book of Proverbs talks a lot about the importance of finding wisdom and understanding. Many people seek wisdom, but few find it. Why? Because they are looking in all the wrong places!

James 1:5 tells us that if we want wisdom, we have to look to God and ask Him to give it to us. And when you do ask God for wisdom, never doubt that He will grant it. Trust that He will give you all the wisdom you need to accomplish the plans that He has for you—at just the right time.

Dear God, I definitely need a lot of wisdom. I'm growing up, and I want to know how to follow You better. I want to serve You and do the right thing. I have a lot of choices to make every day. Please give me the wisdom to make the right ones. Help me to trust You more. Amen.

DAY 33

GOD'S LOVE IS MY SUPPORT

When I said, "My foot is slipping,"
your unfailing love, LORD, supported me.
PSALM 94:18 NIV

Friends may come and go, schools may come and go. . .sports teams, churches, even family members come and go. But as a child of God, you can rest assured that He will always be your constant. It doesn't matter where you are—He's there and He loves you.

His love is greater than anything you or I could ever dream of—it's deeper than the deepest ocean, wider than the span of the earth, and bigger than the universe itself. And on days when you feel alone, His love will support you. Even if the earth crumbled around you, His love would still be there.

So today as you're walking to school or eating your lunch, remember that you've got all the support you'll ever need in the best friend you'll ever have—Jesus.

Jesus, thank You for never leaving me. Thank You for dying for me so that I might live. Help me to lean on You, and help me to be a friend and support to someone else today so I can share what You've done for me. Amen.

DAY 34

CHASE COMFORT

The Lord is close to the brokenhearted;
he rescues those whose spirits are crushed.
Psalm 34:18 NLT

Have you ever lost a loved one or had a falling-out with a friend? Maybe you've gotten into a fight with a family member and feel like things will never be the same. If you have a troubled heart or a burdened spirit, God wants to heal you.

Peace is the gift of God that comforts our hurting souls. Peace is easy to receive when things are going well in life and the future looks bright. But when life presses in and hard times come, peace can seem so far away. The problem is when people chase after peace on their own instead of trusting God to bring them peace.

As Christians, we need to be still and let the truth of God wash over our hurts. Even though stillness is quiet and physically inactive, it is an intentional action that pursues God's peace. Today, quiet your busy mind, and let the peace of God soothe all your hurts.

Father, I cry out to You and wait for Your perfect peace to wash over my pain and heal my heart. Please comfort me in my sorrow. Amen.

DAY 35

THE DREAM GIVER

For we are God's masterpiece. He has created us anew in Christ Jesus, so we can do the good things he planned for us long ago.
EPHESIANS 2:10 NLT

Where do dreams come from? Not nighttime dreams, but the ideas in our heads that just won't go away? . . . Maybe you have dreamed about being a veterinarian since you were little. Or maybe you love to paint or draw. How about the times when you can't stop thinking of visiting other countries or even being a missionary somewhere far, far away? God has big plans for His message to be shared, and it takes all kinds of dreamers to get the job done. If you don't know what your dream is, ask yourself what you are good at and what you love to do. It may not be obvious at first, so ask God to show you the best dream He has for you.

Our dreams are part of who we are, but sometimes we're afraid to think we could do something big. Our confidence needs to grow to catch up with our God-sized dreams. It may take awhile, but if we believe God wants our dreams to come true, we just need to wait for Him to open the doors to make them happen.

Explore your dreams and see where they will take you. With God's help, you can do it. Think big!

Dear God, I want to explore the dreams You have put in my heart. Help me to see the way I should go. Thank You for making all my dreams come true. Amen.

DAY 36

ONLY A PHONE CALL AWAY

Pray without ceasing.
1 Thessalonians 5:17 ESV

Have you ever thought about the purpose of prayer? Do you ever feel like you're praying to the wall instead of to God? Sometimes you may wonder where your prayers even go—if they float away like cartoon thought bubbles into oblivion or if your heavenly Father really is listening to your whispered pleadings.

It might help to imagine that you're talking on the phone when you're praying. God has His ear pressed to the phone on the other end of the line, wanting to listen. . .desiring a connection with you. And you don't have to pray like a pastor at church with big words and flowing sentences. You can talk to God like He's your best friend. A prayer can be a simple and sincere "Help me" or a long monologue about a frustrating day. Even if your mind wanders or you're half asleep, God will still be on the other end of the line, listening to your prayer.

God desires a personal and intimate relationship with you! Allowing Him into your daily life through prayer is a wonderful way to start.

Father, thank You for always listening. I invite You to be a part of my life as my constant companion. Amen.

DAY 37

I DON'T WANT TO!

"And this shall come to pass if you diligently obey the voice of the LORD your God."
ZECHARIAH 6:15 NKJV

Mom thinks your room should be cleaned at the worst possible times. Your friends are waiting. . .your favorite show is on TV. . .you just don't feel like doing it. . .so you put her off. Maybe you choose to ignore her all three times she asks. And if that doesn't work, you head to your room like you intend to obey, but then you start playing a game on your tablet. The next thing you know, Mom is majorly upset and you're grounded. Now what?

God created parents to protect us and teach us to obey. He expects us to learn how to hear and follow through, no matter how we feel. It's the only way He can help us fulfill the plan He has for our lives. There will always be days when our feelings will pull us one way, while in our heart and spirit we know we shouldn't be listening to those feelings. By practicing with small things, like cleaning your room, you will have the ability to make better choices when bigger, more life-altering decisions come along.

God, remind me that I need to obey even when I don't feel like it. I know that learning to obey is a part of growing up. Amen.

DAY 38

GOD KNOWS

You have searched me, LORD, and you know me.
PSALM 139:1 NIV

Sometimes it feels like nobody in the world understands us. That's a pretty lonely feeling. But even when our parents or our friends misunderstand us, we can always talk to God. We never have to worry that He will misinterpret our thoughts or our words. He knows us! He knew us before we were born, and He's been with us every moment of our lives. He knows our thoughts even before we have them.

It's comforting to know God understands us. Sometimes our attitudes are right, but others misunderstand our intentions. If we ask God, He will help us communicate our true feelings to others in a way that they'll understand us better.

Other times, our attitudes may be wrong. We may be angry or hurt or annoyed about something. When we talk to God, He understands, and He helps us get our attitudes right. As long as we come to Him and ask for help, He'll never judge us or make us feel bad about talking to Him. He understands us completely, and He wants to help us live the best lives we can live.

Dear Father, I'm so glad You understand me.
Help me to think like You think. Amen.

DAY 39

THE GREATEST LOVE

Herein is love, not that we loved God, but that he loved us, and sent his Son to be the propitiation for our sins.
1 John 4:10 KJV

There are so many ways and opportunities to express your love to others. You might exchange cards with your friends on a special holiday. You might give your mom a stack of homemade coupons for household chores or hugs and kisses. Maybe you'll make a great big batch of chocolate chip cookies for your dad or pick a beautiful bouquet of flowers to brighten your grandma's day. These are all beautiful expressions of love, but as heartfelt as they are, they cannot come close to the perfect love God has for you.

Did you know that even when your heart was black with sin—when you were hard to love—God gave the greatest possible gift of love? He gave His perfect, holy Son, Jesus, to pay a sin debt that you wouldn't want to pay. What an amazing love that is! Have you accepted it?

Dear heavenly Father, thank You for always loving me. . . especially on those days when I am hard to love. You never let me down, and I am forever grateful. Amen.

DAY 40

A GIANT ERASER

Let all that I am praise the Lord; may I never forget the good things he does for me. He forgives all my sins and heals all my diseases.
Psalm 103:2–3 NLT

Have you ever messed up so badly that you felt like the Lord couldn't forgive you? Here's the good news: God has a giant eraser. Think about your teacher in school, how she takes the eraser and wipes away what she's written on the board so that new stuff can be written down in its place. That's how it is with God. When you mess up (like all people do), you can ask for His forgiveness. Once you ask, He grabs that giant eraser of His and gets to work, wiping away all of that icky stuff from your board. Ah! Doesn't it feel good to have a clean slate, a fresh start?

Don't beat yourself up when you mess up. Just ask for forgiveness and then imagine God wiping away that bad stuff and giving you a chance to replace it with good. He will, you know. So why not stop right now and pray the following prayer:

Lord, I'm so glad You have a giant eraser to wipe away all of my mistakes! Whew! What a relief to know that my mess-ups won't mess up my relationship with You. Thank You for that. Amen.

DAY 41

COURAGE TO FACE THE HARD TIMES

"Be strong and courageous. . .for it is the Lord your God who goes with you. He will not leave you or forsake you."
Deuteronomy 31:6 ESV

What happens when you face a hard time? It won't disappear on its own, so the only option is whether to run from it or face it head-on.

The easiest choice is to run from a difficult situation. Jonah did that when God told him to go to Nineveh. But even during the storm at sea, throughout his time in the fish's stomach, and when he eventually traveled to Nineveh, the Lord went with him. It would have worked best for Jonah to obey immediately; but even though he disobeyed, the Lord did not leave Jonah or forsake him.

God doesn't want you to run from challenges; rather, He wants to face them with you. He inspires you to be strong because He will confront hard times with you. No matter how rough it gets, there's nothing that can make Him leave you. He is with you through it all.

Dear Jesus, I want to be strong and courageous. Help me to face the hard times with determination because I know that You will stay by my side through it all. Thank You for being such a faithful friend. Amen.

DAY 42

THE LORD, YOUR HERO

Though I walk in the midst of trouble, you preserve my life. You stretch out your hand against the anger of my foes, with your right hand you save me.
PSALM 138:7 NIV

Sometimes the world is a scary place. . .and it seems to get scarier every day. Just going to school can feel like you're navigating a minefield. There are so many things you have to watch out for, not only at school, but on the internet, in your neighborhood. . .maybe even in your own home. Sometimes it seems like evil is all around you.

No matter where life takes you, you can be sure that God goes with you. He is the ultimate Dad. He loves you and watches over you every moment of every day. His ears are always open to your prayers (1 Peter 3:12). Because of your relationship with Him, you can be confident that He will keep you safe. When you go to sleep at night, you can sleep peacefully. You don't have to be afraid, because the Lord, your protector, is on the job (Proverbs 3:24).

Dear God, thank You for being my protector. Thank You for loving me and going with me everywhere I go. Thank You for keeping me safe. Even though the world is a scary place, I know I can count on You. Amen.

DAY 43

SOMETIMES LOVE MEANS STOP

The Lord disciplines the one he loves.
HEBREWS 12:6 NIV

There was once a middle-school boy who drew a bright red STOP sign with the word *compassion* scrawled above it in bold, black letters. Compassion means that you feel kindness and concern for someone's trouble. When I saw the picture, I thought, *Wow! That's amazing.* I really liked this boy's insight because sometimes it is compassionate—it shows kindness—to tell someone to stop.

If you see someone running out in the street and a bus is coming, you don't just sit there; you yell for them to stop. This is compassion.

It's the same way with God. Because He loves you, there are times when He will tell you to stop. And sometimes the way He will get you—and me—to stop doing something that is hurtful for us is to discipline us. His discipline is always done in love because He cares for us and He doesn't want us to get hurt, just like you wouldn't want someone you love to get run over in the street.

Sometimes love means stop.

Lord, thank You that You discipline me. I am so very grateful that You don't allow me to do everything I want, especially when You know something is bad for me. I'm glad that You're a good Daddy who cares for me. Amen.

DAY 44

WORDS OF COMFORT

This is my comfort in my affliction,
for Your word has given me life.
PSALM 119:50 NKJV

When your friends hurt your feelings. . .when you feel left out. . .when you're sick or feeling bad. . .remember the one who will never leave you, the one who knows you better than anyone else. Remember that our God wants only what is best for you, and then turn to Him. He is the great comforter. Reread today's verse from Psalm 119, and familiarize yourself with other scriptures about God's comfort. Be assured that He is *always* ready and willing to comfort you.

Dear heavenly Father, my day had a less-than-stellar start—I haven't been feeling well and I didn't feel like going to school today, but I couldn't afford to miss any more days. So I went. Then I found out my friends are having a party and didn't invite me. Oh, they said they thought I was still sick and meant to call me to see if I could come, but now I'm not sure they really want me to. But I want to go, Father. Please give me comfort so that I can quit crying and get past my hurt. And please help me to comfort others when they feel like I do right now. Amen.

DAY 45

IF HIS EYE IS ON THE SPARROW. . .

"Look at the birds of the air, that they do not sow, nor reap nor gather into barns, and yet your heavenly Father feeds them. Are you not worth much more than they?"
MATTHEW 6:26 NASB

God sees the birds as they soar and as they pluck little worms out of the fertile soil, when they make nests for their little ones. . . . If God sees and feeds the birds of the air, you can be sure that He sees and takes care of you! You're worth so much more than flying creatures. God prizes you! You're His child, His creation (see Ephesians 2:10; Psalm 139:13–14; Acts 17:29; Romans 8:16–17).

God understands whenever you're going through a hard time. After all, Jesus came as a human. He suffered every temptation we do (see Mark 1:12–13 and Matthew 4:1–11). He understands. He sees what you're going through, and He's there to help you, strengthen you, and carry you through (see Matthew 6:30; 1 Corinthians 10:13; Philippians 4:13; 2 Corinthians 12:9). He wants you to trust Him and know that He has everything under control. God will never abandon you—no matter what!

God, thank You for loving me. Thanks for understanding, protecting, and helping me. I trust You, Lord. And I will keep trusting You. In Jesus' name I pray. Amen.

DAY 46

READING AND GROWING

Search the scriptures.
John 5:39 KJV

The Bible may have been written centuries ago, but its principles apply to your life today. No matter what situation you find yourself in, God's Word has the answer for how to handle it. Having trouble with a bully? Check out Romans 12:19–20. Struggling with temptation? Read 1 Corinthians 10:13. Whether you're trying to make friends, get along with your family, or be a better student, the Bible has a verse for you. Finding it is the key.

The Bible is a big book with a lot to say. If you're not in the habit of reading it, you can get a little overwhelmed. Start with something familiar, like the creation account in Genesis or the birth of Christ in Luke. Use a highlighter to mark the verses that stand out to you. Write notes in the margins. Most importantly, make a daily effort to read God's Word. You may have outgrown the song, but it's still true that if you "read your Bible and pray every day, you will grow, grow, grow."

Dear God, put a love for the Bible in my heart. Remind me to set aside some time each day to read the scriptures, and most of all, help me to obey what I read. Amen.

DAY 47

JOY IN TROUBLES

Consider it pure joy, my brothers and sisters, whenever you face trials of many kinds, because you know that the testing of your faith produces perseverance.

JAMES 1:2–3 NIV

Did you read that scripture right? Consider it JOY when problems come into your life? *Really?* That's what God's Word says. This doesn't mean you have to act happy and be fake when problems happen. It just means that you "get" the fact that this world isn't perfect and problems will come—and that you trust in God to give you joy, in spite of the bad stuff! Make sense?

Consider this. . . . Let's say you move to a new school and you don't know a single person. You have a not-so-good first day, and you are treated badly by some mean kids. You don't have to be happy about it; but God does want you to remember that He is always with you, and He has you at the new school for a reason. He wants you to be a shining light for Him wherever He allows you to go. Ask Him to give you His joy to make it through, and He will!

Dear Jesus, help me to grow up knowing, loving, and trusting You—even during difficult times. Amen.

DAY 48

ALWAYS, *ALWAYS*

It is God who arms me with strength and keeps my way secure.
Psalm 18:32 NIV

Have you ever been in a situation where you felt lost or alone? A time when you got a panicky feeling in your stomach and you felt vulnerable, like something bad was about to happen? In times like these, it's easy to forget that there is someone who loves and protects you, who will never forget you or abandon you. But your Father in heaven is *always* watching over you, even when it feels like no one is there.

God knows when you are scared or lonely. He knows you better than anyone else on earth ever could, and His love and protection are constant reminders of that. He never tires of hearing from you, and He desperately wants to give you comfort when you need it. He will give you the courage and strength to deal with any situation; you just have to remember to ask.

Whenever you are feeling scared or alone, take a deep breath and talk to the heavenly Father. Tell Him exactly what you are feeling, and give all your worries to Him. He is listening and wants to hear from you—He cares about everything you have to say.

Heavenly Father, thank You for always watching over me and giving me strength when I feel weak. Help me to remember that when I'm feeling lost or scared. Amen.

DAY 49

DO NOT BE AFRAID

For God has not given us a spirit of fear,
but of power and of love and of a sound mind.
2 Timothy 1:7 NKJV

Everyone feels scared sometimes. When do you feel afraid? Is it when you're gearing up for a sports competition or before a big test? Maybe you feel afraid when you're new to something—whether it's a new school, a new class, or a new neighborhood.

The Bible tells us that God has not given us a spirit of fear. He wants us to be courageous. There will be times in life when you have to face things that make you nervous or even scared. And in each one of those experiences, God will be with you. He is *always* right there beside you, cheering you on.

God assures us in His Word that He knows the plans He has for us, and those plans are to bring us hope and a future. . .never to harm us (Jeremiah 29:11). Nothing can touch your life without first being filtered through the fingers of your heavenly Father.

Be strong in Jesus, and when you are afraid, tell Him about it. He will help you face your fears.

God, sometimes I feel so afraid. Help me to remember that You have put a spirit of courage within me. Amen.

DAY 50

THE GOD-HUG

Praise be to the God and Father of our Lord Jesus Christ, the Father of compassion and the God of all comfort, who comforts us in all our troubles, so that we can comfort those in any trouble.

2 Corinthians 1:3–4 niv

Some days it seems like everyone is against us, doesn't it? Friends are mean, and we feel betrayed. Mom gets onto us for leaving our towel on the bathroom floor. Even the dog won't sit in our laps when we call him. On days like that, we feel like there's no hope, no comfort anywhere.

But God, who loves us more than anything, wants to be our comforter. No matter what's going on around us, we can always find that still, small voice in our spirit that says, *"I love you. I'll never leave you. I think you're special, and I want you to trust in Me and have peace."* When we really listen and hear His voice, it feels like a God-hug wrapped around our spirits.

Just as God comforts us, He wants us to comfort others. Today, look for someone who might need comforting, and offer your friendship. It just might make both of you feel better.

Dear Father, thank You for being my comforter. Help me comfort others as You comfort me. Amen.

DAY 51

ME, STRONG?

It is God who arms me with strength and keeps my way secure.
PSALM 18:32 NIV

You may be just a kid, and you might think you are small and weak. But did you know you are also a soldier for the Lord? And that He gives you all the strength you need to face each battle that comes your way? It's true!

The key is to keep your focus on your Savior. Can you imagine yourself running a race? Picture that finish line. . . . Jesus is there, standing with His arms open wide for you.

When you keep your attention on Him and on what *He* has for your life, the bumps, hurdles, roadblocks, and even wars that come your way will be easier to tackle. He's given you a very special set of armor to wear, and He has unlimited strength to help you through even the most difficult of days.

So when you feel weak, don't allow feelings of insignificance to overwhelm you. God has given you *His* strength for each day. And His strength is perfect.

God, thank You for today and even for all the challenges that come my way. Thank You for giving me Your strength. Remind me in the hard times that Your strength is all I need. And help me to keep my focus on You. Amen.

DAY 52

HOW MUCH IS TOO MUCH?

For I am convinced that neither death nor life, neither angels nor demons, neither the present nor the future, nor any powers, neither height nor depth, nor anything else in all creation, will be able to separate us from the love of God that is in Christ Jesus our Lord.

Romans 8:38–39 NIV

Did you ever sin so much that you thought God could never forgive you? That God would abandon you because you'd gone too far? What if you lost your best friend and it was all your fault? What if you told a lie that hurt your brother or sister? What if you stole something or even hated someone in your heart? Would God give up on you? Would He be unwilling to forgive you?

The answer is no! When you say you're sorry to God, He forgives you for all the bad stuff. All those hurtful things are wiped away. Your past becomes like a pile of dirty laundry that gets thrown into the wash. Those clothes come out clean, ready to be worn again.

God not only wants to forgive you, but He hopes to be your best and closest friend.

Lord, forgive me for all the things I've done that make You sad, and help me to live closer to You each day so that I might know Your peace and joy! Amen.

DAY 53

MY ETERNAL HOME

One thing I ask of the LORD, this only do I seek: that I may dwell in the house of the LORD all the days of my life.

PSALM 27:4 NIV

Do you think a lot about your home? It's probably your favorite place to be. . .your room is exactly the way you like it. . .all of your favorite things are exactly where you like them to be, right? Well, do you ever think about your ETERNAL home? If we have accepted Jesus as our Savior, we get to live in heaven with Him forever after our life on this earth is over.

Jesus tells us in John 14:2 that He has gone to heaven to prepare a place for us! He is getting our room ready in heaven. Heaven is a perfect place, and it will be filled with all of your favorite things. So whenever you are having a rough day or feeling down about this life, imagine what life will be like in heaven! Remember: Jesus is getting your room ready!

God, thank You for thinking of me. . .for creating a home in heaven for me. . .for loving me so very much. I am thankful to be Your child! Amen.

DAY 54

NEEDS AND WANTS

"That is why I tell you not to worry about everyday life—whether you have enough food or drink, or enough clothes to wear. Isn't life more than food, and your body more than clothing?"
MATTHEW 6:25 NLT

These days, many families are struggling financially. Mom or Dad may be out of work; single parents are struggling to provide for their kids; the economy has led to an increase in the cost of basic needs that eats away at finances. When you see all of that and can do nothing about it, it can lead to a lot of fear.

It's true you can't do much to change the financial situation of your family right now, but there are things you can do.

First, work on having a great attitude. Let your parents know that you're content with what you have. Next, be creative about ways to stretch what you have, yet still make it interesting. Why not trade outfits with a friend or have a movie night at home instead of going to the theater?

Finally, pray. Pray for the financial situation of your family, and pray for the security your parents feel in God. Be sure to thank God for all of your blessings. When you have a thankful heart, the emptiness fades away.

Lord, help me to remember all of the wonderful blessings You've given me and let me focus on the important things in life, not material things. Amen.

DAY 55

IN HIS CARE

And my God will supply all your needs according to His riches in glory in Christ Jesus.

PHILIPPIANS 4:19 NASB

It's quite easy to confuse wants with needs. Sometimes the line between the two can get a little blurry. But even when there's confusion on our part, God knows what His children need and has promised to provide it.

We should not grudgingly trudge through life, sulking because we don't have the "certain thing" we feel we *need* to have. If there's something that God chooses to equip us with so that we can better serve Him, He will bring it to us.

Because God is our God of unconditional love, He will give us some "wants" too. He is a loving Father who joys in showering blessings on His children.

Trust that He knows what your needs are versus your wants! He owns it all—we only look after it for the time He places it in our care.

Dear heavenly Father, thank You for giving me all that I need. Help me to trust that You will take care of me. Thank You too for the "wants" You have provided. You are so good to me! Amen.

DAY 56

THE COWARDLY LION

"Be strong and of good courage, do not fear nor be afraid of them; for the Lord your God, He is the One who goes with you. He will not leave you nor forsake you."

Deuteronomy 31:6 NKJV

If you've seen *The Wizard of Oz*, you know that Dorothy met several characters on her journey down the yellow brick road. One of those characters was the cowardly lion. He sure seemed like a scaredy-cat, didn't he? Talk about being afraid!

Maybe you've felt like a scaredy-cat at times too. You wanted to run and hide from your troubles instead of facing them. Here's the good news. . . . God will give you the courage to face the things you're scared of. It's true! You can get back on the yellow brick road and walk with courage and confidence, knowing the Lord is walking with you.

Today, if you're struggling to be courageous, ask God to give you His courage. Then look your fears in the eye and say, "You don't scare me anymore!" Watch those fears. . .disappear!

God, sometimes I feel so afraid. I try not to, but I just want to crawl under the covers and hide. Thank You for giving me the courage I need to face the hard things! Amen.

DAY 57

WHEN YOU LOSE A FRIEND

The Lord is close to the brokenhearted and saves those who are crushed in spirit.
Psalm 34:18 NIV

Have you ever lost something that was really special to you? Maybe you lost a favorite toy, a pet, or one of your well-loved books. Everyone loses something that is special to them sometime, but one of the most difficult things to lose is a good friend.

It can be especially hard to lose close friends because we don't think we are supposed to lose them. We expect them to always stay with us. We have to remember that sometimes God brings people into our lives for a long time and sometimes for only a short time.

When they leave, it hurts because you may feel alone or like no one is going to love you again. Maybe you feel angry. Maybe you blame yourself or you blame them for what happened.

No matter how you feel—if you are mad, sad, or frustrated—God cares. When you lose someone special to you, God wants to comfort you. He is always there. He wants to heal your broken heart. Tell Him how you feel, and then listen for His voice. He loves you.

Lord Jesus, it is so hard to lose a good friend. When my heart is broken, help me to trust that You will heal me and help me to keep my heart open so that I can keep loving others. I know You will bring new friends into my life. Amen.

DAY 58

A SPECIAL KIND OF HOPE

Love each other with genuine affection, and take delight in honoring each other. Never be lazy, but work hard and serve the Lord enthusiastically. Rejoice in our confident hope. Be patient in trouble, and keep on praying. When God's people are in need, be ready to help them. Always be eager to practice hospitality.

ROMANS 12:10–13 NLT

There is a recipe for success in these scriptures—a recipe for success in the Christian life. God doesn't give us instruction just to boss us around. He knows that if we can stick to this "recipe," we will be the kind of Christians He calls us to be.

One ingredient mentioned in these verses is hope. Not just any hope, but *confident* hope. There is a difference between plain hope and *confident* hope. You can hope the wind doesn't blow today, but you don't know for sure that it won't. You can hope those shoes you've been wanting will go on sale, but there is no guarantee they will. *Confident* hope is a sure thing. . .like the hope of God's love and a future home in heaven. These things are guaranteed if we have chosen to follow Jesus. We can have this kind of hope all the time. It's a special gift—a gift that God gives to us as a promise.

Aren't you happy to have God's special kind of hope?

Dear Lord, thank You for the gift of hope. Help me to share it with others and show them by the way I live that I have the perfect recipe for life. I will rejoice in the hope You have given me. Amen.

DAY 59

WATCH YOUR WORDS

Don't use foul or abusive language. Let everything you say be good and helpful, so that your words will be an encouragement to those who hear them.

EPHESIANS 4:29 NLT

Sometimes words can hurt much, *much* more than sticks and stones. A scrape on the knee will heal pretty quickly, but wounds that come from hurtful words will stay inside your heart for a lifetime if you let them.

This verse in Ephesians reminds us to watch our words. God wants us to be an encouragement to the people in our lives. He wants us to be helpful and to say things that make Him smile. He doesn't want us to use bad words or gossip about others either. In James 1:26, the Bible tells us that if we claim to be Christians but gossip, our faith probably doesn't mean much to us.

If you've had unkind things said about you, forgive the person who said them and then ask God to heal your heart. If you're the one speaking unkind words, ask God to forgive you and use your words to lift people up instead.

Dear God, please help me to be wise in the way I talk to and about others. Forgive me for unkind things I've said in the past. Help me to honor You with my words. Amen.

DAY 60

HOW HUNGRY ARE YOU?

For he satisfies the thirsty and fills the hungry with good things.
Psalm 107:9 NIV

When you get home from school, are you totally starving. . .so hungry you have pains in the pit of your stomach? Have you ever been that hungry spiritually? Have you ever longed for God so much that you really hungered for Him?

Some people think if they read the Bible once a week, they're good to go. But if the Bible is our spiritual food, we're going to be pretty skinny (spiritually speaking) if we only feast on the Bible once a week. We need to "eat" of it daily! As Christians, we should literally crave God and His Word. We should think about Him with as much joy as we do a candy bar when we're craving chocolate.

If you're less than hungry for more of God, ask Him to increase your spiritual hunger. Once you begin "snacking" on the scriptures, you'll find it's a lot like potato chips—completely addictive! So go ahead—dig into God's Word today. It's full of good stuff!

Thank You, God, for giving me physical food to feed my body. Please increase my spiritual hunger so that I may grow closer to You. Amen.

DAY 61

PLEASE FORGIVE ME

I acknowledged my sin to You, and my iniquity I have not hidden. I said, "I will confess my transgressions to the LORD," and You forgave the iniquity of my sin.

PSALM 32:5 NKJV

When you know you've done wrong—kept the truth from your parents, lied to your friends, cheated on a test, or anything else you know you weren't supposed to do (even in secret)—remember that God knows *all* you do and *nothing* is hidden from Him. But He is a God of mercy and forgiveness. All you have to do is ask!

Dear God, please forgive me for my sin. I thank You for being a forgiving God. I know I was wrong. I know You and my parents love me and will forgive me. I don't know what came over me! And now I can't get it off my mind, and I feel so guilty. You know everything I do, Father—I know I can't hide anything from You. I am so very sorry. Please give me strength and wisdom so I won't disappoint You or my parents again. Amen.

DAY 62

I THINK I CAN; I THINK I CAN!

"Fear not, for I am with you; be not dismayed, for I am your God. I will strengthen you, yes, I will help you, I will uphold you with My righteous right hand."

ISAIAH 41:10 NKJV

Do you ever feel like you just can't do it? Maybe you're struggling in school or you're crumbling under heavy responsibilities. Or maybe the Christian walk is a burden on your heart right now: "Don't give in to temptation." "Stay pure." "Be an example."

You might be tempted to say, "I can't do it!"

You may want to say no when the Holy Spirit is prompting you to invite a friend to church or to tell someone about Jesus. Maybe you want to run away when a friend comes to you for help with a struggle you don't feel equipped to face.

But God promises to be there with you through all of those hard times and to carry your fears. He will give you the strength you need to live out His call in your life, and He'll never ask you to do anything that He won't equip you to do.

Dear God, I want to follow You, but sometimes it's hard. Please give me the strength today to do the things You ask me to do. Amen.

DAY 63

THE REAL HOPE

My soul, wait only upon God and silently submit to Him; for my hope and expectation are from Him.
Psalm 62:5 AMPC

There doesn't seem to be much hope in the world today. The news is full of depressing stories. The friends we once thought would be there through anything turn away. The game that was a sure win turns out to be a loss. The end of the school day can't come fast enough. *Where is the hope?*

Hope is heard in a lot of conversations. "I hope I can go this weekend." Or, "I hope it doesn't rain today." Or, "I hope my mom/dad will let me [fill in the blank]."

But the only real hope comes from Jesus Christ. He is always right there—He doesn't move away or leave us on our own. That's hope we can count on!

He will *be* our true hope and will *give* us true hope—especially in those times that seem to be hopeless.

Dear Lord Jesus, I submit to Your authority and want You to be in control of my life. Thank You for being my true hope and for giving me true hope. In Jesus' name, amen.

DAY 64

THE RIGHT THING —EVERY TIME

. . .because you obey the Lord your God by keeping all his commands that I am giving you today and doing what is right in his eyes.
Deuteronomy 13:18 NIV

Ever had one of those days? You didn't study right after school. Then you had practice. After practice, you went home, ate dinner, helped with the dishes, and then went to your room. Your intentions were good: you did set out your notes and textbook. But, exhausted from a long day, you fell asleep in your school clothes.

Several hours later, you wake up and think, *Oh great! I'm going to flunk my test tomorrow! But there's nothing I can do about it now. I'll study tomorrow, during recess or in study hall.* Defeated, you put on pajamas and crawl into bed for the night.

The following day, things don't go quite as planned. Your gym teacher is testing for endurance, and you lose recess time because you were talking to your best friend in homeroom. When test time arrives, you are scrambling to think of a way to save yourself from the impending F. *Susan always gets A's,* you think. *I could probably cheat off her, and no one would know the difference. . . . But I would know, and my heavenly Father would know. And He wants me to do the right thing—every time.* So with a shrug and a quick prayer—*Thank You, Jesus, for giving me the strength to do the right thing!*—you begin.

God, help me to always do my best to be prepared—and to do the right thing, even when I'm tempted to do what's wrong. Amen.

DAY 65

GIVE HIM YOUR DREAMS

Humble yourselves before the Lord, and he will lift you up.

JAMES 4:10 NIV

I once watched a movie in which a tiny girl held a handful of shiny pennies. An adult approached and held out a five-dollar bill, inviting her to trade. Convinced she had what was best because it looked like the most, she told him no and hugged her pennies close.

This reminds me of how we can sometimes be when Jesus wants to trade what we want for what He wants for us. Maybe He asks us to move to a new school or to join a new club. But we want to hold on to our old thing, like our old school or our old club. We hold on and won't let go because, just like the girl thought her pennies were more, we think that what we have is more.

Remember that God always knows best. Also remember that He will never ask you to give up something without giving something in return that is His best plan. His plan may not always be easy, but it will be right, and you will be happy that you followed Him. If you trust Him, giving up your "pennies" will be easier. Because He made you, He knows what is best for you. You can trust His plan.

Lord, sometimes it's hard for me to give up what I want for what You want. Help me to trust You and not to demand my own way. I love You. Amen.

DAY 66

YOU'RE GONNA LIVE FOREVER!

And this is the testimony: God has given us eternal life, and this life is in his Son.
1 John 5:11 NIV

Someone once said there are only two things you can be sure about: death and taxes. Everybody pays taxes. . .and everybody dies. Or do they?

God never intended for you to die. God created you to be His friend and live with Him forever. But when Adam sinned in the Garden of Eden, death came into the world for the first time. For a long time after that, death had authority over every living thing on the earth. It didn't matter if they were good or bad or worshipped the one true God or not.

When God sent Jesus to die on the cross, Jesus paid the price for Adam's sins and everyone who came after him—including you. Adam may have allowed death into the world. . .but Jesus kicked it out (1 Corinthians 15:21–22). Through Jesus Christ you can have a relationship with the Creator of the universe and cheat death at the same time!

Dear God, thank You for the promise of eternal life I have through Jesus Christ. Thank You for making a way for me to escape death and live a life of joy and peace forever with You. Amen.

DAY 67

GOD'S WORKMANSHIP

For we are His workmanship, created in Christ Jesus for good works, which God prepared beforehand so that we would walk in them.

EPHESIANS 2:10 NASB

You're God's workmanship—His *masterpiece*! God doesn't make mistakes (Genesis 1:31). He made you and didn't mess up in the process. He didn't have a blooper moment.

He knows exactly who you were, are, and will be. He knows why He made you the way you are. And He made you that way for a *reason*!

What if you have a big nose? What if you're fat or skinny, short or tall, blond-haired, brown-haired, red-haired, green-haired, or blue-haired? Everyone is unique and special in their own way. God wants it that way! How boring would it be if everyone looked exactly the same?

God sees you as His workmanship and craftsmanship. He loves you beyond measure, precious one. Trust Him. He knows what He's doing (see Proverbs 3:5; Ephesians 4:20–24; Colossians 2:13–14; 1 Peter 3:3–4).

God, I know that I'm "just right" in Your eyes. Thank You for loving me, covering me with Your fingerprints, and having a plan for me. I love You. Thank You so much. In Jesus' name I pray. Amen.

DAY 68

THE GREAT COMFORTER

All praise to God, the Father of our Lord Jesus Christ. God is our merciful Father and the source of all comfort. He comforts us in all our troubles so that we can comfort others. When they are troubled, we will be able to give them the same comfort God has given us.

2 Corinthians 1:3–4 NLT

To whom do you turn when you're hurt? Sad? Lonely? Afraid? Many times you may turn to your parents, your brother or sister, or friends. God has put these people in your life to help comfort you in times of trouble. God Himself can comfort you too. When you open your heart and pray to Him, don't be afraid to tell Him exactly how you feel.

The Bible teaches us that God is full of mercy. This means that He is compassionate. He wants to comfort His children.

The more you turn to God and feel His comfort, the better you will be able to comfort those around you. When you see someone hurting, you can reach out in love.

God loves you with an everlasting love. When you need to be comforted, tell God. He is always there, and it brings Him great pleasure when you choose Him as your comforter.

God, there are some areas of my life where I am hurting. Be my comforter, I pray. Amen.

DAY 69

WHAT DO I HAVE TO LOOK FORWARD TO?

"For my Father's will is that everyone who looks to the Son and believes in him shall have eternal life, and I will raise them up at the last day."
JOHN 6:40 NIV

Being a tween or teen can be the best. . .and it can also be the worst. The thrills of high school or getting your driver's license are sometimes so hard to wait for. And some days, you can't wait to graduate, be an adult, get a job, get married.

Other days, you wonder if there's anything good at all coming in your future. Is there any point?

There is. And it's so much brighter than the most incredible future you could dream up for yourself. It's eternal life. And God offers it freely to you. Don't you love that? That He sent His Son to die for you and me so that we could live with Him forever. That's love. That's sacrifice.

So no matter where you are today—excited about the future or not—remember that the very best is yet to come. An eternity without pain or sorrow or sadness.

Now that's something to look forward to.

God, thank You for offering me eternal life. Sometimes I don't feel I have much to look forward to, but help me remember that the best is yet to come. Please help me to share that with someone else today. Amen.

DAY 70

ALL PRAYED OUT

Then Jesus told his disciples a parable to show them that they should always pray and not give up.

Luke 18:1 NIV

Do you ever feel like you're all out of prayers? Like you don't have enough energy to speak one more word to anyone, let alone share your feelings with God? Or maybe you're all prayed out because you've been asking God for the same thing over and over again, and you feel like He's either not listening or has decided not to answer.

In Luke 18, Jesus gives us a picture of how He wants us to pray. The widow wears down the judge with her persistent request until one day he finally gives in. No matter what you are praying about, don't give up! Keep talking to the heavenly Father. The process of persistent prayer will change your heart to be more like His. And at times when you feel all prayed out, remember that God is *always* listening and working in your life.

God, sometimes I feel like the lady in Luke 18 when I come to You over and over again about the same thing. I know You hear my prayer, and I trust that You will do what is best for me. Help me not to lose heart but to remember Your love and faithfulness. Amen.

DAY 71

A GIANT TREASURE BOX

My God will use his wonderful riches in Christ Jesus to give you everything you need.
PHILIPPIANS 4:19 NCV

Have you ever waited for Christmas morning, hoping you would get a certain gift? Maybe you asked your parents or grandparents for a new video game or bike. Maybe you secretly hoped for a new gaming system or computer. You planted lots of hints, convinced they would get you what you wanted. Then Christmas morning arrived. . .and no video game! No bike! No gaming system or computer!

Instead of crying "What's up with that?" when you don't get the things you want, why not take your requests to God? The Bible says that He owns everything in the world. He's got a huge treasure box filled with all sorts of unimaginable things!

The cool thing about God is that He doesn't give us what we want; He gives us what we need. Sure, it won't always be some cool gadget or gaming system, but it will always be His very best for you. So pray and let Him know the desires of your heart. Then watch His treasure box open as new gifts—perfect for you—are placed into your hands.

God, I know that I don't always get what I want. Sometimes I ask my parents for things and don't get them. But You know what I really need. Thank You for providing for me! Amen.

DAY 72

LESSON FROM THE SEA

He gave the sea its boundary so the waters would not overstep his command.
PROVERBS 8:29 NIV

Even the ocean has boundaries. When God made the world, He put a limit on those great salty waters. Landlubbers rest easy knowing that no matter how fiercely the waves may surge inland, the waves can only reach so far. If the sea could refuse to obey the rules, imagine the destruction it would cause!

God sees the bright promise of your future. He also knows that poor choices could spoil it. That's why He gave you parents, spiritual leaders, and a conscience. It's why your internet use may be limited and you're not allowed to hang out with certain people.

Staying within your boundaries might mean missing out on some fun. It could even make you unpopular with some of your peers. But when you're tempted to sneak over the line of protection that has been drawn for you, remember that God placed it there for your good. Remember too that when the sea oversteps its bounds, it takes a lot of effort and expense to repair the damage.

Lord, I don't always like the restrictions that my parents and others place on me. Remind me that the rules are for my good, to keep me safe from the dangers of the world. Amen.

DAY 73

WHO COULD KNOW YOU BETTER?

"And the very hairs on your head are all numbered. So don't be afraid; you are more valuable to God than a whole flock of sparrows."
LUKE 12:7 NLT

"Oh, I know her. She sits in the back of my English class." We hear the word *know* all the time. We can say we know about many things or know certain people. And it's true. But there is a different kind of knowing that only God has.

Because He is the one who created you, He knows *everything* about you—from the color of your eyes to the number of hairs on your head and what you want to be when you grow up! He knows you in a way that no one else can. Like the artist who creates a beautiful painting and knows each stroke of the brush and the tiny specks that make it special, God knows each part of you. He is proud of His special creation—the perfect picture of you. He also knows your thoughts and dreams. . .the desires of your heart. God's knowing goes far deeper than we can even understand. And because His knowing is so deep, His love is deep too. And that's the best blessing of all!

Heavenly Father, I sometimes forget that You know me better than anyone ever will. Please help me to be the special person You created me to be. Thank You for knowing me and loving me—no matter what. Amen.

DAY 74

INVITE GOD

"For where two or three gather in my name, there am I with them."
MATTHEW 18:20 NIV

You probably know people who are always ready for a party. They're the ones that make their way to every gathering and are always ready to hang out with anyone and everyone. Social by nature, they enjoy spending time with people and cannot wait for an invitation so they can mingle with others.

God's the same way. He yearns for the time when two or three people gather together to pray, study His Word, offer help to others, or simply spend time together in Christian friendship; and then the Holy Spirit shows up, just like that. He arrives for the smallest of meetings and the biggest of corporate worship services—they're all important to Him.

The next time you seek the presence of your heavenly Father, meet with a friend or family member or two and invite God to join you. He'll be there even before you ask.

God, thank You for showing up whenever I ask. . . before I even ask. I am so thankful that what matters to me also matters very much to You. Amen.

DAY 75

MORE THAN CHERUBS

"I give them eternal life, and they will never perish, and no one will snatch them out of my hand."
JOHN 10:28 ESV

What comes to mind when you think of heaven? Are there any chubby cherubs reclining on clouds and stroking golden harps in your vision? If so, the idea of angelic beings lounging around for all eternity might strike you as. . .well. . .boring.

But if the God who created rainbows and mountains and music and color also created the heavens, then how much more breathtaking and exciting will your eternal home be than earth? As a Christian, you have so much to look forward to. No one really knows for sure what heaven will hold, but you can rest assured that it will be beyond your wildest dreams. There will be infinite joy, overwhelming beauty, and—best of all—you will get to see Jesus face-to-face.

God, thank You for reserving a spot for me in heaven. When I get discouraged or anxious, help me to remember that this isn't my true home. I'm so excited that I get to spend eternity with You! Amen.

DAY 76

DON'T GIVE UP!

God began doing a good work in you, and I am sure he will continue it until it is finished when Jesus Christ comes again.
PHILIPPIANS 1:6 NCV

Have you ever started something that you didn't finish? Maybe you started a craft project and only got halfway done before giving up. Perhaps you joined a sports team but gave up after just a few weeks. Maybe you tried piano lessons but quit after a short time. Perhaps you started putting together a puzzle but never completed it.

We're not very good at carrying through sometimes, are we? Aren't you glad that God is? He doesn't start something and not finish it. That should give you hope! He began a good work in you, and He's going to complete it! He's no quitter! So don't give up, even when you feel hopeless about things. Keep going. God hasn't given up on you, and you shouldn't give up on yourself either. Keep on hoping! Keep on believing! Keep on trying. The Lord is working inside of you right now, at this very moment, and He won't stop, no matter what!

Lord, sometimes I start things but don't finish them. They seem too hard! I give up hope. Thank You, God, for never giving up on me! I want to learn from Your example! Amen.

DAY 77

A FRESH START

He has removed our sins as far from us
as the east is from the west.
PSALM 103:12 NLT

Mess-ups are a part of life. Everybody messes up. *Every single one of us.* Fortunately, God knew that about us before we were ever born, and He decided not to hold our mistakes against us, as long as we are truly sorry.

Sometimes we mess up by accident, like when we drop our lunch box and the contents spill everywhere and we lose our temper about the whole thing. Other times we mess up on purpose. We decide in our hearts that we don't want to clean our rooms, even though Mom has asked us four times already, and so we shut our door and read a book instead. Whether it's an accident or on purpose, God calls those kinds of mess-ups "sin."

But when we realize we've messed up, tell God we're sorry, and sincerely promise to try not to mess up like that again, God wipes the record clean. He forgives us. The verse above says He removes our sins as far as the east is from the west. And since the east and west never meet each other, that's a pretty long way.

Dear Father, I'm sorry for my mistakes.
Thank You for giving me a fresh start. Amen.

DAY 78

A JOYFUL HEART

A cheerful heart is good medicine,
but a broken spirit saps a person's strength.
PROVERBS 17:22 NLT

What does it mean to be joyful? Does that mean God's children will always walk around with smiles on their faces? Will they seem giddy every moment of the day?

Being joyful is the ability to rest in God's goodness, no matter what's going on in life. Not everything that happens will be good, but He will let us rest in Him while we get through it. And that's something to smile about!

Those with illnesses take medicine to feel better, but the Bible says that a joyful heart will have the same results on the body as a good medicine. It can keep a person from having a "broken spirit," which "saps a person's strength." Joy sounds like a much better option!

Whatever today brings, try to keep an attitude of joy. It may change the results of your situation, or it may not. But either way, resting in God and trusting that He will work everything out for His good is always the best way.

Dear Jesus, I want to be a person with a joyful heart. Please help me to trust that You are working good in my life, whether I can see the results right now or not. Amen.

DAY 79

BAND-AID MOMENTS

I will speak with the voice of thanks,
and tell of all Your great works.
Psalm 26:7 NLV

Picture this: You're zooming down the street on your skateboard. You've done this a hundred times, at least. So often, in fact, you're not really paying attention. So instead of watching where you're going, you check out the neighbor's new puppy. Then, *BAM!* You collide with a mailbox. Head trauma and scraped elbows and knees don't bother you as much as the embarrassment of lying on the curb, crying in front of the entire neighborhood. It's a Band-Aid moment in more ways than one. You could limp back home, whining about how life isn't fair. But *you* were distracted by the pup, weren't you? When things go wrong, God often prevents situations from being far worse. What would have happened if that mailbox had been a car?

The next time you encounter a bad situation, try to view it from God's perspective. Your attitude might change from "Life isn't fair!" to "Thank You, God! That was a close one!"

God, help me to see the big picture in my Band-Aid moments. I'm glad You're always there to protect me. Amen.

DAY 80

HE HEARS ME

When the righteous cry for help, the LORD hears
and delivers them out of all their troubles.
PSALM 34:17 ESV

Do you ever wonder if God hears your prayers for help when everything seems to be going wrong? . . . When you feel sick or are depressed? . . . Or when you don't get everything you ask for? . . . Sometimes we forget all that God has done for us or how many prayers He's answered. Remember when you thought you wouldn't be able to play in the soccer tournament? You'd been sick all week and prayed, but you thought God didn't hear. And yet by the time the game rolled around, you were just fine and played one of your best games ever. Or the time when you were scared you'd fail the test and you prayed. . .and you somehow remembered all the right answers and made an A on the test? Thank God for answered prayers!

Dear God, thank You for all the prayers You've answered. Sometimes I forget those times, but please help me to always remember them and know that You do answer my prayers—even if I don't always like the answers. Please help me to remember that You always hear my prayers. Amen.

DAY 81

JOIN THE CLUTTER-FREE CLUB

In his pride the wicked man does not seek him;
in all his thoughts there is no room for God.
PSALM 10:4 NIV

Is your life cluttered? Do you leave the house early in the morning and arrive back home just in time to go to bed? If so, you are probably a member of The Clutter Club. With lots of extracurricular activities, homework, school, and church—there's not much time for anything else.

You know what happens when you have too much clutter in your life? You get stressed out, and then you freak out! One day your best friend says, "Hey, how come you didn't text me back last night?" and you snap, "Hello! I have a million things to do. You're not the center of my world!" Nope. Not good. You need to de-clutter.

There's good news! God is the best organizer, the best planner, and the best at time management. (He did create the whole world in less than a week!) The Bible says to seek Him first. When you do, all of the clutter just seems to fall away, and God supernaturally organizes your day. So ask God to de-clutter your life, and get ready to join a different club—The Clutter-Free Club.

God, please help me de-clutter my life. Thank You! Amen.

DAY 82

THE LORD IS FAITHFUL

But the Lord is faithful, and He will strengthen and protect you from the evil one.
2 THESSALONIANS 3:3 NASB

No matter how difficult the devil tries to make life, God promises that He will be faithful. He'll strengthen you, protect you, and perfect the good work that He began in you (see 2 Thessalonians 2:16–17; 1 Timothy 1:12; Philippians 1:6, 4:13; Ephesians 2:10).

God has given you His armor to unashamedly and boldly wear. Paul says, "Stand firm then, with the belt of truth buckled around your waist, with the breastplate of righteousness in place, and with your feet fitted with the readiness that comes from the gospel of peace. In addition to all this, take up the shield of faith, with which you can extinguish all the flaming arrows of the evil one. Take the helmet of salvation and the sword of the Spirit, which is the word of God" (Ephesians 6:14–17 NIV).

You're given truth, righteousness, the gospel of peace, faith, salvation, and the magnificent Word of God—all of these to wield unceasingly, in faith that God has provided and will protect you.

Father, thank You for keeping me safe. Thank You for protection and peace. Thank You for Your Word, salvation, truth, and righteousness. I will trust You, Lord, with all my heart. In Jesus' name I pray. Amen.

DAY 83

I <3 U

Now this is the confidence that we have in Him, that if we ask anything according to His will, He hears us.
1 John 5:14 NKJV

Is your main means of communication verbal, email, or text message? The majority of us have most of our conversations via text today. It's fun; it's easy; it's fast. You can send pictures, notes, even videos.

What if God texted you? How would you feel about that? Would you feel like He took a shortcut if you wrote to Him with a deep need and He wrote back: IDK?

Did you know God hears every word you speak and every need on your heart? And what's better is that He replies with an active response. *Every single time.*

He either meets that need by giving you exactly what you asked for, or He meets it with a *no* or sometimes a *maybe*. But even in the *no* and the *maybe* there is still action. He decides what's the very best for us, and He is going to provide that even if it means saying *no*. And He never texts it in all caps.

Dear God, please help me to accept the no's and the not-yets with grace. Thank You for always hearing me and responding to me. Amen.

DAY 84

GOD PROVIDES

"Look at the birds of the air; they do not sow or reap or store away in barns, and yet your heavenly Father feeds them. Are you not much more valuable than they?"

MATTHEW 6:26 NIV

Do you ever look at what others have and feel jealous? Maybe you wish you had the nicest name-brand clothes or the newest smartphone. Perhaps a neighbor's big house or expensive car causes your family home or car to seem shabby in your eyes.

The Bible promises that God takes care of His children. He cares for the birds, providing food for them in nature. Will He forget about His children? No way!

You may not always have everything you *want*, but consider all of your *needs* that God meets every day. Ask Him to help you be content. It's a dangerous thing to always want more. Some children grow into adults who are never satisfied. They are constantly on the lookout for the next thing that might bring them happiness.

True happiness doesn't come from our belongings but from a genuine relationship with God. Start today by thanking Him for the way He provides all that you need. Then challenge yourself to say a prayer of thanksgiving whenever you begin to feel even the slightest tinge of jealousy.

Thank You, Lord, for Your many blessings. Amen.

DAY 85

A SPECIAL MESSAGE

The people read it and were glad for its encouraging message.
ACTS 15:31 NIV

Are you happy, sad, excited, or disappointed? Celebrating or feeling depressed? Lonely, loved, worried, nervous? . . . No matter what you're feeling, God's Word *always* has a message for you—a message that will help you with anything and everything you care about, whatever's on your mind. Your life is important to the one who created you!

So pick up your Bible, and get reading! Set aside a special time of day to spend with the one who loves you more than anyone or anything. Highlight, underline, or circle the passages that speak to your heart.

When you're through spending time in God's Word, you'll have time to reflect and write in a journal. And the best part? . . . You'll find yourself growing closer to the heavenly Father *every day*!

God, please help me to stay faithful, spending time in Your Word every day. Thank You! Amen.

DAY 86

IN THE GARDEN

You will always harvest what you plant. Those who live only to satisfy their own sinful nature will harvest decay and death from that sinful nature. But those who live to please the Spirit will harvest everlasting life from the Spirit.

GALATIANS 6:7–8 NLT

Do you like growing things? In school you probably learned about planting seeds and watching them grow. Jesus liked to use "gardening" illustrations in the Bible to help people understand what He was teaching too! John chapter 15 is a good example of one of these illustrations. Jesus says, "Yes, I am the vine; you are the branches. Those who remain in me, and I in them, will produce much fruit" (John 15:5 NLT).

You can learn a lot by hanging out in a garden. But if you're not a big fan of digging in the dirt, just soak in all the beautiful flowers and plants that God created. View them as reminders that God wants you to do the right thing and grow into a young person who harvests "love, joy, peace, patience, kindness, goodness, faithfulness, gentleness, and self-control" (Galatians 5:22–23 NLT).

God, thank You for the many different kinds of plants and flowers in Your creation. Use them to remind me of Your teachings to do the right thing and grow into the kind of person You created me to be. Amen.

DAY 87

A MAN OF HIS WORD

If we are faithless, he remains faithful,
for he cannot disown himself.
2 Timothy 2:13 NIV

Believe it or not, there are some things God can't do. God can't lie. He can't sin. He can't break a promise. God is perfect in every way. He is always with you, always hears you, always knows what you are going through, and always has the answer. God would never do anything to violate His perfect nature. He is good, all the time, in every situation. If He were to do or be anything else, He would not be God.

That's good news for believers. If God says He will always be with you. . .He will. If He says He will protect you from your enemies. . . He will. If He says He will provide for your needs. . .He will. God is a Man of His Word. What He says He will do. . .He does!

Dear God, none of the people in my life are perfect. Sometimes even the people I love the most let me down. Thank You, Father, that You NEVER let me down. Thank You for being a Man of Your Word who keeps all of His promises. Amen.

DAY 88

GOD WON'T BREAK HIS PROMISES

Let us hold unswervingly to the hope we profess, for He who promised is faithful.
HEBREWS 10:23 NIV

Do you ever wonder if God really saved you? If He's really there? If He really has a plan for you? Does He truly know the number of hairs on your head? Does He care about every single little thing that happens to you? Did He really know you before you were born?

It's easy to doubt God in our humanness. We are imperfect, so it's hard to understand how He can be perfect and all-knowing, all-powerful, all-present, and love us so much that He sacrificed His own Son to die for us.

But in Titus 1:2, we get a huge affirmation—God doesn't lie!

When you learn how to study the Bible, you learn that scripture doesn't contradict itself, and scripture always backs up scripture. So when God says He will never leave you nor forsake you—it's true. When it says that you are fearfully and wonderfully made—it's true.

Other people may break their promises, but God won't. He doesn't lie.

God, I sometimes find myself doubting the truth of Your Word. Please forgive me and help me to remember Your promises. I love You, Lord. Amen.

DAY 89

FORGIVEN: NO MORE BAD LABELS

If we confess our sins, he is faithful and just and will forgive us our sins and purify us from all unrighteousness.

1 John 1:9 NIV

Have you ever done something wrong and felt like you have been labeled “bad,” “not worth keeping,” or “not worth loving”?

Sometimes when we sin, people will stick a label on us. They will say we are bad, but God always forgives, and He always gives us second chances.

In Exodus 2:14, after Moses killed a man, a Hebrew made fun of him and said, “Who made you ruler and judge?”

More than forty years later, God did send Moses to rule and deliver His people. Acts 7:35 says, “He [Moses] was sent to be their ruler and deliverer by God himself. . . .”

What is wonderful is that even though Moses had done something bad, God still used him. God didn’t let a bad label stick to Moses. He forgave him. Then God sent him to be a ruler and deliverer over the Israelites.

Remember that if you did something wrong today, it doesn’t have to be your label tomorrow because God forgives you and He will still use you.

Lord, I am so grateful You never say that You won’t forgive me because I sin, You always give me another chance. And You will always give me things to do for You. Amen.

DAY 90

WHERE IS GOD?

"I will never fail you. I will never abandon you."
HEBREWS 13:5 NLT

There are lots of things that we know exist, even though we can't see them. Things like the air, our beating heart, love, and even the sun on a cloudy day. We often take these things for granted but still trust they are there.

When the wind blows, we know it's the movement of the air that we need to breathe. When we feel our pulse, we are reminded we have life. When the clouds part and the sun shines, we feel its warmth.

So how do we know that God is always around? The Bible tells us He is with us all the time, but how can we be sure? Is believing what the Bible says enough? Sometimes. When we have some sort of evidence, we are satisfied. God provides evidence in many ways, but the most precious proof is when He speaks the truth to us personally. When we know God in a personal way, He will speak softly to our hearts, telling us He is there. He will always be there to answer questions and hear our cries twenty-four hours a day.

He will *never* leave you. Learn to listen for His voice.

Dear Father, I know You are with me, and I want to hear You speak to me. Help me turn to You when I am in trouble. Thank You for being by my side every minute of every day. Amen.

DAY 91

JUST TRUST!

God, treat us kindly. You're our only hope. First thing in the morning, be there for us! When things go bad, help us out!

Isaiah 33:2 MSG

Have you ever lost hope, been so disappointed and discouraged that you just didn't think it was possible for things to get better? Everyone has moments like this at some point in their lives, and it's at those low points that God wants to reach out and give you hope. Having hope means that even if your situation doesn't get better immediately, you have complete faith and trust that God is still in control and will work things out. Holding on to hope and trusting that God will take care of you isn't easy; it takes patience and time. But if you do put your hope in the Lord, He will give you a peace that passes all understanding and joy in any situation.

Whenever you feel discouraged or hopeless, take the time to tell your heavenly Father and ask Him to fill you with hope. God loves His children and wants the absolute best for you. He wants to bless you with His peace and joy. Just ask, and He will provide.

Dear God, I don't know why I'm going through this situation, but You do. Please help me get through it and to put all my hope in You. I trust that You are in control and will give me peace and joy in any situation. Amen.

DAY 92

GOT THE GIGGLES?

May the God of hope fill you with all joy and peace as you trust in him, so that you may overflow with hope by the power of the Holy Spirit.

ROMANS 15:13 NIV

Have you ever had this happen: you're with your friends and you get the giggles. One person starts laughing. . .and then another. . .and then another. Before long, everyone is cracking up! That's kind of how it is when you let the joy of the Lord take over your life. Even when you're going through a tough time, God's joy can bring a smile to your face. It's true! And your smile can be contagious! Others see it and start smiling too. Before long, the joy that's inside of you has spread to the people around you! Everyone is soon feeling better.

So don't worry about the tough stuff you're going through. Just ask God to give you His joy so that you can laugh your way through the tough times. He will do it! And when He does. . .watch out! Your joy might just spread like wildfire!

Lord, I don't always feel joyful. Sometimes I get sad. But now I know that I can ask for Your joy and You will put a smile on my face! I'm so glad! Amen.

DAY 93

GOD IS ALWAYS WITH ME

"And the Lord, He is the One who goes before you. He will be with you, He will not leave you nor forsake you; do not fear nor be dismayed."
Deuteronomy 31:8 NKJV

Are there days when you are afraid of just about everything? Afraid of going to class on your first day at a new school? Feeling tongue-tied when the teacher asks you to tell the class a little about yourself? Or what about the time you were late for class and got sent to the principal's office? What about the day you embarrassed yourself by giving the wrong answer to a question the teacher asked you? When any of these things happen, remember that God loves you; and He will *always* be with you. He doesn't want you to fear a thing!

Dear God, please help me never to forget that You go before me—You know all that I am doing and all that will happen to me. Please help me to remember that I don't need to be afraid or worried about what will happen because You are always here with me and will never leave me. Amen.

DAY 94

HEAD SCRATCHERS

We don't yet see things clearly. We're squinting in a fog, peering through a mist. But it won't be long before the weather clears and the sun shines bright! We'll see it all then, see it all as clearly as God sees us, knowing him directly just as he knows us!

1 Corinthians 13:12 msg

Have you ever tried to understand—really, truly understand—God? Little kids ask their parents, "Who is God's mommy?" and "Could there ever be a rock so big that even God couldn't lift it?" The answers to these questions go against everything we know as humans: God doesn't have a mommy; He has always been there. God can lift the biggest rock that there ever could be.

God's love for us sinful humans is just as confusing. How can the Master Creator love His creation so much that even when Adam and Eve sinned, God said, "Yes, you messed up. But I love you so much that I have a plan for us to be together." That plan is Jesus.

Someday in heaven the fog of confusion will lift. We'll understand God's will and His plan for all of creation. We'll know why He answered our prayers the way He did. And we'll fully understand how big His love is for us.

God, while it's impossible to understand everything about You. . .for now I will just trust You with all my heart. Amen.

DAY 95

HELLO? ARE YOU THERE?

He has never let you down, never looked the other way when you were being kicked around. He has never wandered off to do his own thing; he has been right there, listening.

PSALM 22:24 MSG

At the end of a hard day, after dealing with bullies, temptations, and stresses of life, it's comforting to walk in the front door of your own home, isn't it? The soothing smells of comfort food. The familiar sounds of Mom tinkering in the kitchen. It's comfortable. It's always there, and you trust it will always be the same.

That's how it is with God. He promises that He is always there with us and that He will never change. Sometimes it's hard to believe that because we can't see Him. But we do hear His voice in our hearts when we pray; we feel His presence when someone offers comfort in His name; and we feel Him surrounding us when we praise Him.

Today let God reveal His presence to you. Be aware of what He's doing in your life right now.

Father, please show Yourself to me today. Help me see You clearly. Thank You for never leaving me alone. Amen.

DAY 96

DO-OVER

Count yourself lucky, how happy you must be—
you get a fresh start, your slate's wiped clean.
PSALM 32:1 MSG

Video games are addictive. From old-school PAC-MAN to the very latest in gaming technology—there's nothing quite like getting the highest score or advancing to the next level. But when you get blown up or eaten in the very first minute or two, it can make you so mad, right? If you're not too far into the game and nobody is watching, do you ever just restart the game?

In real life, we don't get many do-overs. When you say something hurtful to your best friend, you can't rewind and start again. So isn't it nice that with God we always get to start over? No matter what we've done, God still loves us and forgives us. Psalm 103 says that He has removed our sins as far from us as the east is from the west. The Bible also says that He doesn't even remember our sins anymore. In other words, we get to wipe the slate clean! All we have to do is tell God we're sorry, and then we get to start over and move forward with our heavenly Father. With God, we always win!

Lord, thank You for forgiving my sins and giving me a new beginning. Amen.

DAY 97

FATHER KNOWS BEST

Your Father knoweth what things ye have need of.
MATTHEW 6:8 KJV

"But I prayed about it! Why didn't it work out?"

If you've ever asked this question, then you know how disappointing it is when your prayers go unanswered. No matter how many promises and miracles there are in the Bible, the one you're looking for is the most important. And if it doesn't show up, you might find yourself wondering if there really is a God who listens and cares.

Rest assured that God hears His children each and every time they call. But like all good parents, your heavenly Father decides whether or not your petition is a good one. Some answers to prayer are delayed until the timing is right. Other prayers are denied because they don't fit into God's plan for your life. And sometimes God thrills your heart by opening the windows of heaven and pouring out blessings.

Before you pray for something, ask yourself if your desire is a godly one. If it is, then wait patiently to see what God will do. Remember that when you trust Him with your life, everything will work out for the best.

Dear God, thank You for loving me enough to choose what's best for my life instead of spoiling me with what I want. Amen.

DAY 98

ESCAPING TEMPTATION

No temptation has overtaken you that is not common to man. God is faithful, and he will not let you be tempted beyond your ability, but with the temptation he will also provide the way of escape, that you may be able to endure it.

1 Corinthians 10:13 ESV

There are many different temptations. Some are really big ones. Others are quite small. Some are easy to avoid. Then others trap you. . .and sometimes they trap you over and over again.

Jesus was tempted by Satan while He was on earth. So He knows what it's like to be faced with a really difficult choice. But unlike His creation, He didn't give in to temptation.

The Bible says that you will be tempted. You'll be stuck in that moment when you know what you should do but pause to decide what you will actually do. It's in that split second that God wants you to know there is an escape—a right choice to make. He will be faithful in helping you overcome it. Just look to Him!

Dear Jesus, You understand what it's like to be tempted, so I know it's not unfamiliar to You. Please give me the strength to overcome temptation. Thank You for always making a way for me to get through it. In Your name, amen.

DAY 99

JUST BE YOU!

I praise you, for I am fearfully and wonderfully made.
Wonderful are your works; my soul knows it very well.
PSALM 139:14 ESV

Dr. Seuss wrote, “Today you are You, that is truer than true. There is no one alive who is Youer than You.” And that’s a fantastic thing! God created each of us to be unique on purpose! Not even identical twins are exactly alike. They have different likes and dislikes. One may have more freckles. The other might need braces. God made us all just the way He wanted us to be.

Take a few minutes and open your Bible. Read the rest of Psalm 139. Ask God to help you understand these verses and believe them. Print out the words and hang them on your wall or on your bathroom mirror as a special reminder that God made you to be YOU! He doesn’t want you to change to be more like one of your friends. He gave you special gifts and talents and ideas that nobody else has! Be thankful and use them to honor Jesus!

Dear God, thank You for the gifts and ideas that You have given me. Help me not to be afraid to be myself. Show me how to use my personality to bring You joy! Amen.

DAY 100

DANGEROUS!

The LORD will watch over your coming and going both now and forevermore.
PSALM 121:8 NIV

Have you noticed that being alive is dangerous? You get sick. Your friends have accidents. Your grandparents grow old. But God cares about each of us. So much so, He even has the hairs on your head counted. He knows everything there is to know about you, and He watches over all your comings and goings.

The Bible doesn't guarantee us a perfect life here on earth. In fact, Jesus said we will have many troubles, but the Lord is right here with us. He may not sweep away every misery or heal every wound, but He has promised to give you strength to handle whatever life throws at you.

God can take something that was meant for evil and turn it into something good. He is the master at turning shadows into a sunrise. We can rest in that promise until He takes us home to be with Him for eternity.

Jesus, help me to trust in You—that no matter what happens each day, I know You'll stay beside me, helping me with every choice I make and every step I take. Amen.

DAY 101

GOD'S MASTERPIECE

For we are God's masterpiece. He has created us anew in Christ Jesus, so we can do the good things he planned for us long ago.
EPHESIANS 2:10 NLT

What exactly is a masterpiece? The dictionary defines it as "a person's greatest piece of work" or "an example of skill or excellence."

Artists paint. Sculptors sculpt. Musicians compose. Many of them dedicate their entire lives to creating a *masterpiece*, the work of art for which they will be remembered.

Now think about everything that God created—He created the entire world! Imagine that. Every flowering tree, each unique animal, the brilliant stars, and the clear blue water were designed by your heavenly Father.

But none of that brought Him complete satisfaction. It was not until He created humankind that God had crafted His greatest work, His *masterpiece*. We were created in order to bring glory to our Creator. When you begin to worry about your appearance or wonder if you have enough talent, remember that God made you to be just as you are. And you are His masterpiece!

Heavenly Father, I don't feel so special sometimes. Sometimes I feel quite ordinary. Help me to remember that I am perfect in Your sight. I am Your masterpiece. Amen.

DAY 102

YOU CAN DO IT!

"The Lord is my strength and my defense; he has become my salvation. He is my God, and I will praise him, my father's God, and I will exalt him."

Exodus 15:2 NIV

Ever have one of those weeks when you feel like everything has come crashing down on you at once? You've got a big test to study for, practice that you can't miss, a paper to write for language arts, and you're totally behind in math. It makes you want to pull your hair out and scream, "I CAN'T DO THIS!"

The truth is. . .you probably can't. Not by yourself, that is. The great thing is you don't have to because you are never alone. You've got God on your side. The Bible says you can do all things through Christ who strengthens you (Philippians 4:13).

Take a few minutes every day to spend time with God in prayer and worship. When you do, you'll find you really can do everything you need to do because God will give you the strength you need right when you need it (Isaiah 40:31).

Dear God, sometimes I get overwhelmed with all the stuff I'm supposed to do. Help me to remember that my strength comes from spending time with You and giving all my cares to You. Thank You for being a loving God who gives me strength. Amen.

DAY 103

THE WAGES OF SIN

For the wages of sin is death, but the free gift of God is eternal life in Christ Jesus our Lord.

ROMANS 6:23 NASB

There are consequences to every decision you make—good consequences and bad.

We certainly haven't earned eternal life, treasures in heaven, or even *anything* good at all. But God has given us a gift—a marvelous and undeserved gift. He sent His one and only Son to earth so that you could be saved from eternal suffering.

Jesus was born in a stable, despised and rejected by His own people, beaten and hung up to die on a rugged, splintery cross—even though He was sinless.

His sacrifice was no small undertaking. The devil didn't want Jesus to go through with His purpose. We can safely assume that he made it as hard as possible. But Jesus persevered through everything—because He loves the world and everyone in it (John 3:16). He extended His grace to *everyone* so we can have hope for a future of *everlasting* bliss where we can worship Him and live to the *absolute* fullest.

Father, I can't comprehend why You sent Jesus to die for me. I can't even begin to imagine what it was like. But I thank You with everything in me. In Jesus' name I pray. Amen.

DAY 104

EAT YOUR SPINACH!

He gives strength to the weary and
increases the power of the weak.
ISAIAH 40:29 NIV

Remember that old cartoon *Popeye the Sailor Man*? Popeye got his strength from eating spinach. Just one can. . .and *BAM!* His muscles popped out, and he could take out any of his enemies!

There are some days when we just don't feel very strong. We're spiritual wimps! But we don't have to stay that way. We can get strong in a hurry, and it doesn't even require eating a can of spinach or working out at the gym! All we have to do is pray and read our Bibles, and God builds our spiritual muscles! In other words, we get strong from the inside out.

Do you need to be strengthened today? Reach for your Bible and swallow down as much as you can! Write your favorite verses on pieces of paper and put them on your bathroom mirror. Memorize them and say them out loud. Before long, you'll be the strongest kid in town!

God, sometimes I get so tired! I don't even want to get out of bed in the morning. Thank You for giving me the strength to keep going, even when I really want to pull the covers over my head! Amen.

DAY 105

LEARN TO USE YOUR SWORD

Study to shew thyself approved unto God, a workman that needeth not to be ashamed, rightly dividing the word of truth.
2 Timothy 2:15 KJV

In Ephesians chapter 6, we're given the rundown of the amazing armor of God that is available to each and every believer. Isn't it cool to know that He's provided that for us? We have a way to stand firm every moment of every day.

But all too often, we hide behind our shield of faith because we're doing good just to survive the attack of the enemy, right? Guess what? God's given us a sword as well. And one we're supposed to be using.

The sword is the sword of the Spirit, which is the Word of God. We need to be studying the Word, hiding it in our hearts, so that we are ready to use it when God calls us to.

Why not try to commit a verse to memory each week? Or spend a couple extra minutes each day in a short Bible study. It's amazing what can be accomplished if you just give that little bit of extra to God each day.

Lord, I want to know You better, and I want to study Your Word so that I can be prepared to serve You better each day. I want to be a kingdom worker who has no need to be ashamed. Amen.

DAY 106

A HOPEFUL TOMORROW

Why are you cast down, O my soul? And why are you disquieted within me? Hope in God, for I shall yet praise Him for the help of His countenance.

PSALM 42:5 NKJV

On those days when you think there is nothing left to hope for, or when you feel down and out of sorts—maybe the day didn't turn out quite like you had hoped, or something you'd been wishing for fell through—remember to look to the one true hope. God will always give you new hope for a new day. After all, He gave each one of us the hope of eternal life in heaven with Him through His precious Son, our Savior. How can we have a down day when we think of that?

Dear God, I didn't make that A like I thought I would. And I was late for one of my classes. Now I have to do extra work, which means I won't get to spend time with my friends this afternoon. And tomorrow isn't looking good either—I feel so frustrated inside, mostly at myself. Please help me to get past this down feeling and be able to hope again like I did this morning. Amen.

DAY 107

DOES GOD LIKE ME?

"The LORD your God is with you, the Mighty Warrior who saves. He will take great delight in you; in his love he will no longer rebuke you, but will rejoice over you with singing."
ZEPHANIAH 3:17 NIV

You have probably heard a lot about how much God loves you. But *love* and *like* are a little different, right? Do you think God likes you?

Pastor and author Dr. Charles Stanley says this: "Yes, God likes me. He approves of me. He likes spending time with me. He likes being with me. He likes hearing me when I pray to Him, and He also enjoys talking with me through His Word. I believe He loves me. He knows I make mistakes, but He sees my heart and my desire to know Him better each day."

When you come to know Jesus as your Savior, God washes all your sins away and He sees you as the perfect kid you are. And you can say with confidence: "God likes me!" He rejoices over you, and the Bible says He even sings about you! You are liked. You are loved. You are His!

Dear God, wow! This makes my heart smile. Thank You for loving me. . .and for liking me just the way I am. Thank You for Jesus. Thank You for seeing me as perfect. I love You. I like You a whole lot too. Amen.

DAY 108

GOD'S YEARBOOK

See what great love the Father has lavished on us, that we should be called children of God!

1 John 3:1 NIV

Right before the end of every school year, the yearbook comes out. It's so much fun to flip through the pages and see all of your friends and find out who looks like they just climbed out of bed. And secretly, you're hoping you're not one of them.

Did you know God has His own yearbook too? If you turn to the year you were born, your face would be there. He picked that specific moment in time for your birth. He wanted to create you exactly at that moment so you could be right where you are today. He continually looks through His book and says to the angels, "Isn't My child wonderful? Look how smart and kind! This is My child, whom I love so much!"

God enjoys celebrating your life as much as you do. He takes pride in all you do and say. . .in your adventures and how you handle your challenges. He doesn't even care if you're the one in the school yearbook with bedhead. You are His treasure!

God, thank You for adding me to Your yearbook. I celebrate life with You and plan to make the best of today. May all I do and say be pleasing to You. Amen.

DAY 109

CHANGED PLANS

"For I know the plans I have for you," declares the LORD, "plans to prosper you and not to harm you, plans to give you hope and a future."
JEREMIAH 29:11 NIV

You're getting ready to leave for vacation. You've packed, fed your fish, and went to bed early so you could be up at the crack of dawn. Your sleeping bag is waiting by the back door. Your backpack has a flashlight, whistle, and crackers. You can't wait!

When you come downstairs the next morning, your parents tell you that something has come up—something that will keep you from your camping trip. Your grandmother has fallen and will need their help getting around for the next few weeks.

Instead of telling Mom and Dad that you understand, you stomp upstairs and throw your suitcase. Its contents spill out all over the floor. After putting all of your stuff back in order, you realize how horribly you've behaved. You ask your parents to take you to see your grandma—and after seeing her, you realize how much worse her fall could have been. And you give thanks to God for your family. . .and for plans that can change when others are in need.

God, I know You have plans for me—and Your plans aren't always my plans. And thanks for always understanding how I feel. Amen.

DAY 110

HERE'S HOW GOD SEES YOU

So Peter went over the side of the boat and walked on the water toward Jesus. But when he saw the strong wind and the waves, he was terrified and began to sink.

MATTHEW 14:29–30 NLT

VeggieTales creator Phil Vischer wrote a rhyming script called "A Snoodle's Tale" about a small, unique creature struggling with self-image. The snoodle feels unloved, unwanted, and unimportant because of his differences and because of the way others are treating him. Eventually, the snoodle's creator shows him a picture of what he really looks like and says, "Here's what you look like. Here's how I see you. Keep this in your pack, and you'll find it will free you from all of the pictures and all of the lies that others make up just to cut down your size."

When you take your eyes off of Jesus—just like Peter did—your self-image will begin to sink. You'll feel "less than." You'll feel unloved. Your differences will stick out. Your faith will grow weak. But when you keep your eyes on Christ, you'll begin to see yourself as He sees you! Perfect. Just right! Fully capable of serving Him and loving others too!

God, thank You for creating me just the way I am. Help me to keep my eyes on You so that I can see myself just as You see me. Amen.

DAY 111

WHERE'S YOUR PLAYBOOK?

All Scripture is inspired by God and is useful to teach us what is true and to make us realize what is wrong in our lives. It corrects us when we are wrong and teaches us to do what is right. God uses it to prepare and equip his people to do every good work.

2 TIMOTHY 3:16–17 NLT

If you have ever played a sport, you probably had to look at a rule book or game plan written by your coach. You studied the rules and learned how to play the game before you actually competed against another team. You then practiced what you learned, hoping to come out a winner.

We all want to be good at following Jesus and doing His will for our lives. And the best way to know how to play on His team is to read His rule book, the Bible. We can try to live as Christians on our own, but it's so much better with His Word to guide us. He is our coach, and we need to understand how He wants us to play the game.

Take a few minutes each day to read God's Word. It will guide you, play by play, to be the best at whatever He has planned for your life.

Jesus, thank You for being my coach. I know I can win in the game of life with Your encouraging guidebook. Amen.

DAY 112

GOD SAID IT, AND HE MEANT IT

He who began a good work in you will carry it on to completion until the day of Christ Jesus.

PHILIPPIANS 1:6 NIV

Do you ever worry that your salvation isn't real? Do you ever lay awake at night and worry that you've somehow disappointed God and He's turned away from you? Or maybe you worry that you never really surrendered your life to Him in the first place?

Sometimes, if you've grown up in a Christian home and you've been going to church for years and years, doubts can set in about whether or not your faith is real. Maybe you worry that you're only a Christian because of your parents. Maybe you worry that you're just not good enough.

But God's Word is true. He said that when you turned to Him, He gave you a new identity. You are a new person in Christ. He doesn't play games with that. He is not a liar. He promises that He'll finish the work He started in you. You can trust Him.

Dear God, please forgive me for doubting the finished work of Your salvation. Help me remember Your promises and know that I am a new creation in You, and no one can take that away from me. Amen.

DAY 113

MY LIFE GPS

For we are His workmanship, created in Christ Jesus for good works, which God prepared beforehand so that we would walk in them.

EPHESIANS 2:10 NASB

There are many decisions to be made in life. Who should you choose as your closest friends? What extracurricular activities should you participate in? And later in life, should you go to college? Where should you get a job? Will you ever get married?

Wouldn't it be awesome to have a life GPS to figure it all out? It could tell you which paths to avoid, which turns to make.

God is our GPS. He sees the whole picture. He knows every detail of every life. His children are referred to as His "workmanship" in the Bible. You were made to love Him and to do good works that only you can do!

Don't get overwhelmed because you don't have all the answers yet. Stay close to Jesus. He will let you know His plan for your life in His perfect timing.

Dear Father, thank You for creating me and making me a special "workmanship." Help me to listen to You and to obey You so that I can do the works You have created me to do. In Jesus' name, amen.

DAY 114

THE FAVOR FACTOR

Surely, Lord, you bless the righteous;
you surround them with your favor as with a shield.
Psalm 5:12 NIV

If your father were the principal of your school, wouldn't you expect special treatment? Wouldn't you expect him to allow you unlimited hall pass privileges? Wouldn't you expect all of the teachers to be nicer to you, simply because you were his kid? Of course you would, because you'd have favor with the guy in charge.

Well, guess what? You *do* have favor with the guy in charge—*God*! The Bible says that He has crowned your head with glory and honor and favor. He loves showering you with favor because He adores you.

You can walk in the favor of God all the time. Here's all you have to do. Start thanking God for His supernatural favor. Every morning before you head off to school, thank God that you have favor with your teachers, your principal, your coaches, your peers, your parents, and anyone else you might encounter. Then watch your life begin to change for the better. It's amazing, really. Once you start praising God for His supernatural favor, you'll begin to see more of it in your life. So start praying and praising, and enjoy the favor of God today!

Lord, thank You for Your favor. Amen.

DAY 115

A TRUE FRIEND WILL TELL YOU THE TRUTH

"No longer do I call you servants, for the servant does not know what his master is doing; but I have called you friends, for all that I have heard from my Father I have made known to you."
JOHN 15:15 ESV

If I asked you to describe your best friend, how would you do it? What qualities about him or her do you like best?

When I think about one of my very best friends, one of the things I love is that she will always tell me the truth. If I am cranky and have a bad attitude, she may tell me that I need to trust God. When I need to hear something from the Bible to help me with my life, she is honest. That's one of the things I love about her: she tells me the truth in love.

Jesus is a best friend who will tell you the truth. His truth will protect you and guide you. He will never lie to you.

If you want a best friend who will tell you the truth and help you if you are going the wrong way, Jesus is this kind of friend. He loves you more than anyone can. Just open your heart to hear Him.

Lord, thank You that You want to help me in every area of my life. I know that You will never lead me in a way that will hurt me. There is no one more faithful. Amen.

DAY 116

WHICH ROAD SHOULD I TAKE?

"I say this because I know what I am planning for you," says the LORD. "I have good plans for you, not plans to hurt you. I will give you hope and a good future."

JEREMIAH 29:11 NCV

If you've ever been on a road trip, you know what it's like to follow a map. Sometimes we come to a fork in the road and don't know which way to go. If we don't pay attention to the map, we can get lost in a hurry!

Did you know that God has a spiritual road map for your life? The Bible gives you all the directions you need. When you come to a fork in the road—and you don't know which way to take—His Word will give you answers. And remember, you can always pray and ask Him to guide you if you're really feeling lost. He will! Just listen closely to His still, small voice. He wants to show you the correct road, one that will lead you to a place of safety and peace.

God, I don't always know which road to choose or which direction to go. When I feel mixed up and lost, You always guide me. Thank You for helping me choose the right road! Amen.

DAY 117

HAPPINESS VS. JOY

But let all who take refuge in you rejoice; let them sing joyful praises forever. Spread your protection over them, that all who love your name may be filled with joy.
PSALM 5:11 NLT

Most children have learned the popular song "If You're Happy and You Know It." Remember clapping your hands, stomping your feet, or nodding your head along with the song to show your happiness?

But what about times when you don't feel happy? Life certainly has its fair share of sad days, doesn't it?

The great thing about being a child of God is that instead of just happiness, which is temporary, you have permanent joy in your heart. A relationship with Jesus Christ brings a peace that non-Christians simply don't have access to, no matter how hard they may look for it. It's a peace found only in Christ, and it comes with a bonus gift of joy!

Even on your most difficult days, spend some time in prayer or worshipping the Lord, and you will feel that deep-down joy well up in your heart. Try it!

Thank You, God, for planting joy deep down in my heart! May others be pointed to You when they see my joy bubbling up, even in hard times. Amen.

DAY 118

A LOVED CHILD OF GOD

For you are all children of God through faith in Christ Jesus. And all who have been united with Christ in baptism have put on Christ, like putting on new clothes. There is no longer Jew or Gentile, slave or free, male and female. For you are all one in Christ Jesus.

Galatians 3:26–28 NLT

God made you, and He loves you unconditionally. It's been said that "God is no respecter of persons." And that simply means that we are all equal in His sight. He loves you just as much as He loves your friend, your mom, and your pastor. Nothing you do could make Him love you more. And nothing you do could make Him love you less. We are children of God because of what Jesus Christ did for us on the cross.

When you start feeling down, remember how much God loves you. The Bible tells us that His love is unfailing! Psalm 13:5 (NIV) says, "But I trust in your unfailing love; my heart rejoices in your salvation." That's a good verse to memorize for those days when you're feeling bad about yourself. Never forget that you're a child of God and you're loved!

God, I sometimes forget who I am. Help me to remember that I am Your child and that You love me more than anyone else ever will. I rejoice in You! Amen.

DAY 119

DUMPY DAYS

The Lord hath comforted his people.
Isaiah 49:13 KJV

For every cheerful day you have, there's bound to be a dumpy one waiting just around the corner. A day when everything is boring, every*one* is annoying, and you feel like shouting, "Leave me alone!"

God knows all about those kinds of days. As the Father of many children, He's watched a lot of kids grow up. You're not the first to sulk over something trivial or to cry. . ."just because." Thankfully, as God's child, you have a great advantage. You can climb into the lap of the great comforter and let it all out on His big shoulder.

The next time you're in a foul mood that you can't seem to snap out of, take some time to pray. Sneak away to a private place where you can talk to God out loud, without being interrupted or overheard. Tell Him what's troubling you, and ask Him to fill you with His comfort. You'll be amazed at how much better you feel.

Lord, I'm so glad that You understand me even when I don't understand myself. Remind me of that when I'm feeling moody and unhappy, and help me cast my cares on You. Amen.

DAY 120

PROMISES KEPT

The believer replied, "Every promise of God proves true; he protects everyone who runs to him for help."
PROVERBS 30:5 MSG

Do you ever find it hard to keep promises? Do you think most people do? What about God? Do you wonder about the promises He made to His children? Are you afraid that someday He won't be there for you? If so, reread the verse above. God keeps His promises *always*. He cannot break them any more than He can lie. He is God, and He never breaks His Word. His promises are true for those who lived long ago, all the way up to the present, and even into the future. That means they are for you and your children and even your children's children! They are for everyone who believes in Him. Trust Him. Run to Him!

Dear God, please help me to remember that You always keep your promises, that You will guide and protect me. Please help me to keep my promises, even when it's hard to do. And help me remember to run to You for help every time I need it. Amen.

DAY 121

BETTER THAN HAPPY

In him our hearts rejoice, for we trust in his holy name.
PSALM 33:21 NIV

Being a child of God has its perks. One of them is joy. We're talking full-out JOY that has nothing to do with how well you're doing in school, whether you have a best friend, or if you got the part you wanted in the school play. It's a joy that doesn't depend on everything going your way.

Being a Christian doesn't mean that your life will never have any challenges. In fact, Jesus made it clear that you can expect some troubles in this life. But you don't have to worry because He HAS overcome the world (John 16:33).

When things seem to be out of control, just know that God is at work in ways you can't see. You don't have to be happy about the troubles in your life, but trusting God can give you joy in spite of them.

Dear God, thank You for the joy that comes from knowing You. Sometimes my life doesn't go the way I'd like it to, but I know that I can trust You to help me through even the toughest times. Thank You that You are always with me and You give me joy. Amen.

DAY 122

THE FINGERPRINTS OF GOD

For You formed my inward parts;
You wove me in my mother's womb.
PSALM 139:13 NASB

When you look in the mirror, what do you see? Messy hair, imperfect skin, big ears?

Or do you see strands of hair numbered by God, a heart loved by the Savior, eyes to see His creation, and skin covered in the Father's fingerprints?

You're not only God's uniquely made child, but you're created in His image (Genesis 1:27)!

God doesn't make mistakes. "God saw *all* that He had made, and behold, it was *very* good" (Genesis 1:31 NASB, emphasis added).

You're not a piece of trash to be thrown into the garbage. You're not a blunder or a mess-up. You're a child of the Most High God (Romans 8:15–16)! He loves you (John 3:16; Romans 5:8; Ephesians 2:4–5), and He has plans for you (Ephesians 2:10).

Lord, thank You for creating me as I am. Thank You for loving me no matter how sinful I am or how ugly I may feel. Thanks for Your unending and magnificent love. In Jesus' name I pray. Amen.

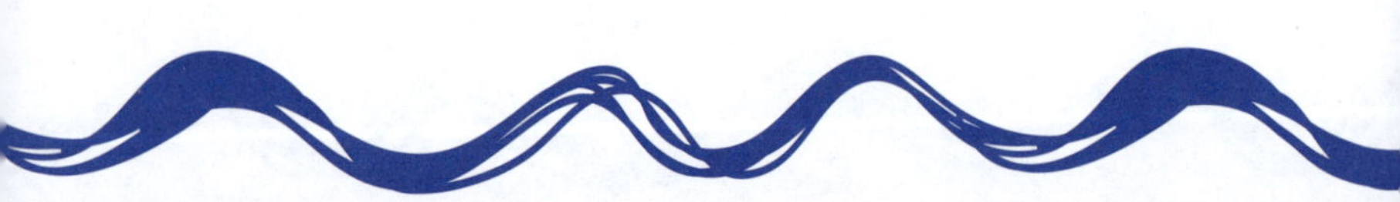

DAY 123

DOWN IN THE DUMPS

Be full of joy always because you belong to the Lord. Again I say, be full of joy!
PHILIPPIANS 4:4 NLV

When you've scored poorly on a test, gotten into a fight with a friend, or disappointed a parent, it can be really hard to dig yourself out of the dumps. The world seems like it's been turned upside down, and everything and everyone is against you.

There is only one way out of this hole. God has given you the incredible ability to be joyful at all times. The key is to have faith in knowing you are His. God is watching over you; He will forgive your sins; and He has prepared a special place for you in heaven. What amazing things to be joyful about! If you trust God to do these things for you, He can help you climb out of the pit and view the day with fresh eyes and a happy heart.

God, thank You for giving me so much to be joyful about. Help me to turn my eyes away from earthly troubles when they bring me down and to instead trust in You to rescue me. Amen.

DAY 124

WHAT MAKES YOU STUMBLE?

"Jeremiah, say to the people, 'This is what the Lord says: "When people fall down, don't they get up again? When they discover they're on the wrong road, don't they turn back?" ' "

Jeremiah 8:4 NLT

Did you know you can hurt yourself just as much by tripping on a stone as you can by trying to jump over a big rock? We often think that the little stone can't bother us much—that the big rock is the thing to avoid. But the little stones are sometimes hidden and can be even more dangerous. When we're just walking along, not really watching our step, those little stones can really trip us up.

That's the way it is when we try to make good choices. We worry about the big stuff—the things we know for sure are not right for us. But if we don't pay attention to the "little" bad choices we make, pretty soon they will become mountains that block our view of God.

Always choose well in the little things, and the big decisions will be easier.

Dear Lord, help me to be more careful of little stones as I walk the path of life. I want to make the right small decisions and be ready for the big ones. Thank You for guiding me each step of the way. Amen.

DAY 125

IN THE MIDDLE OF THE MESS

Can anything ever separate us from Christ's love?
Does it mean he no longer loves us if we have trouble
or calamity, or are persecuted, or hungry, or destitute,
or in danger, or threatened with death?
Romans 8:35 NLT

Think about those times when you've asked yourself, "How in the world did this happen to me? I've done everything right, and I still ended up hurt and disappointed." Sometimes life just isn't fair. Bad things can and do happen to good people. It started way back when Adam and Eve were tempted in the Garden of Eden. They introduced sin into the world and, from that point on, everything changed. God had a choice at that point. He could have said, "I've had enough of these people I created! I'm walking away!" But He chose a different route and stuck with us. Why? Because He loved us then, and He still loves us today.

So when bad stuff happens, God has already made His choice to stick with you; but you have to make the choice to stick with Him. Don't blame Him for what Satan has done to our world. Instead choose to look for the ways He loves you. He's there somewhere. . . just reach out to Him.

God, I don't understand why some things happen, but I promise to look for Your love in the middle of the messes. Amen.

DAY 126

DON'T BELIEVE THE BULLY

Out of my distress I called on the LORD; the LORD answered me and set me free. The LORD is on my side; I will not fear. What can man do to me?

PSALM 118:5–6 ESV

Eleanor Roosevelt said, "No one can make you feel inferior without your consent." That means it's your choice whether or not you allow someone else to make you feel like you don't matter. That person might think he or she is better than you, but it won't really make a difference unless you actually start believing it yourself.

Bullies like to act like they're better than everyone else. But remember this the next time you come across a bully: hurting people hurt people. More often than not, a bully is just a kid (or even a grown-up) who has had a lot of hurts in his or her life and who hasn't yet experienced the love of Jesus. You might not be the one to give them the help they need, but you can pray for them whenever they come to mind.

Dear God, there is a bully in my life that really bothers me and makes everyone else feel bad. Please help. This person must be hurting, and I pray that the bully will come to know You as Savior. Amen.

DAY 127

MY LORD KNOWS ME BETTER THAN I KNOW MYSELF

Even before there is a word on my tongue,
behold, O Lord, You know it all.
Psalm 139:4 NASB

Did you ever long for a best friend who knew you so well that they could finish your thoughts or sentences? Someone who understood when you were sad, without you even having to say a word? Someone who would always be there to comfort you, no matter how badly you treated them? A friend like that is a treasure indeed.

You have a friend like that waiting for you. God knows everything about you. The good, the bad, and even the ugly. But you know what? He loves you, flaws and all. He won't ever turn His back on you; He'll always be there. He's there in the happiest times and in the saddest. When you're all alone, and when you're surrounded by people. And He wants you to know that you can talk to Him anytime you want. He'll never be too busy for you.

God, thank You for being my best friend.
Even when others fail me, You'll always be there.
Help me to be Your light to others. Amen.

DAY 128

TAKE A DEEP BREATH!

Though you have made me see troubles, many and bitter, you will restore my life again; from the depths of the earth you will again bring me up.

Psalm 71:20 NIV

What a terrible day! You missed five words on your spelling test. You sang off-key in music class, and the girl beside you laughed. When you were drawing with your colored pencils in art class, three of them broke. You lost your lunch money—and you have no idea where. You left your math homework at home. And, as if that wasn't enough. . .on the walk home from school, your backpack strap snapped, sending your books sailing because you hadn't zipped it shut! Whew!

Take a deep breath. God made you. He wants to fill your heart with joy. He knows everyone will have a bad day from time to time. Just remember that He made you with power, love, and a sound mind. Then thank Him for it!

God made you in His image. And God doesn't make mistakes.

Lord, I'm so happy You made me. I know Your love is eternal. Even when I have a bad day, Your guidance is important to me. Tomorrow is a new day. Thank You for fresh starts! Amen.

DAY 129

FAKE IT TILL YOU MAKE IT

Create in me a clean heart, O God,
and renew a steadfast spirit within me.
PSALM 51:10 NASB

You know the type. They pretend to be one person, act like someone completely different, but deep down they're nothing like either of those people. Fakers, right?

It's easy to pretend to be someone else for a short while. You carefully choose every single word and action, but it will never last. You can never keep up with the charade, because even if you try to hide from your true self, eventually it will come out.

God wants nothing more from you than for you to be authentically, truly Christlike. That doesn't mean you can be perfect; no one is. But it does mean that you strive for honoring Christ with your words and your actions. God can help you do that authentically.

If you want to be pure and righteous on the outside, you need to be pure and righteous on the inside. That's what it means to be true to yourself and honor God.

Dear God, please forgive me for the things I do that are not like Jesus. Help me walk in truth today and always. Amen.

DAY 130

LOVE ONE ANOTHER

"So now I am giving you a new commandment: Love each other. Just as I have loved you, you should love each other. Your love for one another will prove to the world that you are my disciples."
JOHN 13:34–35 NLT

Jesus gave the disciples a command at His last supper with them. He told them to love one another. It sounds so simple; yet it isn't always an easy command to follow. He told the disciples that their love for one another would prove to the world that they were His followers.

The same command holds true for us today: *Love one another.* What does this look like in your life? Loving your parents includes treating them with respect and obeying them. Loving your brothers and sisters means putting them first and not always fighting for your own interests. Loving your classmates calls for going the extra mile. Treat others with kindness—*always*.

But what if someone doesn't treat you in a loving manner? What a great opportunity for your reaction to stand out! You will be known as a Christian when you show love, just as the Savior first loved you.

Jesus, I want to be loving, but often I fail. It's so hard to put others before myself. Help me, Lord. Amen.

DAY 131

DO YOU FEEL INADEQUATE?

"So do not fear, for I am with you; do not be dismayed,
for I am your God. I will strengthen you and help you;
I will uphold you with my righteous right hand."
Isaiah 41:10 NIV

Has God placed a dream in your heart? When you think about your dream, do you feel excited? Or do you feel like you can't accomplish it? If you feel like you are unable, be encouraged! It's actually great that you know you can't do it all on your own because then you know that you have to lean on God to help you. Then, when you succeed, He will get the credit. This is why God likes to use people who can't do stuff in their own strength. He likes to give His strength to people who can't accomplish their dreams on their own.

Lord, thank You that You give me strength to accomplish the dreams You have for me. Thank You that I don't have to be perfect; You will help me. I am excited about the strength You will give me to accomplish Your plans for my life. Amen.

DAY 132

READY AND WAITING

Don't worry about anything; instead, pray about everything. Tell God what you need, and thank him for all he has done.

Philippians 4:6 NLT

Have you ever tried to get the attention of someone who has ear buds in their ears? You can yell and holler, but if they're busy listening to something else, they're just not going to hear you.

There are very few people who we can name who will listen to us anytime. And even if they're willing, they may be on a telephone call or be unavailable at some point.

But God isn't like that. He is ready to listen anytime. At school, before an exam. On the bus, on the way home from school after a hard day. At 3:00 a.m., when you just can't sleep. The instruction we have is to not worry, but rather pray. You can run to a friend, to your mom, or to someone else for help, but first take it to God. He will hear you and will give you what you need.

Dear heavenly Father, thank You for listening to me right now and for always being ready to listen. You're never too busy or too distracted to give me Your attention. Thank You for all You have done. Amen.

DAY 133

HELLO, GOD. . . ARE YOU THERE?

The Lord is near to all who call on Him, to all who call on Him in truth. He will fill the desire of those who fear Him. He will also hear their cry and will save them.

Psalm 145:18–19 NLV

Have you ever called someone on the phone and they didn't answer? Maybe you left a message, but they didn't return your call? Isn't it cool to know that God always answers when you call? In fact, He's waiting on your call right now! You don't even have to have a phone to talk to Him. All you have to do is just open up and share your heart. You don't need a special place or a special time. He's there, around the clock!

Not only does the Lord hear you, but He cares about what you're telling Him. He's on your side. So next time you really wish someone would listen to you, forget about calling a friend on the phone. Call on the best friend of all, the one who's always there when You need Him. He can't wait to hear from you! C'mon, give Him a call! What are you waiting for?

God, I'm so glad You hear my prayers!
You're always there for me, ready to listen.
Thank You for caring so much about me. Amen.

DAY 134

COURAGEOUS

Be strong, and let your heart take courage,
all you who wait for the Lord!
Psalm 31:24 ESV

What are you most afraid of? The first day of school? Being the new kid? Being the last one picked for the kickball team? Maybe you're nervous about a big test coming up. There are many things in this life that can make us feel anxious, that can make us want to pull the covers over our heads and never come out.

But God doesn't want us to feel afraid. When we place our trust in Him, He gives us courage. No matter what we may face, God wants to face it with us. He will never leave us alone, and if we ask Him to help us, He will. We just have to hold our heads high and trust Him.

Sometimes He helps us by giving us wisdom for how to handle a situation. If something is truly dangerous, He may give us courage to tell a trusted teacher or other adult. If something is just scary, like making new friends, He might give us courage to be the first one to reach out in friendship. Whatever we face, God will never leave us to face it alone.

Dear Father, thank You for giving me courage
to face whatever may come. Amen.

DAY 135

DO YOU REALLY LOVE GOD?

If anyone boasts, "I love God," and goes right on hating his brother or sister, thinking nothing of it, he is a liar. If he won't love the person he can see, how can he love the God he can't see? The command we have from Christ is blunt: Loving God includes loving people. You've got to love both.

1 JOHN 4:20–21 MSG

These are some strong words in the book of First John. Basically, if you say you love God and act with hatred toward another kid at school, or a bully, or a family member—*or anyone at all*—the Bible says you can't possibly love God. You may be angry at people, but to truly hate someone else is not possible for someone who has Jesus in their heart.

Are you struggling to be nice to someone else? Ask God for help. Are you angry with a certain person pretty much all the time? Ask God to forgive you for your anger and help you to see that person just as He sees them.

God, please forgive me for my anger. I don't want to hate people. I want to see the best in them—just as You see them. But there are some people who really get on my nerves. Help me to be nicer. Show me how to act with kindness in my heart. Amen.

DAY 136

SAY WHAT?

"Love your enemies, do good to those who hate you, bless those who curse you, pray for those who mistreat you."
LUKE 6:27–28 NIV

"The way you laugh is embarrassing!" yells Macy, the girl who always finds something ugly to say about you. "Seriously, I would never laugh if I sounded like that."

You try to ignore her, but she keeps coming at you.

You're so mad you could just, just. . .pray for her.

Say what?

I know. It seems totally weird to pray for someone who constantly hurts your feelings and enjoys being mean to you. But it's what Jesus says to do. In His Word, He says to pray for your enemies. He doesn't say you have to like it, but He does say you have to do it.

So the next time someone acts ugly toward you, don't fight back. Instead, pray for that person. You probably won't feel like praying at that very moment, but do it anyway. You may have to do it through gritted teeth; but if you'll do your part, God will do His. He may not change your enemy's actions, but He will change the way you feel about that person. So determine today to pray—especially for your enemies!

God, please help me to love my enemies the same way You do. Amen.

DAY 137

ALL WRAPPED UP

"God blesses those who mourn, for they will be comforted."
MATTHEW 5:4 NLT

Don't you just love a fluffy blanket? Especially on a cold winter night in front of the TV. Add a glass of milk and some warm chocolate chip cookies, and you are feeling good. Comfort. . .everyone savors the feeling.

There are many things in the world that make us feel frightened or angry. We might be mixed up and not know where to turn. All we really want is to feel better. So we search for someone or something to make that happen. Maybe it's a friend's voice on the phone, a hug from Mom, or your favorite music. . .whatever makes you feel safe and secure.

We need even more comfort when we are sad. When someone dies or a bad thing happens, God is ready to give us peace like a warm fuzzy blanket. He comforts us like no one or nothing else can. He wants His children to come to Him and snuggle up close.

The next time you need comfort, run to the heavenly Father and let Him wrap you up in His loving embrace.

Dear God, there are times when I need a hug from You. Thank You for sending Your comfort just when I need it most. Help me to be a comfort to others too. Amen.

DAY 138

DREAMING OF PARADISE

"What no eye has seen, nor ear heard, nor the heart of man imagined, what God has prepared for those who love him."
1 Corinthians 2:9 ESV

What do you think heaven looks like? A fluffy place filled with harp-playing angels or a lush garden with flowers and waterfalls? How about a golden city with pearly gates somewhere in the clouds? Maybe none of those images fit your idea of heaven. That's okay. Dream away! Make it as wonderful as you can imagine. Because no matter how awesome you paint it, the real thing will be a million times better.

The human mind is limited to the things of this earth. . .and this life. God's imagination goes far beyond that. His creating power has no limits. So when the Bible says that heaven will be a paradise, you can be certain that it's something you don't want to miss out on.

God has promised heaven to those that love and serve Him. Are you ready to go there? Now would be a great time to search your heart and make sure.

Lord, I don't know what heaven will be like, but I know I want to spend eternity there. Guide me through this life, and prepare me to meet You someday. Amen.

DAY 139

IS ANYONE THERE?

The Lord hears when I call to Him.
Psalm 4:3 nasb

It can be so frustrating to call someone and not be able to reach them. The line rings and rings, and you keep hoping for them to pick it up. You leave a message. You send a text. And you still can't reach them. Wouldn't it be nice if everyone were available exactly when we needed them? But in our all-too-busy world, that doesn't happen often. We have to leave messages and wait for the person to call us back.

With God, though, He's always available. Day or night. Twenty-four hours, every day of the year. He never takes a vacation. And you can rest assured that He always hears us. The Bible is full of verses that back that up. He made you, He cares about you, and the coolest part? He's just waiting for you to call on Him. He longs to hear from you.

So next time you're struggling, call your heavenly Father. He'll *always* be there with a listening ear.

God, thank You so much that You are always with me. Thank You for always being right there, waiting to answer my call. Thank You for always listening. And remind me to keep the communication lines open all day. Amen.

DAY 140

EN GARDE! (ON YOUR GUARD!)

I have hidden your word in my heart that I might not sin against you. . . . I delight in your decrees; I will not neglect your word.
Psalm 119:11, 16 NIV

You? In a fight? You would never! . . . But you are. You may not realize it, but you ARE in a fight. It's not a physical fight. It's spiritual (Ephesians 6:12). And to win, you need to be really good at using the sword of the Spirit—the Word of God (Ephesians 6:11).

Of all the pieces of armor listed in Ephesians 6, only one is for fighting—the Word of God. But like any weapon, you have to know something about it to be able to use it. A Bible that sits on the shelf gathering dust is a useless weapon.

Reading God's Word daily is like practicing your fighting skills. As you hide His Word in your heart, you'll find yourself growing stronger in your faith. When the enemy tries to tempt you, you'll have no trouble holding him off because your sword of the Spirit will be ready. *En garde!*

Dear God, I am so thankful that You have given me Your Word as a powerful weapon. Help me to learn to use it effectively. Help me to hide it in my heart so that I will not sin against You. Amen.

DAY 141

A WHOLE PILE OF BIRTHDAY PRESENTS

For you created my inmost being;
you knit me together in my mother's womb.
Psalm 139:13 NIV

Have you ever felt like nobody really understands you or even "sees" the real you? Everybody feels that way sometimes. When a friend takes the time to know who you are, it's better than a whole pile of birthday presents. God is that friend who "sees" you and "knows" you because He's the one who made you—the one who formed you.

God knows your happiest day and your darkest fear. The things that make you cry when you're all alone or the things that make you smile or laugh out loud. He knows your innermost secrets and your biggest dreams. He even knows your favorite flavor of ice cream with all your favorite toppings.

God not only understands you, but He wants you to be the very best version of you. That takes seeing and knowing to a whole new level!

Lord, thank You that You know me inside and out. Thank You for loving me enough to help me become all that You created me to be. Amen.

DAY 142

A SNEAK PEEK

You are my hiding place and my shield; I hope in your word.
PSALM 119:114 ESV

If you haven't noticed, the Bible is gigantic. If you attempt to read it, the thin pages and tiny print may be discouraging. There are a lot of numbers and hard-to-pronounce names. You might even be wondering if the Bible could in any way relate to your life.

God's Word may seem like a long, boring, and confusing book, but it really is God reaching out and speaking to you in your everyday language. In the pages of the Bible, the Creator of the universe allows you a sneak peek into His intimate interactions with humanity. He chose to give you a book that would help guide you and give you insight into His character. And best of all, you get to read about the life of His Son, Jesus, who walked the earth, healed the sick, embraced children, and loves you unconditionally.

So when the Bible begins to seem dull or unimportant, just remember that it is God desiring to comfort, teach, and connect with you through His words.

God, thank You for giving me a sneak peek into Your character and promises. Please help me learn how to study and understand Your Word. Amen.

DAY 143

EVEN WHAT YOU DON'T SAY

For God is greater than our worried hearts and knows more about us than we do ourselves.

1 John 3:20 MSG

You might tell your best friend *most* of what is going on in your life, but there are probably things you don't tell him or her. Really, aren't there things you couldn't talk about, even if you tried? How do you tell your best friend about that shaky feeling you have—when you can't seem to pinpoint what is causing you to feel so out of place? How do you describe the fact that your day seems off and nothing feels secure, but on the surface everything looks just fine? Feelings are not always easy to talk about until you figure out where they are coming from.

God knows everything about you—including all your features and characteristics *and* what you can't say out loud. He spent the entire time you were in your mother's womb molding and shaping you, right down to the number of hairs on your head. It's more than okay for you to sit down with Him and say, "Look, God, I feel insecure and I don't know why. Can You show me?" Trust the one who made you to help you sort it out.

God, thank You for understanding who I am. I'm grateful I can come to You when I don't have answers. Amen.

DAY 144

DON'T BE GREEDY, HELP THE NEEDY!

Use your hands for good hard work, and then give generously to others in need.
Ephesians 4:28 NLT

Jesus wants us to help other people who are in need. This is easy to forget because you may live in a place that doesn't have a lot of really poor people—people who don't have anything to eat and who sleep on the streets. We don't see those people on a daily basis. But there are still very real needs that people have in your community.

And since it is so easy to forget about the needy, we get caught up in the things we want that we don't have. New shoes. A better phone. Better clothes. Having nice things is okay, but if they are the most important thing in your life, that's called greed. The Bible says in Luke 12:15 (NIV): "Watch out! Be on your guard against all kinds of greed; life does not consist in an abundance of possessions."

Christmas is a time where churches sponsor clothing and food drives, and that's wonderful. But those same people have needs all year long. Call your church and find out how you can help the needy in your community today.

Dear God, please give me Your eyes to see the needs in my community. Amen.

DAY 145

TO GROW OR NOT TO GROW?

In this you greatly rejoice, even though now for a little while, if necessary, you have been distressed by various trials, so that the proof of your faith, being more precious than gold which is perishable, even though tested by fire, may be found to result in praise and glory and honor at the revelation of Jesus Christ.

1 PETER 1:6–7 NASB

Are there times when you get so overwhelmed that persevering just doesn't seem possible? There's no easy way out. . . . You can't give the mouse a click to turn off the trouble and walk away from your problems.

Why does God allow you to go through hard things? Why doesn't He just stop the painful things from happening?

First Peter 1:6–7 gives an answer: the Lord loves you, dear one. He is testing your faith, which is more precious than gold, so that it may result in praise at the revelation of Jesus.

You're not alone in the hard times (see 1 Peter 5:8–10; Matthew 28:20; 1 Corinthians 10:13). Trust Him. He knows what He's doing.

God, thank You for difficulties and hard situations. I know that You're using them to help me grow. I really want to learn, Lord. And if the way to do that is by persevering in the hard times, then I'll trust You and "press on toward the goal for the prize" (Philippians 3:14 NASB). In Jesus' name I pray. Amen.

DAY 146

HE LOVES ME ANYWAY

Jesus replied, "Anyone who loves me will obey my teaching. My Father will love them, and we will come to them and make our home with them."

John 14:23 niv

You gather around the kitchen table with your family. Dad opens his Bible and reads the Ten Commandments. He reminds you to always obey God's rules. But you wonder, *What if I don't obey them? Will God stop loving me?*

That night, you go to your room. You read over the Ten Commandments again. You get on your knees and say your prayers. Then you snuggle up in bed, finding comfort in knowing and trusting that the heavenly Father loves you—*no matter what!*

You will always try your best to obey God's commandments, which is just what He wants you to do. But if you ever fail, He will love you anyway. And He'll gently guide you back to His embrace. Oh how He loves you!

God, thank You for loving me. No matter what, Your love is all-forgiving and Your Word is unfailing. Amen.

DAY 147

WHO KNOWS YOU BEST?

"And he pays even greater attention to you, down to the last detail—even numbering the hairs on your head! So don't be intimidated by all this bully talk. You're worth more than a million canaries."

LUKE 12:7 MSG

Are you ever amazed at how well your parents know you? They seem to know what you think or what you are about to say before the words leave your mouth. Well, God knows you even better. He made you—He even knew you before you were born! And when the unexpected happens, always remember that the same God who knows you so well is also going to take care of you. You are His child, and He will see you through everything that comes your way.

Dear God, please help me to always remember that You know everything that happens to me—good or bad. And You will protect me and guide me. Please remind me that You know what is going to happen to me even before it ever does. And that You know how to help me when I don't know how to help myself. Thank You for always taking care of me, Father. Amen.

DAY 148

ON HIS MIND

What is man that You are mindful of him,
and the son of man that You visit him?
PSALM 8:4 NKJV

Do you have big plans this weekend? Is there a big event coming up or something exciting that you've been planning for a while? There are always things going on, filling your mind with details, anticipation, and anxiety. Your thoughts are revealed in the words you say, and they both show the condition of your heart.

That same thing is true for God. He has thoughts, and those thoughts come out through His words, and His thoughts and words reveal the condition of His heart. The cool thing is that God's thoughts are constantly about you and what's best for you. He is focused on protecting you, guiding you, providing for you. . .and loving you. He thinks about you all the time. And He talks about you too. In fact, the Bible is His Word to you.

Do you think about Him? Today, let your thoughts be centered on the one who loves you most. Let your words reveal your thoughts as you talk to other people about Him. Those thoughts and words reveal the true condition of your heart.

Dear God, please help me to control my thoughts today and let them be about You. Help me remember to speak truth to others and to keep my heart turned toward You. Amen.

DAY 149

FORGIVENESS

But God showed his great love for us by sending Christ to die for us while we were still sinners.
Romans 5:8 NLT

One of the greatest things about God is that He knows all of our flaws, and yet He loves us unconditionally. Yep, God loves you when you mess up or make a mistake. And there is nothing—*absolutely nothing!*—you can do to cause Him to stop loving you.

The Bible says that God sent His Son, Jesus, to die for us *while we were still sinners*. He didn't wait for us to clean up our act. He sent Jesus to pay the price for our sins. He knows us, and He loves us just the way we are.

Think about the grace that God pours out on you as He forgives your sins. Do you show grace to other people when they make mistakes? One way that others can see God in you is through forgiveness. Choose to forgive today!

God, thank You for Your forgiveness. Help me to be forgiving too. Amen.

DAY 150

HONOR YOUR PARENTS

Honour thy father and thy mother, as the Lord thy God hath commanded thee; that thy days may be prolonged, and that it may go well with thee, in the land which the Lord thy God giveth thee.

Deuteronomy 5:16 KJV

Maybe your parents are totally great. Yours is the house where all the kids want to spend their time. On the other hand, maybe you feel like your parents are trying to rule your life. Or it could be that your mom and dad fall somewhere in the middle.

The truth is that no parent is completely perfect. Parents are human just like you are. For the most part they are trying to help you become a mature young person. Even though you might not like everything they say or do, you must remember that God has a reason for putting you together. He expects you to honor your parents—to respect and obey them.

When things go well, thank God. If you are struggling, turn your situation over to God. You might be surprised to discover that it's you who needs to change.

Above all, honor your parents, and enjoy God's blessings that follow.

Heavenly Father, thank You for my parents. While I'm not perfect and neither are they, You have set us in this family—together—for Your purpose. Help me to obey and to show them honor. Amen.

DAY 151

LIVE TO GIVE!

"Love your neighbor as yourself."
LEVITICUS 19:18 NIV

Esther Kim and Kay Poe made national news in 2000—not for their great Tae Kwon Do skills, but for their strong friendship. Esther, then twenty, and Kay, then eighteen, had been best friends and competitors in Tae Kwon Do since they were very young. When the two buddies discovered they would have to fight each other for the last remaining spot on the 2000 US Olympic team, they dreaded the match.

Then the unexpected happened. Kay dislocated her kneecap just before the finals and could hardly stand for the final match against her best friend. Moments before the two friends were supposed to compete, Esther forfeited the fight so that her best friend could claim the final spot on the Olympic team.

Esther may not have earned a spot on the Olympic team that year, but she gained recognition as a champion of love. The Bible tells us that love is not selfish or self-seeking, but that's one of those verses that is much easier to read than live. Ask God to help you put others' needs above your own. Look for ways to be a better friend. Live the love!

God, please help me to live to give, and help me to love my friends the way You love me. Amen.

DAY 152

INTEGRITY AND TRUTH

Jesus said to the people who believed in him, "You are truly my disciples if you remain faithful to my teachings. And you will know the truth, and the truth will set you free."
John 8:31–32 NLT

Since you were little, you've always been reminded to tell the truth, right? But did you know that telling the truth is not just about obedience?

Jesus is actually the source of all truth. And knowing Him—knowing about *real* truth—will set you free. When you know true freedom in Christ, you can live a life based on honesty and integrity. Integrity is knowing the right thing to do and doing it, even when nobody else is looking.

Mark Twain said, "Always tell the truth. That way, you don't have to remember what you said." When you make daily choices that honor God, such as being honest and trustworthy, you don't have to ever worry about being caught in a lie. And that's a freeing feeling!

Jesus, help me to be faithful to Your Word. Thanks for teaching me right from wrong. Help me to make wise choices, even when nobody is looking. I know You are always looking, and I want to honor You with my life. Amen.

DAY 153

WHAT TO WEAR

"And why do you worry about clothes? See how the flowers of the field grow. They do not labor or spin. Yet I tell you that not even Solomon in all his splendor was dressed like one of these."

MATTHEW 6:28–29 NIV

Do you ever worry about whether or not your clothes measure up to your friends' clothes or if your stuff is as cool as theirs?

If you do, that's normal. We all think about that stuff sometimes. And the great thing is, God understands how we feel. He wants us to have everything we need, and He will often find cool ways to see that we get them.

Whether it's through hand-me-downs, or bargain finds at a thrift store, or through parents who have the money to buy us brand-new things, God loves to take care of us. And He loves to see us smile because we feel good about ourselves.

Oh, He may not always give us every single thing we want. But He knows what we need, and He will provide it, if we just ask Him and trust Him with the results.

Dear Father, thank You for providing me with everything I need. Help me to appreciate the things You provide. Amen.

DAY 154

HEAVENLY LANGUAGE

Sound speech, that cannot be condemned.
TITUS 2:8 KJV

Can you tell a Hispanic accent from a British one? A French from an American? How about a Southern accent versus one from the Midwest? The difference in speech is pretty remarkable, isn't it? But most remarkable of all is the difference between a Christian accent and a worldly one.

A true child of God glorifies their Creator in every aspect of their life. . .including the way they talk! The speech of the world is laden with four-letter words and off-color humor. And the worst part is that bad language is contagious. The more you hear it, the more natural it may become for you to slip into the habit yourself.

While you can't entirely avoid hearing the world's language, you can limit what goes into your ears. Surround yourself with godly friends and influences. Choose your music carefully. Avoid television shows and movies that have bad language in them. And if you have friends who curse, ask them to try not doing so around you. Most of all, keep tight control of your own thoughts and speech. Remember that you represent God. . .and He is always listening!

Dear Father, I know that You don't want me to use bad language. Help me to always keep my speech pure so that I can glorify You. Amen.

DAY 155

DROP ANCHOR!

This hope we have as an anchor of the soul,
a hope both sure and steadfast.
HEBREWS 6:19 NASB

Do you ever feel like you're floundering? Like you're on a ship lost at sea just rowing in circles? Sometimes life can be that way. You're not sure what direction to go, you're tired, you've lost hope that you'll ever see the horizon. School, music, youth group, activities. . . choices about which sports to play, what you want to do with your life—it can all be overwhelming.

And let's face it—it's tough. But there is hope. And it's in the Lord. Just as the anchor on a boat holds it steady, God is the anchor of your soul, and He's offering you *His* hope. And His hope is true and everlasting. Allow Him to anchor you. Seek Him in everything you do, and He will guide you toward an even greater future.

So when you're lost, when you're tired and afraid, sometimes it's best to drop your anchor down and rest in Him. He's longing to take care of you.

Lord, sometimes I feel so lost. The choices and decisions I have to make overwhelm me, and I'm not sure which way to go. Please be my anchor. Thank You for Your hope. Help me to rest in You and turn to You for all the decisions in my life. Amen.

DAY 156

STREETS OF GOLD, *REALLY?*

The twelve gates were twelve pearls; each gate was made from a single pearl. The street of the city was of pure gold, transparent as glass.
REVELATION 21:21 GNT

Not many of us understand what God is trying to show us about heaven in the Bible, especially when we read the descriptions in the book of Revelation. What kind of place is heaven? Are there really streets of gold and pearly gates? Sounds too good to be true, doesn't it?

We are Christians because we choose to believe what God tells us. And He tells us that He is preparing a special place in heaven for us. If He said it, it's 100 percent true. All the details—including the streets of gold and pearly gates—really don't matter much. We can simply trust that heaven will be perfect because we know it's been created by a perfect God—the very same God who sent His Son, Jesus, to save us.

Think of how much God loved us—enough to make a beautiful home for us to live in forever. Everyone wants to know they will have an eternal home. And who wouldn't want to dwell in the most beautiful place we could possibly imagine?

Have you picked heaven as your eternal home? It's never too late. Jesus is waiting for you to say yes to heaven.

Heavenly Father, I can't imagine what heaven looks like, but I believe You have made a home for me there. I'm so grateful that You accept me as Your child and that I get to spend eternity with You. Amen.

DAY 157

GOD IS ALWAYS WITH ME

I will be with you always, even until the end of the world.
MATTHEW 28:20 CEV

On occasion a small child or a pet will shadow someone they love. They follow close behind, chasing at the leader's heels. It can be fun for a time, until the leader wants a little bit of freedom. Then they may try to escape from the sight of the follower.

Sometimes we take the position of the leader in our relationship with God, with Him "along for the ride." When we want a taste of freedom, we try to dodge Him so that He can't see what we're doing. But He is always there, so all that has happened is that we have grieved the God who has promised to always be with us—even until the world ends.

Since God is our constant companion, it would work best for us to give Him the leader position and follow where He leads. He will never try to get away or "lose" us. He wants us to be following closely, maintaining a close relationship with Him.

Dear Jesus, You have promised to always be with me. No one else shows that kind of devotion. Thank You for loving me so much that You want to be with me! Amen.

DAY 158

DOING THE IMPOSSIBLE

A hard worker has plenty of food, but a person who chases fantasies has no sense. . . . Work hard and become a leader; be lazy and become a slave.

PROVERBS 12:11, 24 NLT

Good, hard work has always been valued. God wants us all to work hard at whatever He has given us to do. Hard work can seem daunting at times, but it is accomplished by taking it one step at a time. Saint Francis of Assisi said, "Start by doing what's necessary, then what's possible; and suddenly you are doing the impossible."

This verse from Proverbs also talks about becoming a leader. If you're shy, this may sound a little scary to you. But you're already a leader if you think about it! Aren't there other kids in your life who look up to you? Maybe a younger brother or sister. Or a neighbor. Or the little kids you help with at church.

Whatever you decide to do, work at it with all your heart. Other people are looking up to you. So don't cut corners. Don't be lazy. Work hard, and soon you'll be doing the impossible!

God, I've never really thought of myself as a leader, but I guess I am! Help me to be a better one and a hard worker for those who look up to me. Amen.

DAY 159

YOU PROMISED!

"God is not a man, that He should lie."
NUMBERS 23:19 NKJV

The last few times you promised your mom you would do the dishes right after your favorite TV show, did you do it? Most of us would honestly say, "Well, sometimes I did, and sometimes I didn't."

But when God makes a promise, it's not the same. The Bible is full of promises that He's kept and *still keeps* consistently today. His track record is worthy and full of integrity. At times we may start to believe He is not going to keep His promises, at least where we are concerned. But chances are, we don't realize He's simply not going to keep a promise in the way we expect Him to. Maybe we are looking for immediate comfort or escape from a situation when it is actually in our best interest to go through the hard stuff. God knows what's best, even when we don't.

So the next time it feels like God's not going to keep a promise, trust that He sees the bigger picture. He's there and working through all the details to give you only the best results!

God, help me to be patient as I wait on You. I know I need to trust that Your promises will happen in Your way. Amen.

DAY 160

WANT TO HANG OUT WITH ME?

You hem me in behind and before,
and you lay your hand upon me.
PSALM 139:5 NIV

Have you ever had a friend say, "Hey, let's hang out together"? You make plans to do something, like go to the movies or have a sleepover, but then your friend ends up doing something else instead. Man, that can really hurt! Doesn't your friend want to spend time with you?

God isn't like that. The Bible promises us that He is standing next to us at all times. He never leaves us, no matter what! He's the best sort of friend!

Are you lonely today? Need someone to hang out with? Why not hang out with the King of kings and Lord of lords? He will wipe away your loneliness and remind you that you are loved. Best of all, He's already there, right beside you, waiting for you to say, "Hey, let's hang out together!"

God, I'm glad You're never too busy to hang out with me. I get a little lonely sometimes, but You're the best friend in the world because You always say yes when I need someone to spend time with me. Thank You, Lord! Amen.

DAY 161

WATCH YOUR MOUTH

From the fruit of their lips people enjoy good things,
but the unfaithful have an appetite for violence.
Those who guard their lips preserve their lives,
but those who speak rashly will come to ruin.
Proverbs 13:2–3 NIV

Words are powerful. They are so powerful that God used them to speak the world into being. By doing this He demonstrated a spiritual law. . .the power of the spoken word.

Your words have power too. When you say something out loud, the same spiritual law that was in effect when God created the world is still at work. Your words have the power to build up or tear down, to bless or curse. The Bible says your words are so powerful they actually have the power of life and death (Proverbs 18:21).

Because words are so powerful, it's important to use them well. Some people (even Christians) who don't understand this lead empty, defeated lives because they are speaking all the wrong things. "I'll never get this right!" "My parents are the worst!" "My life is the pits!"

What are the right things? Whatever God's Word says. No matter what the situation, always make sure you find out what God's Word says about it. Then YOU say what GOD says. "I can do all things through Christ!" "The Lord cares for me because I trust Him." "By His stripes I am healed."

Dear God, help me to remember the power of my words. Teach me to use them well. Amen.

DAY 162

ETERNAL PERSPECTIVE

Work willingly at whatever you do, as though you were working for the Lord rather than for people. Remember that the Lord will give you an inheritance as your reward, and that the Master you are serving is Christ.

Colossians 3:23–24 NLT

An eternal perspective. What in the world does that mean? That is the idea behind this verse summed up in two, easy-to-remember words. Having an "eternal perspective" means that you realize all the work you do right now—your schoolwork, your chores at home, how you treat others—it all means something to God! And not just for right now. . . It means something for all eternity.

God is always with you and watching over you. He sees the choices you make. He sees inside your heart, and He knows and understands why you do certain things. When you remember this and realize that doing your math homework can be pleasing to God, it changes how you do things! You're working for God and not for your teacher! You're taking out the trash for God and not just your mom!

God, thanks for watching over me and guiding me. Help me to do my work, remembering that it is ultimately for You. Amen.

DAY 163

GOD'S DESIGN

For you created my inmost being; you knit me together in my mother's womb. I praise you because I am fearfully and wonderfully made; your works are wonderful, I know that full well.

PSALM 139:13–14 NIV

Does God make mistakes? Did He somehow mess up by not making you look just like someone else? Do you think He was disappointed when He saw how you turned out? If you answer this question honestly, it gives a good insight into what you believe about God. . .and about yourself.

God made your body, and He designed your face exactly how He wanted it. He knew you before anyone else ever even saw you. He thinks you're perfect. It doesn't matter how much you weigh, how tall you are, or the kinds of clothes you wear. You are His beloved. And what's best is He knows your heart and loves you still.

Thank Him for making you a masterpiece, perfect in every way. Know that truth, and let it bathe you with confidence.

Dear God, please help me to love myself so I can be a reflection of You to those around me. Amen.

DAY 164

MY GUIDE

So I say, let the Holy Spirit guide your lives.
Then you won't be doing what your sinful nature craves.
GALATIANS 5:16 NLT

Is Jesus in your heart? Have you ever taken the time to fully commit your life to Jesus Christ? If you have said yes to Him, then the Bible tells us the Holy Spirit—the Spirit of God Himself—comes and lives inside of you (2 Corinthians 1:21–22) to guide you, to help you know right from wrong, and to encourage you every day of your life.

We all mess up. And without someone to guide us, we would be lost forever. Jesus says, "I am the way and the truth and the life. No one comes to the Father except through me" (John 14:6 NIV).

If you have never asked Jesus to come and be the center of your life, what's stopping you? You can talk to God anytime, anywhere. Even in the quietness of your own heart.

Dear Jesus, I know I've messed up, and it's pretty clear that I need some help. Please forgive me and come into my heart. Wash away my sins and make me new. Thank You for loving me so much that You gave up Your life to save me. Thank You for a fresh start. Thank You for being my guide. Amen.

DAY 165

HE KNOWS YOU—AND LOVES YOU

You have searched me, Lord, and you know me. You know when I sit and when I rise; you perceive my thoughts from afar. You discern my going out and my lying down; you are familiar with all my ways. Before a word is on my tongue you, Lord, know it completely.

Psalm 139:1–4 NIV

As you lie down on the picnic blanket, you search the sky and are reminded that God knows you.

He was with you when you had a terrible fight with your best friend. He knew you would say you're sorry and ask for forgiveness. He was with you when you ice-skated all around the rink holding on to your dad's hand. Then He watched you try and try again until you were able to skate on your own.

God knows every little thing about you. . .your every thought. . . He knows the sins you have already committed and the sins of your future. And He loves you. He knows your heart.

And His arms will surround you in love and protection forever.

God, I'm so happy You know me. The color of my hair and eyes were Your design. You have predetermined my height and weight. I want to be as tall as You want me to be, Lord. Thank You for letting me be me. Amen.

DAY 166

DOES GOD REALLY CARE?

We are afflicted in every way, but not crushed; perplexed, but not despairing; persecuted, but not forsaken; struck down, but not destroyed; always carrying about in the body the dying of Jesus, so that the life of Jesus also may be manifested in our body.

2 Corinthians 4:8–10 NASB

You're so precious in the sight of God. Every move you make, every breath you take, every thought you think. . .He knows it all.

God's in absolute control. No matter what you're going through, God sees it. He knows your pain. He's got plans for you like you could never imagine. And He's *always* with you (Matthew 28:20).

A flower goes dormant in the winter but comes back to life in the spring. It wasn't dead. . .just asleep as the Lord worked on it. And so it is with you. During those times of "winter," let Him carry you, and just rest in His strong and capable arms as He strengthens your heart and helps you grow.

Father, thank You for taking care of me. Thank You for knowing me, my thoughts, my fears, my dreams, my everything. . .every hurt and every pain, every tear that falls and every sickness. I'm in total awe that You care so much about me. Thank You. In Jesus' name I pray. Amen.

DAY 167

READ THE INSTRUCTIONS

All Scripture is inspired by God and is useful to teach us what is true and to make us realize what is wrong in our lives. It corrects us when we are wrong and teaches us to do what is right. God uses it to prepare and equip his people to do every good work.
2 Timothy 3:16–17 NLT

Have you ever opened a brand-new board game and tossed aside the instructions? You find that you don't know how to set up the game, what the rules are, or most importantly, how to win! Soon you find yourself reading the instructions so that you can play the game correctly. It takes a little bit of time, but in the end it's worth it.

The Bible is God's instruction book for life. If you jump into life without reading scripture, you won't know God's will or His ways. You may start out on a wrong path. You won't receive the warnings that His Word contains for your good. And you certainly won't win in the Christian life.

Your heavenly Father has provided guidance and truth in the Bible. Take the time to read the instructions today!

Thank You, Lord, for giving me instructions for life. Create in me a love for scripture, I pray. Amen.

DAY 168

OBEY? NO WAY!

For God is working in you, giving you the desire and the power to do what pleases him.
PHILIPPIANS 2:13 NLT

Your dad tells you to get to bed by 9 p.m. because you have early morning practice the next day, but you decide to go to your best friend's overnighter anyway. You want to obey your dad but not enough to miss a great party, right? Your mom asks you to clean your room before heading off to hang out with your friends, and you say, "Sure, I'll do it later." But later never comes. You want to obey your mom but not enough to actually clean your room, right? If this sounds familiar, you may have an obedience problem.

Obedience is a tough one. But here's the good news: if you're a Christian, God is constantly working on your heart so that you'll want to obey Him. He will never give up on you. He doesn't dwell on your disobedience. Instead, He sees you through eyes of love. The more you understand His love, the more you'll want to obey God and others in your life. Ask Him to help you, and remember today is a great day to obey!

God, help me to become more obedient. Amen.

DAY 169

GOD LOVES ME

God's love, though, is ever and always, eternally present to all who fear him, making everything right for them and their children.
Psalm 103:17 MSG

Are you ever afraid that you're not good enough for God's love? That maybe something you've done or something you've said will make Him stop loving you? Or maybe you are just unlovable?

The truth is God doesn't ever stop loving because we are unlovable. In fact, His love is something we can count on and always trust to be there. If we do wrong, all we need to do is ask His forgiveness, and He will give it to us because He loves us. God will help us do better and make things right again for us if we turn to Him. Know that God loves you. . .and that He always will. You can count on it!

Dear God, thank You for loving me always. Please help me to remember that You love me even when I know I'm not acting in a lovable way. Please help me turn to You and feel Your love. Amen.

DAY 170

I'M FORGIVEN

As for our transgressions, You forgive them.
PSALM 65:3 NASB

No matter what you've done—God sent His Son to pay the price for your sins. You are forgiven.

Did you get that? As long as you have accepted His free gift of salvation, you are forgiven. For *everything.*

Even after you're saved, it's all too easy to mess up. And sometimes the guilt overwhelms you. But you are still forgiven. It's often harder to forgive ourselves than it is to understand that Almighty God loves and forgives us. So don't fall into that trap.

There will be days when you stand strong to temptation, and there will be days when you fail. But praise God, He is there, loving you, wanting to pick you up and dust you off. Confess your mistakes to Him and bask in His amazing grace. You are forgiven!

Heavenly Father, I'm so sorry for all the times I've failed You. I'm sorry for my sin but so thankful for Your forgiveness. Please help me to stand strong today in the face of temptation, and help me to share Your forgiveness with someone else today. Amen.

DAY 171

A THANKFUL HEART

Always give thanks for all things to God the Father in the name of our Lord Jesus Christ.
EPHESIANS 5:20 NLV

Bad days? We all have them. And you've been there with. . .the haircut that didn't turn out like you wanted, the reprimand from your teacher for talking in class, the less-than-perfect grade on your spelling test, and the bruised knees from your embarrassing trip over your chair in Sunday school.

We can't always control things that go wrong, but what we can control is our reaction to those things. So the next time you have a bad day, think about the wonderful things in your life—like your fantastic family, your cuddly pet, your best friend, your bedroom that's decorated just the way you like it—and you'll find yourself bouncing back fast from your sour mood.

And last but not least, thank God for all the good stuff in your life. He'll be happy to hear from you!

God, when things don't quite go my way, instead of feeling sorry for myself, help me to think of everything that's good—there are a lot of wonderful things in this life of mine! Thank You for blessing me! Amen.

DAY 172

YOU HAVE A HISTORY

"Fear not, for I am with you; be not dismayed, for I am your God. I will strengthen you, yes, I will help you, I will uphold you with My righteous right hand."

ISAIAH 41:10 NKJV

Can you remember some really great seasons in your life? You got just what you wanted for your birthday. . . . You were invited to the best party of the year. . . . It was easy to see how God laid His hand on your life and blessed you magnificently.

If you think a little longer, you can also recall when things were downright awful. You flunked a class. . . . Maybe you broke your leg or lost your best friend. During those times, it wasn't as easy to see God's blessings.

When life gets tough, it pays to remember our history with the heavenly Father. Then we can begin to see that even though we flunked that class, God provided understanding parents and teachers who helped us get back up and try again. We can be thankful that it was only a broken leg and not something worse. By remembering the ways He protected and sent support, we can gain the courage to move through to the next great season in our lives—and we can feel grateful for what we have *right now*.

God, thank You for all You do for me—even if life does get a little tough at times. Amen.

DAY 173

STAR LIGHT, STAR BRIGHT

Become blameless and pure, "children of God without fault in a warped and crooked generation." Then you will shine among them like stars in the sky.

PHILIPPIANS 2:15 NIV

Have you ever looked at the sky at night? If you live in the city, chances are that you can't see very many stars. But if you get away from the streetlights of town and gaze at the same sky, you'll be amazed. Millions of stars, like scattered diamonds, shine in the heavens, brightening the darkness.

As God's child, you are like one of those twinkling stars. His light shines within you, visible to all who see. And each time you tell the truth. . .each time you show kindness to others. . .each time you obey God's Word, your light shines brighter. And just like the stars in the sky, you are most visible when surrounded by darkness. When others do the wrong thing, but you stand up for what's right, your tiny glow becomes a beacon.

So don't be afraid to do what's right, even if no one else does. Remember that you are a glittering diamond in the night sky. Keep on shining!

Heavenly Father, please help me to shine my light brightly for You. I want to be an example to others so they can come to know You too! Amen.

DAY 174

RAINBOWS AND PROMISES

He will keep his agreement forever;
he will keep his promises always.
Psalm 105:8 NCV

Remember the story of Noah? After a long time in a boat with a bunch of animals, God brought him and his family safely to land. The first thing they did was offer their praise to God for His goodness. God was pleased with their sacrifice, and He placed a rainbow in the sky as a sign of His promise that He would never again flood the earth.

God's promises aren't just for long ago though. He has made promises since then and will keep every single one. He will not break any of them.

When we become God's children, He promises to love us, protect us, guide us, and then take us to heaven to live with Him forever when our time on earth is done. What amazing promises!

We can always be certain that whatever He says, He will do. Remember that the next time you see a rainbow!

Dear Father, thank You for the many promises You have given to us in the Bible. I know that You will be faithful to keep Your Word. Help me to faithfully keep the promises I make too. In Jesus' name, amen.

DAY 175

WHAT'S SO SCARY?

"I am leaving you with a gift—peace of mind and heart. And the peace I give is a gift the world cannot give. So don't be troubled or afraid."
JOHN 14:27 NLT

There are lots of scary things in the world. Perhaps your own dark room scares you. Or maybe a bad dream that wakes you up in the middle of the night. When you were small, remember how you felt when you lost sight of your parents in a store? . . . Scared enough to cry, right?

Fear comes when we think there isn't anyone or anything to protect us. In situations that are new to us, we often need someone to lean on to keep fear away. The Bible tells us that God is always near and that we can depend on Him to take care of us. The more we know what the Bible has to say, the more we will trust Him to rid our hearts and minds of fear.

The worst part of fear is that it can hold you back from becoming the kid God created you to be. It isn't part of His plan for you to be stopped in your tracks because you're feeling afraid and alone. He will help you fight the battle; all you need to do is ask for His protection and peace. Then clear your mind, and get to work on becoming who He wants you to be! You have nothing to fear with God beside you!

Dear Lord, I get scared sometimes and don't know what to do. I don't like feeling afraid, and I ask You to help me in those times. Thank You that You are always with me and helping me be who I was meant to be. Amen.

DAY 176

HOPEFUL

May the God of hope fill you with all joy and peace as you trust in him, so that you may overflow with hope by the power of the Holy Spirit.

ROMANS 15:13 NIV

Let's face it. Some days are just rotten, and it seems like things will never get any better. When that happens, we feel like crawling in a hole and pulling the earth in around us. It's a pretty crummy feeling to have no hope.

But with God, we always have hope for a better future! We can know, without any doubt, that things will get better for us. God loves us, and He has good things in store for us. We can dream. We can imagine. We can plan for the future. And we can do those things because of that one little word: *hope.*

No matter how bad things may seem, we can be certain there are good things coming our way. We can even talk to God about these things and tell Him our hopes and dreams. He loves us, and He wants to give us the secret desires of our hearts.

Dear Father, thank You for giving me hope. When things seem hopeless, help me to trust in Your love for me. Amen.

DAY 177

SHINE OR GRUMBLE?

Do all things without grumbling or disputing, that you may be blameless and innocent, children of God without blemish in the midst of a crooked and twisted generation, among whom you shine as lights in the world, holding fast to the word of life.

PHILIPPIANS 2:14–16 ESV

You have a choice each day—to either shine for Jesus or grumble and complain. Every day of your life there will be plenty of things for you to complain about. There will also be many blessings to be thankful for. You can focus on blessings, or you can complain about problems. What kind of person do you want to be around? One who shines? . . . Or one who grumbles?

God's Word tell us that "His divine power has given us everything we need for a godly life through our knowledge of him who called us by his own glory and goodness" (2 Peter 1:3 NIV). This means that when we accept Jesus as our Savior and choose to follow Him, God gives us everything we need to make good choices. . .to choose to shine!

God, please help me to be a kid who shines for You! There are lots of times I want to grumble and complain, but please help me to focus on my blessings and not my problems. Amen.

DAY 178

COUNT ON IT!

Through His shining-greatness and perfect life,
He has given us promises. These promises are of great
worth and no amount of money can buy them.
2 PETER 1:4 NLV

How many times have you used the words "I promise"? Probably hundreds, right? We're always promising to do things. Sometimes we keep those promises, and sometimes we don't. Nothing makes you feel worse than having a friend or loved one break their promise to you. We've all gone through it. Our parents promise that we'll go to the movies or maybe a theme park. Then something happens, and the plans get canceled. Usually it's nobody's fault, but it still stinks!

God never has to say, "Oops! I said it, but I didn't really mean it!" You'll also never hear Him say, "Well, I told you I would do that, but then I changed my mind." See, with God, what He says is what He will do. In other words, He always keeps His promises! If you want to know more, read your Bible. It's loaded with great promises just for you!

Dear Lord, I feel like so many people have broken their promises to me! They say one thing and do another. I'm so glad You never go back on Your promises. Thanks for giving me Your Word, Lord. Amen.

DAY 179

PRECIOUS, UNCOUNTABLE THOUGHTS

How precious are your thoughts about me, O God. They cannot be numbered!
PSALM 139:17 NLT

Who knows you? I mean *really* knows you? Who can you be yourself with? Who can you laugh with until you cry? But even in thinking about that person, there are certainly a few things they *don't* know about you—and probably a few things you would rather them *not* know about you.

There is a friend who knows everything—*everything*—about you and loves you more than anyone else can. He not only made you, He knows all about you, and the number of His thoughts about you cannot even be counted!

You are precious to your Creator. There is nothing He does not know about you, yet despite any flaws, He wants you. He has big plans for you. And He loves you more than you can ever imagine!

Dear heavenly Father, thank You for creating me and for Your love for me. Some days I don't feel worthy of that love, but help me to remember that I don't have to do anything or be anything to earn Your love. Thank You for Your precious thoughts of me that are too many to count! Amen.

DAY 180

GOD HAS A PLAN

"For I know the plans I have for you," declares the LORD, "plans to prosper you and not to harm you, plans to give you hope and a future."
JEREMIAH 29:11 NIV

Do things ever seem to go wrong and just keep going wrong for you? You didn't get the part in the play or the spot on the team you wanted so badly. You couldn't go to the party you'd been looking forward to for weeks. You came down with a virus and missed too much school, and now your grades are suffering. Life's not always easy, but remember God has good plans for you. He will see you through the tough times and get you past any illnesses and disappointments. He has a plan for better days ahead, so trust Him. He knows the plans for your future, even if you don't.

Dear God, thank You for Your plan for me. A plan that will give me hope and keep me looking ahead to the future You have in store for me. Help me to remember that You do have a plan, even if I don't know what it is right now. Amen.

DAY 181

HEIRS FOR ALL ETERNITY

If you belong to Christ, then you are Abraham's descendants, heirs according to promise.
GALATIANS 3:29 NASB

A "covenant" is an agreement or promise made. In Genesis 15, God made His covenant with Abraham. Genesis 15:17–18 (NASB) says, "There appeared a smoking oven and a flaming torch which passed between these pieces. On that day the LORD made a covenant with Abram." God sealed His covenant by passing between the halves of Abram's offering. Passing through the pieces was like saying, "Cross my heart, hope to die." God was telling Abraham that He'd die before He would break His covenant.

We're not just heirs, we're children of God through our faith, we've "received adoption" (Galatians 4:4–6). He's preparing a place for you in heaven and will fulfill His covenant to you. He will *never* abandon you (2 Corinthians 4:8–18). God always keeps His promises, and He will never leave you to wander in this dark world alone.

Lord, thank You so much for making me an heir through my faith in Your Son, Jesus. Help me to live freely, but not take my freedom for granted (Galatians 5:1, 13). In Jesus' holy and precious name I pray. Amen.

DAY 182

CHOOSING YOUR FRIENDS

The righteous choose their friends carefully,
but the way of the wicked leads them astray.
PROVERBS 12:26 NIV

Ever walked on a balance beam? It's tricky, isn't it? At first, young gymnasts require a coach to "spot" them as they try to keep their balance walking along the beam. Later, it becomes easier for them to stay focused and centered on their own.

Would it be easy to pull up a friend onto the balance beam to walk with you? No way! It would be next to impossible! And yet, how easily that friend could cause you to stumble and take a fall right off the beam. Just one tap of a finger might be all it would take.

The same is true in life. As you choose your friends, choose wisely. How easy it is to lose our way and be led down wrong paths by friends whose hearts do not belong to Christ.

It's good to be kind and loving to everyone, but it's so important that your closest companions love Jesus. You won't seek to cause each other to fall down, but instead you can spot one another on the balance beam of life.

Lord, I want to thank You for Christian friends who encourage me to walk in Your ways. Amen.

DAY 183

ALL THINGS FABULOUS

And my God will meet all your needs according to the riches of his glory in Christ Jesus.
PHILIPPIANS 4:19 NIV

Stores are loaded with all things fabulous, aren't they? When you walk by those racks and shelves filled with cool clothes and gadgets and shoes, it's all so tempting. You find yourself wanting something so desperately that you convince yourself you really *need* it. . .that your life won't be as fun or meaningful without it. And so you buy it.

Sometimes you use what you've purchased and truly enjoy it. But many times it just ends up at the bottom of your drawer or stuffed in the back of your closet. And you sometimes even wonder why you bought it in the first place. That's the nature of buying things. Stuff goes from treasure to trash way too fast, and the thrill of buying has to be repeated over and over and over.

Fortunately God cares more about you than to just give you everything you want. God gives you everything you need, and that promise won't ever fade or tarnish or be forgotten at the bottom of a drawer!

Lord, thank You for giving me everything I need. And forgive me that sometimes when I'm so busy asking You for more, I forget to thank You for what I already have. Amen.

DAY 184

YOU CALL. . .HE ANSWERS

I sought the Lord, and he answered me;
he delivered me from all my fears.
Psalm 34:4 niv

God hears you when you pray. Every single time. He hears the prayers you whisper at night, the ones you think in your head, and the ones you say right out loud. He always hears you.

God always answers too, even though it may not seem like it. Because God is more interested in your character than your comfort, the answer may not be the one you were hoping for. Sometimes the answer is "no." Sometimes the answer is "wait." And sometimes the answer is "yes," but you don't recognize it because it doesn't look the way you thought it would.

No matter how God chooses to answer your prayer, just know that He WILL. His ways are not our ways (Isaiah 55:8). You have to trust that He knows what is best. Just believe Him for the best because that's what He wants to give you. Anything is possible (Mark 9:23)!

Dear God, sometimes when I pray I feel like my prayers don't reach You. But no matter how I feel, I choose to believe what Your Word says. When I call on You, You will answer me and deliver me from all my fears. Thank You for being a God of answers. Amen.

DAY 185

IT'S NOT MY PROBLEM!

Help each other in troubles and problems.
This is the kind of law Christ asks us to obey.
GALATIANS 6:2 NLV

We all have troubles from time to time. Turning a book report in late. Missing the school bus. Losing homework. Arguing with brothers and sisters. Disagreeing with Mom and Dad.

How do you feel when you have troubles of your own? Lonely? Helpless? Afraid? Worried? You probably have at least one if not all of those feelings. Now imagine what you would do if you had no one to talk to. . .no one to help you through a tough time. Handling your problems all by yourself would make your troubles seem even bigger, wouldn't it?

Even though we may want to turn and run away from someone else's problems, we are called to follow God's example and reach out to help others in their time of need. Whether they need a listening ear, a shoulder to cry on, an extra set of hands to complete a big chore. . .we can pitch in and let God's light shine through us.

God, sometimes I just want to shout out, "It's not my problem! Why should I help? It has nothing to do with me!" But then I remember what You want me to do. Thank You for being an example of reaching out to others in need. Amen.

DAY 186

STANDING ON THE PROMISES

My eyes stay open through the watches of the night,
that I may meditate on your promises.
Psalm 119:148 NIV

You lie in bed with your eyes wide open. You reflect on the day. . . .

It had rained all afternoon. Just as the rain had turned to a light sprinkle, you glanced out your bedroom window and spotted the most brilliant rainbow you'd ever seen. You ran outside to get a better look and saw that the rainbow spanned from one side of the sky to the other—a vibrant burst of color: red, orange, yellow, green, blue, indigo, and violet. A beautiful reminder of God's unfailing promises and amazing love for you!

Standing on the promises of Christ my King,
Through eternal ages let His praises ring,
Glory in the highest, I will shout and sing,
Standing on the promises of God.

Are you standing on His promises?

God, thank You for Your peace, rest, and love. Your promises are within my soul. I am standing on Your promises! Amen.

DAY 187

LIFE IS HARD, BUT GOD IS GOOD

For just as the sufferings of Christ are ours in abundance, so also our comfort is abundant through Christ.

2 Corinthians 1:5 nasb

Ever need a do-over? Your locker won't open; you step in a mud puddle in your new shoes; you get a bad grade on a history paper; you fall on your face in front of half the school. . . .

On those days when you just want to give up because the world has thrown everything at you that it possibly can, remember that Christ suffered for you as well. That's another way our God is so amazing. He understands every hurt, every tear, every horrible event in your life because He's been there. He was publicly humiliated, battered, beaten, spat upon, and hung on a cross.

When you're in the middle of a trial, remind yourself to turn to Him. His comfort is the only comfort you'll ever need, and it is abundant. There's plenty of it for every day of your life.

God, I need Your comfort. And it's so nice to know that You understand all the hurt and pain in my life. Thank You for Your sacrifice, and thank You for always being there for me. Help me to smile through the trials and keep my focus on You. Amen.

DAY 188

FIGHT THE URGE TO FIGHT!

Do not repay anyone evil for evil. Be careful to do what is right in the eyes of everyone.
ROMANS 12:17 NIV

"You are such a loser!" your friend yells.

"I'm not the loser. YOU are!" you scream back. "I can't believe I was *ever* your friend."

Ever been there? Ever been so mad at one of your friends that you screamed ugly, hurtful things at him or her? Or how about your siblings? It can be especially hard to get along with your sisters and brothers because you spend so much time together. Sometimes you get sick of them, right? Fights happen.

But fighting, which is also known as "strife," is a very *serious* subject. James 3:16 tells us that where strife is, every evil work is also there. Being in constant strife is like inviting the devil into your home. It's like saying, "Yo, devil. Come on in and make yourself comfy. Oh, and bring all of your evil buddies along—like jealousy, fear, bitterness, and unforgiveness." Don't let strife camp out in your life. Instead, fight the urge to fight! You'll be so glad you did.

God, help me to walk in love, not strife. Help me to be a peacemaker in all of my relationships. I love You. Amen.

DAY 189

CAN YOU HEAR ME?

But when you ask him, be sure that your faith is in God alone.

JAMES 1:6 NLT

You just got out of the shower and realized there are no towels in the bathroom. "Mom!" you yell at the top of your lungs, "I need a towel!" The problem is, you don't have a clue where Mom is at the moment. She could be right down the hall and your towel will be on the way as soon as you speak; but she could be outside weeding the flowerbeds and not hear you at all.

At times, it can feel the same way when we talk to God. We pray for a friend to pass his or her test, and by His miracle she does. Then on another day, we pray for other friends in trouble and hear nothing. Is God outside weeding the flower beds too?

Hearing God's voice isn't always easy. A lot of noise fills up our lives. If you need an answer, make sure you find some alone time and practice listening for His instruction. Most of all, be patient. . . because His answer comes in His timing—not ours.

God, I need to hear Your voice today. I commit to finding a place where just You and I can hang out for a while. Amen.

DAY 190

HE MADE ME

Your hands have made me and fashioned me; give me understanding, that I may learn Your commandments.
PSALM 119:73 NKJV

In this world we live in, it is sometime hard to grasp the fact that our God made us. That He made us each unique, and that He knows everything about us. He knows our weaknesses and our strengths; He knows when we do wrong and when we do right. He knows everything that has happened and everything that will happen to us. And we owe Him everything. We should want to do His will always. But to be able to do His will, we need to know His commandments and follow them. He will help us. All we need to do is pray for understanding.

Dear God, please help me learn Your will and understand it deep inside my heart so that I can do the things You want me to do. I want to please You in all ways. It's the least I can do. You made me, You gave me life. You protect me and care for me. Help me to always remember that. Help me to know Your will, Father. Amen.

DAY 191

TEMPTATION NATION

No temptation has overtaken you that is not common to man. God is faithful, and he will not let you be tempted beyond your ability, but with the temptation he will also provide the way of escape, that you may be able to endure it.

1 Corinthians 10:13 ESV

Temptation is everywhere. Temptation to do the wrong thing. Temptation to cheat on a test. Temptation from girls and boys at school—or even friends at church! When you choose to follow Jesus, the devil gets angry! The enemy will do whatever he can to try and trip you up!

So what's a kid who loves Jesus to do? Ephesians 6:10–11 (NIV) gives us the answer: "Be strong in the Lord and in his mighty power. Put on the full armor of God, so that you can take your stand against the devil's schemes."

Every morning, put on the full armor of God, knowing that you are headed into battle. Remember, God is faithful, and He will always give you an escape! Be on the lookout!

God, help me to be strong in You today! Cover me with Your power, and protect me from the devil's plans. Help me do the right thing and always stand up for what I believe in. Amen.

DAY 192

WHEN JOY IS HARD

Consider it pure joy, my brothers and sisters, whenever you face trials of many kinds, because you know that the testing of your faith produces perseverance. Let perseverance finish its work so that you may be mature and complete, not lacking anything.

JAMES 1:2–4 NIV

It's easy to feel joy when things are going right. When we make an A on a test, or get invited to sit with the cool kids at lunch, or our parents notice what a great job we did cleaning the kitchen, we feel happy. But what about when everything goes wrong?

The Bible tells us to rejoice *even then*! That sounds plain crazy. But when we think about it, it's the hard times that build our character. It's the hard times that help us grow up and become mature. It's the hard times that teach us love, patience, and kindness.

Next time things seem to be going all wrong, take a moment and thank God. Let's remind ourselves that God must be doing something pretty special. And let's smile, knowing God's plans for us are always good, even when they don't seem good at the time.

Dear Father, help me to be joyful even in the hard times. Thank You for caring about who I am tomorrow and not just about how I feel today. Amen.

DAY 193

GOD'S LOVE FOR ME

The person who has My commands and keeps them is the one who [really] loves Me; and whoever [really] loves Me will be loved by My Father, and I [too] will love him and will show (reveal, manifest) Myself to him. [I will let Myself be clearly seen by him and make Myself real to him.]

JOHN 14:21 AMPC

It's rather easy to love someone who loves you back. It's the ones who have hurt or offended you who are the difficult ones to love.

But God loved us before we ever knew Him. He loved us when we knew Him but didn't love Him back. We hurt Him and offended Him, yet He kept on loving us.

Finally, the day came that we repented and told God that we chose to love Him. As God's children, we profess our love for Him, but we don't always show it. The Bible says that the person who really loves Him will obey Him.

Dear God, I do love You. I want to obey Your commands to show You that my love for You is genuine. Thank You for loving me when I'm not very lovable and for promising to always love me. In Jesus' name, amen.

DAY 194

PURE JOY!

Celebrate God all day, every day.
PHILIPPIANS 4:4 MSG

Think about some things you'd like to have. . . . Pretty easy, right? Maybe you've been wanting a new pair of jeans or shoes. Or maybe you'd like to have a brand-new smartphone. We always have a ready list of "stuff" that would make us just a little happier, don't we?

But have you ever made a list—an A to Z, everything-that's-good-in-your-life list? From the simple to the big stuff—sunshine, your favorite food, your lovable (but occasionally annoying) sister or brother, your friends, your bike, your house, your favorite family vacation spot—you have too many blessings to name!

While we often tend to think about all of the things we don't have, the fact is every moment of the day, no matter where you look, you can find at least one item to thank God for—one blessing in your life. Now that's reason to celebrate. . .all day long!

God, help me to think about all the wonderful things You have given for my enjoyment—not just "stuff," but the things in my life that really matter. You've blessed me with so much that I could have an "I've-been-blessed celebration" every day of the week! Thank You! Amen.

DAY 195

REJOICE. . .ALWAYS?

Rejoice always, pray without ceasing, in everything give thanks; for this is the will of God in Christ Jesus for you.
1 THESSALONIANS 5:16–18 NKJV

Your best friend moves away. Your pet dies. Your parents separate.

There are events in each of our lives that are terribly difficult to bear. Doesn't it seem almost cruel that Paul wrote to the Thessalonians, telling them to rejoice and give thanks *always, in all things*? And yet he went so far as to say it was God's will for them.

Jesus knows there are times when your heart hurts. He understands that you don't always feel like jumping for joy. But what He does want you to know is that He is always there. He wants your fellowship with Him through prayer to be constant. He calls you to trust Him to work good things from the bad in your life.

So even on your worst day, *pray* to God. *Thank Him* even for the hard times. Hard times lead you to the foot of the cross, which is a great place to be. *Rejoice* that you are not alone but that you belong to a heavenly Father who will lead you through every trial.

Father, I trust You to work all things together for good in my life. I thank You, even in the hard times. Amen.

DAY 196

HE IS ALWAYS WITH ME, PART ONE

The LORD is my rock and my fortress and my deliverer, my God, my rock, in whom I take refuge; my shield and the horn of my salvation, my stronghold.
PSALM 18:2 NASB

The Lord God—your heavenly Father, the beginning and the end, the author and the healer—is watching over *you*! He's your rock, your fortress, your deliverer, your refuge, your shield, your stronghold! His arms are stretched open wide ready to embrace you and shelter your soul.

When the strong winds blow, when the water rises up high above you, when your enemies encamp around you, He's here to hold you tight and keep your heart at peace (John 14:27).

Can you imagine that? Can you imagine God standing here with His arms open wide? He is calling you, dear one (John 10:3)! Run into His arms. Take His outstretched hand, and don't let go! When the devil "prowls around like a roaring lion" (1 Peter 5:8 NASB), keep your eyes on your glorious Lord. He's your Savior. And He's always here.

Lord, thank You for watching over me. Thank You for being my shelter, fortress, and shield. I love You, Lord. Please help me to keep my eyes on You. In Jesus' name I pray. Amen.

DAY 197

HE IS ALWAYS WITH ME, PART TWO

Do you not know that you are a temple of God
and that the Spirit of God dwells in you?
1 Corinthians 3:16 NASB

You're a temple of God Most High! Your prayer is the altar, your heart is the sacrifice, and your tears are a precious anointing unto Him.

The Spirit of God Himself dwells in you, and He'll never leave you. You were bought at a price, beloved child. The price of Jesus' blood on the cross.

Romans 8:15–16 (NASB) says: "For you have not received a spirit of slavery leading to fear again, but you have received a spirit of adoption as sons by which we cry out, 'Abba! Father!' The Spirit Himself testifies with our spirit that we are children of God."

God's our Father, and we're His children. He's here with us and in us. And just like a loving father, He guides and directs us through His Holy Spirit (John 14:16; John 16:13; Romans 8:26).

Lord, thank You for giving me Your Holy Spirit. Thank You for helping me and for giving me Your Word. Please help me to keep my focus on You and never forget that You're always with me. In Jesus' holy name I pray. Amen.

DAY 198

BEES AND GOD'S PLAN FOR ME

For we are God's handiwork, created in Christ Jesus to do good works, which God prepared in advance for us to do.

Ephesians 2:10 NIV

Have you ever seen bees buzzing around beautiful flowers? The job the bees are doing is quite amazing.

When a bee visits a flower, yellow pollen rubs off on her tiny belly. Then she visits the next flower, where the pollen drops into that flower. This is called pollination. Without pollination from bees, many plants wouldn't grow fruit.

Isn't it incredible that God has given even the tiny bee an important job to do? I once read that every three mouthfuls of food we eat are because there was some fuzzy bee somewhere doing her job.

It makes sense that if God has a plan for the tiny bee, He has a plan for you too. And even though the bee is small, what she does is not insignificant.

Lord, sometimes I might doubt that You have a plan for my life. But I know if You care about the bee, You care about me. I choose to trust that You will slowly unroll Your plan for me. In the meantime, I choose to walk with You each step and trust You for what happens. Amen.

DAY 199

FORGET ABOUT IT!

It's wise to be patient and show what you are like by forgiving others.
PROVERBS 19:11 CEV

When a friend hurts your feelings, it's likely you will be angry—maybe even a little sad. You might even hold on to your hurt feelings for a while. After all, friends aren't supposed to hurt each other, are they?

No doubt about it, forgiving your friend will be hard. But this could be the perfect opportunity to reflect God's amazing love into the life of someone else—a way for your friend to see God through your actions. After all, God's Word gives us this bit of wisdom: "Dear children, let's not merely say that we love each other; let us show the truth by our actions" (1 John 3:18 NLT).

Talk to God and ask Him to take away your hurt feelings, and then ask Him for His help in extending forgiveness to your friend. And after you forgive them, forget about it. God will be delighted!

Heavenly Father, sometimes my emotions can be hard to manage—especially when I'm hurt by something my friends do or say. Forgiving others definitely isn't easy. But when I open my heart to Your Word and extend forgiveness, I know it makes You happy. Amen.

DAY 200

CREATED FOR A PURPOSE

Always do your work well for the Lord. You know that whatever you do for Him will not be wasted.
1 Corinthians 15:58 NLV

You are not an accident. God created you to have fellowship with Him through Jesus Christ, and He has a special assignment for you to carry out in your lifetime.

The world's view is that all life on this planet happened by accident. People who go along with that theory believe everything that happens is random chance. No plan. No order. No blessing. Can you imagine?

But the Bible says God made you for a special purpose. Nothing, good or bad, happens to you that God has not allowed. Even if something happens that seems bad at first, God can turn it around so that it is good for you in the end.

Knowing you have a purpose is like having a vision of where you're going. The Bible says that when "people can't see what God is doing, they stumble all over themselves" (Proverbs 29:18 MSG). But you won't stumble because you know God has a plan and a purpose. . . just for you.

Dear God, thank You for creating me with a purpose in mind. Help me to know what that purpose is and to be obedient to Your plans for my life. Amen.

DAY 201

GOD WILL FORGIVE YOU—ALWAYS!

"Come now, let's settle this," says the Lord.
"Though your sins are like scarlet, I will make them as white as snow. Though they are red like crimson, I will make them as white as wool."
Isaiah 1:18 NLT

Have you ever messed up big-time and thought, *Uh-oh, now I've done it. I feel so bad about what I've done. I wonder if God will ever forgive me?*

Maybe you told a lie. Maybe you cheated on a test at school. Maybe you were mean to your best friend.

While all of us will occasionally make mistakes and fail to be "perfect," it's a comfort to know that God has promised in His Word to forgive us—*no matter what*. He loves each of us so much that there's nothing we could do to cause Him to turn His back on us—no matter how big or bad our sin may seem.

Need forgiveness from God? Simply ask, and you'll have it!

God, if I ever find myself doubting Your love for me, I will remember this: Your love is so perfect that when I tell You that I'm sorry, You'll always wrap Your arms around me and whisper, "I forgive you." Amen.

DAY 202

DO I REALLY NEED IT?

And my God will supply all your needs according to His riches in glory in Christ Jesus.
PHILIPPIANS 4:19 NASB

Our society is filled with things. Commercials, billboards, the mall. . . all of it telling you about the latest and greatest hot-ticket item. And a lot of times, it's easy to get caught up in wanting things, saying that you *need* them. Especially when your friends come over with their new smartphones, laptops, clothes, shoes. . .you name it.

But God doesn't want us to be caught up in this world and the stuff. He wants us to know that He's everything we need. And He will supply our needs.

Remember that next time you tell your mom about something that you "just gotta have." God loves to bless us with extras all the time, but don't get greedy and caught up in things. This world is not your home, and in heaven you'll be surrounded by the Lord's treasures. So store up your treasure in heaven, and know that God will supply what you truly need.

God, as I struggle with things that I want, help me to focus on others' needs and how I can help meet them. Help me to be thankful for everything that I have and to remember that You supply all my needs. Amen.

DAY 203

WHAT ABOUT ME?!

Let us not become weary in doing good, for at the proper time we will reap a harvest if we do not give up.

Galatians 6:9 NIV

You volunteer your free time at the local animal shelter. You donate new and used books, clothes, and toys to charity every year. And you regularly visit the retirement home and play games with lonely residents. That's in addition to the little unremembered acts of kindness you do throughout the rest of the year. And to be honest, you're getting a little worn out from all this "doing good" stuff. You even find yourself wondering if it's worth all the effort.

If we focus on others instead of ourselves, we'll begin to see the effect of our good deeds. And God will have a hand in that. He sees what we're doing to make a difference in the lives of others; and He promises that we will experience something good because of it. While people may overlook or forget our kindnesses, isn't it wonderful to know that God never will? Today, ask the Lord to give you the strength and energy you need to keep up the good work. And then wait and see what good things He brings your way!

God, I'm so sorry that I sometimes get tired of doing nice things for others. Please forgive me. Help me to notice all the wonderful things that happen when I do something good for someone else. Amen.

DAY 204

RESTORE THE LIGHT

O Lord, how long will you forget me? Forever? . . .
Turn and answer me, O Lord my God!
Restore the sparkle to my eyes, or I will die.
Psalm 13:1, 3 NLT

Do you ever wonder if maybe—just *maybe*—God has forgotten about you? Maybe you have a big problem at school or in your family and nothing seems to be getting better. . .even though you've been praying about it for a L-O-N-G time! So much that your smile isn't as big as it used to be and the light is gone from your eyes.

King David in the Bible felt just like this. And if most Christ-followers are honest, they've all felt the same way a time or two in their lives. But you know what? The truth is that God hasn't forgotten about you! God tells us in His Word that His ways are not our ways (Isaiah 55:8). His timing is perfect, and His plan for you is good. He is always working everything out for your good and His glory (Romans 8:28)—even when it doesn't seem like it. Check out the rest of Psalm 13 to see what David decides to do about his feelings!

God, sometimes I feel forgotten. Please help my faith to grow so that I trust You more. Please bring back the light to my eyes—the light that comes from my hope in You. Amen.

DAY 205

THE BOOGEYMAN

Do not be overcome by evil,
but overcome evil with good.
Romans 12:21 niv

When you were little, did you lay in bed at night with the covers tucked tightly around you? Did you pull them up to your chin and shiver, worried that the boogeyman was going to come out from under your bed and *get you*? What did you do about it?

If you cried out to your parents for help, they likely told you to think about other things— pray, sing a song, or fill your mind with something silly. Diversion was the best way to resist the boogeyman.

When you're tempted to do wrong, think of that temptation as the boogeyman. In order to resist it and turn from the sin, you need to fill your life and your mind with holy and righteous things that will distract you from the temptation of sin. Your enemy will throw temptation at you, but it's your job to resist it. When you do that, sin will flee.

Dear God, please help me to keep my mind from evil and focused on Your holiness. Help me resist sin and temptation so I can stay rooted in Your truth. Amen.

DAY 206

CALL YOURSELF "MASTERPIECE"

For we are God's masterpiece. He has created us anew in Christ Jesus, so we can do the good things he planned for us long ago.
EPHESIANS 2:10 NLT

Do you think of yourself as a masterpiece? God certainly does! Search Google for "10 most valuable masterpieces in the world." The first thing you'll notice is how the entire world recognizes that a masterpiece is worth a fortune. That's how God sees you! He knows you are not ordinary or average—because He created you. You are an original. He designed you just as you are for a purpose. As you scroll through the paintings on Google, you'll see that each one has its own prominent brushstrokes and color. No two are alike!

Today is a great day to start recognizing your value. Throw out those thoughts that say, *I'm just average. I'll never do anything special.* And instead, choose to tell yourself the truth. Every day, remind yourself, "I was made by the artist who paints only masterpieces. His brushstrokes set me apart from everyone else. He filled my personality with original colors. I am special to Him!"

God, thank You for painting me with such artistry! I look forward to what You have planned for my life. Amen.

DAY 207

BEING STRONG

Look to the Lord and his strength; seek his face always.
1 Chronicles 16:11 NIV

Has anyone ever told you to keep your chin up, hold your shoulders back, and be strong? That sounds like good advice. But sometimes it's hard to be strong, especially when things aren't going the way we want. Sometimes we just want to cry, or throw a fit, or give in to peer pressure. Being strong isn't always easy.

But God says we don't have to be strong on our own. If we look to Him, He'll be strong for us. He'll give us the strength we need to be nice when others are mean. He'll give us the strength we need to say no when others try to get us to break the rules. He'll give us strength for all sorts of things we may face in this life.

God's strength is unending, and He's never far away. For as long as we live, if we look to Him and ask Him for help, He will always, *always* give us the strength we need.

Dear Father, help me be strong when I need to be. Remind me that You are always there, giving me strength when I ask for help. Amen.

DAY 208

GOD'S AWESOME WORKMANSHIP

Thank you for making me so wonderfully complex!
Your workmanship is marvelous—how well I know it.
PSALM 139:14 NLT

What is the last thing you created? A science fair project? A painting? Something to eat? How difficult was it to make? Did it take a lot of time and effort?

With only His words, God created the sun and moon, stars and planets. He spoke into existence all animals and plant life. And for the grand finale, God created humanity. He effortlessly spoke Adam into being. And then He chose to create Eve to be a helper for Adam.

Not too long ago, God crafted you. He caused you to develop in a very safe place until the day you were born. In those few months, He fashioned your body and began its functions. He made you unique, with the qualities that make you the person you are. If you ever question your worth, just think of the workmanship He displayed in creating you. He is intentional in what He creates, so you were made specifically by the God of the universe. You are special!

Dear Jesus, thank You for making me according to Your plan. Please help me to remember how special I am and how marvelous Your works are. In Your name, amen.

DAY 209

CAN YOU HEAR ME NOW?

The Lord has heard my plea;
the Lord will answer my prayer.
Psalm 6:9 NLT

Did you know that God knows your voice? He really does! He knows exactly who you are when you pray; and not only does He hear you, but He listens to *everything* you have to say. It's all important to Him!

Like our earthly parents, God has a special ear when it comes to listening for His children. He wants to hear from us anytime, anywhere, and for any reason. Your prayers matter to Him as though you were the only child He had. Think of a parent who proudly watches their child in the school play. Their words ring out like music to the parent's ears. That's the way it is when God hears us call out to Him.

There's no need to worry that He might not pay any attention to you, even if you don't always know what to say. Your prayers please God, and He listens. When He hears the cries of His children, He sends His love and protection.

After you have prayed, be still. It will then be your turn to listen.

Dear Lord, thank You for hearing my prayers and listening to my voice. Help me to have more faith that You will answer my cries for help. Amen.

DAY 210

GOD HAS MADE A WAY

Jesus said to him, "I am the way, the truth, and the life. No one comes to the Father except through Me."

John 14:6 NKJV

Have you ever been lost? Maybe your mom or dad made a wrong turn and you found yourselves lost in an unfamiliar city or neighborhood. But then the GPS gets you back on track. "Turn around as soon as possible," it says. Everyone snickers as the machine makes it so obvious that you've lost your way!

Wouldn't it be crazy to turn off the GPS at that point? And yet, so many people do just that to Jesus every day. They tune Him out. They choose their own paths. But on our own, we are simply unable to find God.

Long before you were born, the Father made a way for you. He sent His only Son, Jesus, to die on a cross for your sins. Jesus is the only way to the Father. To know God and to spend eternity with Him in heaven, you must know His Son.

If you're on a road that leads away from Jesus, turn around as soon as possible. God has made a way for you to come to Him.

Come into my heart, Jesus, and forgive me of my sins. I want to follow You. Amen.

DAY 211

JUMP IN! THE WATER IS JUST FINE

"But since you are like lukewarm water, neither hot nor cold, I will spit you out of my mouth!"
REVELATION 3:16 NLT

Have you ever jumped into a swimming pool in the late spring? The water was so cold your teeth chattered nonstop, right? Even your goose bumps had goose bumps! But then an amazing thing happened—the water didn't feel cold anymore. Why? Because you got used to the temperature!

Do you know that sin is the same way? When you first enter the "sin pool," you'll immediately want to get out. It won't be pleasant. But the longer you remain in the "sin pool," the easier it becomes to stay there. Suddenly, telling lies about your friends doesn't seem so awful. Or cheating on your language arts test doesn't seem so bad.

Sin has a funny way of fooling you into thinking "it's okay" to sin a little, but the Bible says differently. In fact, it says that God wants to spit out a lukewarm Christian from His mouth. So don't get used to sin. You have to choose between the world's way and God's way. Jump into God's way. C'mon in! The water is fine!

Lord, please help me to stand my ground when it comes to my beliefs. I want to be red hot when it comes to You. Amen.

DAY 212

THE FLIP SIDE

"Do to others whatever you would like them to do to you. This is the essence of all that is taught in the law and the prophets."
MATTHEW 7:12 NLT

Mark Twain said, "Keep away from people who try to belittle your ambitions. Small people always do that, but the really great ones make you feel that you too can become great." The flip side is just as important: do what you can to make those around you feel they can become great! Be an encourager. Not just with your close friends, but treat *everyone* just like you want to be treated.

Jesus wants us to understand about the flip side. He talks a lot about not judging others when we have sin in our own life that needs to be dealt with first (see Matthew 7:1–5). He wants us to love and be considerate of others, even if we might disagree sometimes. Ask God to help you respond to others in a way that would make Him smile.

And whenever you're in a weird situation, remember the flip side: How would you want to be treated at a time like this?

God, please give me the courage to do the right thing. Help me think of others first and treat them like I would want to be treated. Amen.

DAY 213

LIFE EVERLASTING

"For God so loved the world that He gave His only begotten Son, that whoever believes in Him should not perish but have everlasting life."

John 3:16 NKJV

Sometimes we get so caught up in this earthly life that we forget to think about the everlasting life we will one day have in heaven. Our eternal life is where our focus should be—even now!—and we should always be looking forward to that day when we meet Jesus face-to-face. God wanted us to have a life with Him so much that He gave His only Son, Jesus, to die that we might live! It should be on our mind every morning, every evening, all day long.

Dear God, thank You for sending Your Son, Jesus. . . for loving us so much that we might have eternal life—the promise of life in heaven with You! Please help me keep my focus on the life that truly matters, the eternal life I will have someday because of Your amazing gift. Amen.

DAY 214

GOD'S GARDEN

And the Lord God planted a garden.
Genesis 2:8 KJV

Digging out weeds, picking off bugs, watering, pruning, fertilizing. . . there's always something to do in a garden. The reward of all that sweat and toil is beautiful and satisfying not only to the one doing the hard work but to everyone who sees it.

Growing up in God's garden is the safest and happiest place to be. Plenty of sunshine and rain along with constant protection mean that you have every chance to grow up healthy and beautiful. But God's ways of cultivating can also be uncomfortable at times, especially if you need a lot of pruning or tend to attract pests. You may be tempted to run wild rather than endure His methods of shaping you.

Plants left to themselves don't remain lovely for long. They are eventually choked by weeds, devoured by insects, or crushed by careless feet. You're far better off submitting to the hands of your wise and loving Creator than trying to develop on your own. Have patience, dear one. It may be a lot of work, but God's flowers always grow up wonderfully!

Lord, You make all things beautiful. Help me to be patient and submissive while You cultivate me into a blossom worthy of Your love. Amen.

DAY 215

REPLACE JUDGING WITH LOVING

"For in the same way you judge others, you will be judged, and with the measure you use, it will be measured to you."
MATTHEW 7:2 NIV

It's not easy to put yourself in someone else's shoes. And the Bible warns to be careful when you judge someone. When you judge someone without understanding their situation, you'll often be put in a very similar situation during your lifetime. That's what "the measure you use will be used on you" means. Sometimes God allows things like that to happen so that you can understand and forgive those toward whom you harbor bitter feelings.

The mean girl at school? She might have a really bad home life, and she only knows how to express herself through anger. The boy who smells bad and wears dirty clothes? His dad may have lost his job, and they can't afford deodorant. Or maybe their water was even shut off! You just never know. So pray for others and be careful how you judge them.

Dear God, please help me not to judge others. I want to be a loving example of You to everyone I see each day. Help me not to avoid people I don't understand, and please give me wisdom to know how to act around them. Amen.

DAY 216

YOUR FUTURE'S SO BRIGHT, YOU'RE GONNA NEED SHADES!

"For I know the plans I have for you," declares the LORD, "plans to prosper you and not to harm you, plans to give you hope and a future."
JEREMIAH 29:11 NIV

So what are your plans for the rest of your life? Got it all figured out? No? That's okay. Even if you don't have a plan yet, God does.

God's plan for you was established long ago. He wants you to prosper and have a bright future. He's already given you all the gifts and talents you're going to need. But guess what? You can choose to go along with God's plan. . .or not. God isn't going to force you to follow His plan even though He knows it's the best one. The choice is yours.

The Bible says if you commit whatever you do to the Lord, your plans will succeed (Proverbs 16:3). As you plan your future, ask God to guide your choices. Let Him know that you want His plan to be YOUR plan for the future. Then you'll have it made in the shade!

Dear God, as I make choices about my future, I want to make sure they are the right ones. Please guide me and help me to know the plans You have for me. I choose to go along with Your plan because I want Your best for me. Amen.

DAY 217

THE COMPANY YOU KEEP

Do not be joined together with those who do not belong to Christ. How can that which is good get along with that which is bad? How can light be in the same place with darkness?
2 Corinthians 6:14 NLV

Young people often try to fool themselves (and their parents) into believing that they won't be influenced by the bad behavior of others. So eager to fit in, they will deny the fact that the language, activities, and behaviors of their friends will have an influence on them.

Jesus doesn't ask His children to isolate themselves. In fact, He wants us to be part of the world around us. But we should be shaping the world, not letting the world shape us.

We can only impact the world when we strive to solely be "joined" or united with people who share our love for Jesus and our goal of pleasing Him with our lifestyle. If you feel that those types of people are difficult to find, pray that God would lead you to ones who will build you up and with whom you can live as an example to others.

To stay in God's light, ask Him to give you wisdom in choosing your friends.

Heavenly Father, please help me choose my friends wisely. Lead me to others who will positively influence my Christian walk. Amen.

DAY 218

COWARDLY LION OR COURAGEOUS WARRIOR?

Therefore, being always of good courage, and knowing that while we are at home in the body we are absent from the Lord—for we walk by faith, not by sight—we are of good courage.
2 Corinthians 5:6–8 NASB

Sometimes it's really hard to stand up and be strong and courageous, but God is calling you to do it for Him! You're not like the cowardly lion who looks fierce on the outside but is really timid on the inside. You're God's warrior. You are a child of the king! And no matter how big or small you are, whether you are quiet or loud, God wants to use you in His divine plan. He's calling you to muster up courage because you have it.

Take courage in every situation. You might be able to stand up for someone who's being bullied, to tell the truth—even when it's the unpopular thing to do, or to audition for that part you thought you were too scared to try out for. The possibilities are endless when you draw on the courage of the Lord.

God, sometimes I'm so scared of trying something new or even doing what's right. Please help me to see that You have given me courage. And I don't have to be afraid. Amen.

DAY 219

HOPE-GIVER

Do any of the worthless idols of the nations bring rain? Do the skies themselves send down showers? No, it is you, Lord our God. Therefore our hope is in you, for you are the one who does all this.

Jeremiah 14:22 NIV

It's 7 p.m., and your dad still isn't home from work. You're beginning to worry. You look outside, and the rain is coming down so fast that water rushes down the street and the storm drain is overflowing. The street begins to look more riverlike with every passing minute.

Mom notices that your worry is beginning to spiral out of control, and she reminds you of the hope-giver, Jesus, who holds everything in the palm of His hand—even the raging storm outside. She reminds you that Jesus is only a prayer away and that He alone can calm your fears and the storm.

Another hour goes by. You notice the swing set has toppled over and the backyard looks like a swimming pool. You can't even see the fence at the end of your yard. But now instead of fear, you have hope in your heart—hope because of the ultimate hope-giver!

Shortly after, you hear the garage door go up. Dad is safe and sound—praise God!

Lord, thank You for my family. And thank You for giving me hope, even in situations that seem hopeless! Amen.

DAY 220

GOD UNDERSTANDS

Be ye doers of the word, and not hearers only.
JAMES 1:22 KJV

"Kali, let me see your math homework," said Courtney.

Kali stared at her friend. "Why?"

"I forgot all about it last night," said Courtney. She dug a pencil from her backpack. "I need to copy yours before class starts."

"But—I mean. . ."

Courtney glanced at the classroom door. "Hurry! Mr. Perez will be here any minute!"

Kali bit her lip. "I can't."

"Why not? You didn't do it either?"

"No. I did it. But I can't let you copy it. Don't you remember? We talked about this in Sunday school last week. Cheating is the same as stealing."

A guilty flush crept across Courtney's cheeks. "I know, but—Kali, I have to get this done. I'll get in big trouble if I miss another assignment. God understands that."

Kali considered for a moment. Then she looked at her friend.

"Courtney, friends don't ask friends to disobey God. You and I both know it's wrong to cheat. *That's* what God understands."

Dear Father, I never want to make excuses to sin against You, no matter what others do. Give me boldness to stand up for what's right, even if those I have to stand up to are my friends. Amen.

DAY 221

KNOCK, KNOCK!

Be anxious for nothing, but in everything by prayer and supplication with thanksgiving let your requests be made known to God. And the peace of God, which surpasses all comprehension, will guard your hearts and your minds in Christ Jesus.

PHILIPPIANS 4:6–7 NASB

Do you have a tendency to worry? Have no fear, everyone does!

But God tells us *not* to worry—*not* to be anxious—but to come to Him in prayer with thanksgiving. You can call on the name of the Lord with confidence—and thankfulness!—that He hears you.

What if you don't know the "right words to say"? Romans 8:26 says, "The Spirit also helps our weakness; for we do not know how to pray as we should, but the Spirit Himself intercedes for us with groanings too deep for words." You don't have to say long, eloquent words and phrases for God to hear and/or answer your prayer. All He asks is that you come to Him (Matthew 11:28). Today's verse says He even gives you the gift of peace that "will guard your hearts and your minds in Christ Jesus" just for calling on Him.

Father, I'm so thankful that I can call out to You with the assurance that You hear me—and help me! Thank You for Your love and for giving me Your Holy Spirit. In Jesus' holy name I pray. Amen.

DAY 222

MY FUTURE

Do not conform to the pattern of this world, but be transformed by the renewing of your mind. Then you will be able to test and approve what God's will is—his good, pleasing and perfect will.

ROMANS 12:2 NIV

I can remember wondering as a child what God had in store for my future. Would I be tall or short? Would I have a successful career? Would I stay in my hometown or move across the country?

I've been a grown-up for a long time now, and I still wonder about many things that relate to my future.

The truth is, God has a beautiful plan for each of us. And His plan includes this: He wants us to be like Him. He doesn't, under any circumstances, want us to mess up our lives by leaving Him behind and becoming like the world.

We may not know the details of our future, but we can be assured about God's most important plan. He wants to make us beautiful in spirit. And He will do what He needs to do to bring about that plan.

Dear Father, thank You for making good plans for my future. Help me to fulfill Your plans by becoming more like You. Amen.

DAY 223

MY STRENGTH COMES FROM GOD

"Don't panic. I'm with you. There's no need to fear for I'm your God. I'll give you strength. I'll help you. I'll hold you steady, keep a firm grip on you."
ISAIAH 41:10 MSG

Have you ever had a hard time standing up for what you know is right? Or saying no instead of going along with the crowd? Do you feel weak when you must make a decision to go against the crowd? Do you worry that your friends might desert you if you don't go along with them? Remember that God is with you in every situation—offering you His strength when you need to be strong, to help you stand up for what is right. Lean on Him. He will always give you the courage to do what is right.

Dear God, please give me the strength and courage to do what is right. Please help me to trust that You are always in my corner, keeping me strong and steady. Please help me to make decisions according to Your will and not go along with the crowd when I know I shouldn't. Please help me to encourage my friends to lean on You too. Amen.

DAY 224

A MEGA BESTSELLER

All Scripture is God-breathed and is useful for teaching, rebuking, correcting and training in righteousness.
2 Timothy 3:16 niv

What is the Bible, anyway? And what's the point of reading it? Maybe thinking about reading the Bible makes you want to yawn. Maybe you think the Bible is just a book about ancient characters who don't have anything to do with you. It's easy to think that way—at first glance. But if you dig a little deeper, you'll find life in those pages. Stories packed with every kind of drama imaginable, bigger in scope than any 3-D IMAX experience. You'll also discover people just like you.

Bible folks may not have driven cars, or watched TV, or eaten pizza, or texted anyone, but their hearts were just the same as yours. They looked up at the same night stars and wondered if the God who made them was real, if He loved them as much as He claimed to, and if He had a plan for their lives.

God was faithful to those ancient people, just as He is faithful to you today. Not only can you learn from the people you meet in the Bible, but God's Word is a mega bestseller—and it's helpful for guidance in everything that matters most in life.

Lord, please give me the desire to read Your living Word, the Bible, so that I might grow strong in my faith. Amen.

DAY 225

BUT YOU PROMISED!

God's way is perfect. All the LORD's promises prove true.
PSALM 18:30 NLT

God has given us lots of promises. He is such a good and loving God who knows we need the hope of His promises in times of trouble. He is our heavenly Father who wants to give us all good things in His time.

The thing about promises is that they are no good unless they're kept. God *always* keeps His promises, but sometimes we get tired of waiting for them to come true. We want God's promises on *our* time instead of trusting Him for His perfect timing. And in our selfishness, we run out of patience.

Why is it so hard to wait for God's promises? Maybe it's because we're used to getting everything on demand. We have fast food, instant entertainment, and a short drive to the store.

But we must remember that the best things come from God, and sometimes we need to be patient until He's ready to deliver on His promises. It means choosing what He wants for us instead of choosing what we think we should have and when. It's always better to wait for the best instead of settling for second best. God's way is perfect, and He will prove it!

Jesus, please help me to have patience. I want to wait for all the good and wonderful promises You have for me. I believe You have only the best in store for me. Thank You for proving Yourself through Your promises each and every day. Amen.

DAY 226

MAKE THE BEST OF IT

Dear brothers and sisters, when troubles of any kind come your way, consider it an opportunity for great joy. For you know that when your faith is tested, your endurance has a chance to grow.

JAMES 1:2–3 NLT

It's been said that the happiest people don't have the best of everything, they just *make* the best of everything! The Bible tells us that trouble is going to find us in this life. And that can be a bit discouraging if you think about it too much. But don't let it get you down! Jesus says, "I have told you these things, so that in me you may have peace. In this world you will have trouble. But take heart! I have overcome the world" (John 16:33 NIV).

Here's what you need to focus on instead: when you're facing difficult situations, Jesus Himself will come alongside you to help you through it. He will give you peace, and you will feel closer to God during the hard stuff (see Psalm 34:18)! Praise Him!

God, please give me the strength to make the best of everything that I face in life. Thanks for being faithful to me and giving me peace. Help me trust You 24-7! Amen.

DAY 227

MORE THAN JUST MUSCLES

In your strength I can crush an army;
with my God I can scale any wall.
Psalm 18:29 NLT

While it's true that most guys have more muscle than most girls, it doesn't necessarily mean either is stronger. There are more aspects to strength than muscles alone. What about choosing to do the right thing when your friends are doing the opposite? How about standing up for a friend? When you have the strength to be loyal or to say no, you are one of the most powerful people in your circle. You are demonstrating strength in character.

God has given you unique strengths so that you can overcome the challenges that come your way. It won't always be easy. Even strong people will have moments of weakness, but you have a partner and friend in God. He will always be there to hold your hand and strengthen your heart during the battles. By being strong in character, you are flexing *your* kind of muscles!

God, please show me each of my strengths. I want to be able to use them to fulfill the purpose You have for me. Thank You for giving me more than muscles! Thank You for giving me strength of character. Amen.

DAY 228

THAT YOU MAY *KNOW*

I write these things to you who believe in the name of the Son of God so that you may know that you have eternal life.
1 John 5:13 NIV

When you flip a coin, you don't know whether it will land on "heads" or "tails." When you put a coin into a gumball machine, you can't predict the color of gumball that will plop into your open palm when that magical little metal door is lifted. There are some unknowns in life. . .and there are some knowns.

You can find absolute truth in the pages of God's Word. One of those truths is that, as a believer in Jesus, when you die, you will go to heaven to live forever with God.

Unlike flipping a coin, your eternal life is not a wish or a chance. It is a promise, something to hold on to. It is for sure. When writing the book of 1 John, the apostle did not say, "I write these things to you who believe in the name of the Son of God so that you may HOPE that you have eternal life." Nor did he write, "that you PROBABLY will have eternal life." He wrote, inspired by God, "that you may KNOW that you have eternal life " (emphasis added).

Thank You, God, that I know I have eternal life through Jesus. Amen.

DAY 229

ON EARTH, IN HEAVEN

"If I go and prepare a place for you, I will come back and take you to be with me that you also may be where I am."

John 14:3 NIV

God has made a way for sinners to have a relationship with Himself. He sent His Son, Jesus, to earth to take our punishment. He died for our sins rather than require that we suffer for them ourselves, as we deserve.

Because He loves His followers so much, He has prepared a place for us to live with Him forever. That should not be the reason we repent—simply to avoid hell and make it to heaven. But it is a blessing we will experience, living with Him in a place where there will be happiness and joy forever.

Throughout the days that God has appointed for us to live on the earth, we are to live for the Lord. What we do here should be for the purpose of pointing others toward Him. And then, when our days here are done, we will be united with our Savior to begin our forever with Him.

Dear Father, I know I need to be doing the work You have for me while I'm on earth, but I'm really looking forward to being in heaven with You for eternity too. Amen.

DAY 230

BETWEEN SUNDAYS

Teach them to your children, talking about them when you sit at home and when you walk along the road, when you lie down and when you get up.

DEUTERONOMY 11:19 NIV

Sundays are special days to get together with other Christians to worship God and study the Bible, but it's the things we learn and the decisions we make during the week that make all the difference in life.

Jesus taught through stories how God's ways are important for everyday life—not just for Sundays. God has a way for making everyday things—like arguments with a sibling, bullying in the school hallway, and struggles through team practice—easier, if we are willing to learn.

Much can be discovered through reading your Bible, but God also designed life so that we can learn from other Christians how we should react in different situations.

If you have Christian parents, watch them and ask them for advice. If you have not been blessed with Christian parents, ask a pastor or Sunday school teacher for help finding a mentor. Many Christian adults are happy to take time to help you learn God's ways.

God, thank You for the good Christian influences You have placed in my life. I am grateful for each one of them. Amen.

DAY 231

HUNGRY FOR LOVE

But you, Lord, are a compassionate and gracious God, slow to anger, abounding in love and faithfulness.
Psalm 86:15 NIV

Do you remember the last time you were really hungry and your stomach growled?

Just as your stomach gets hungry when it doesn't have food, your emotions can get hungry too. Just like your stomach craves food, you were made to crave love.

Some kids get so hungry for love from a parent, or someone else who is special in their lives, that they will do anything to get it, even if it means that they allow someone to hurt them.

When you are hungry for love, remember God loves you more than anyone can. Also remember that He created a "love hole" inside of you that He wants to fill with Himself. He created you to give and receive love to others, but no matter how well others love you, there will always be an empty place inside you that can only be filled by Jesus.

Lord Jesus, I want and need love. I thank You that You made me for love. Help me so that when I feel the need for love, I don't try to get it in ways that aren't good for me and don't glorify You. Help me to turn to You for the love that I need. You are the only one who can fill me up. Amen.

DAY 232

MY IDOL

Little children, keep yourselves from idols.
1 John 5:21 KJV

TV shows hold contests to pick the best singer, survivalist, cook, designer, model, businessman, even bride in the land. Every viewer judges them, looking for the very best qualities that stand out above all others. But the winner's moment of fame is often that—a moment—and soon we've forgotten their names.

An idol is anything in your life that is held up above God or that gets more of your attention than God.

God is firm when He tells us that we are to put nothing before Him. No person, nothing you own, no hobby or activity you enjoy should ever push God out of first place in your life. He should be the first friend you call, the last person you talk to at night, your most prized possession, and your biggest insurance toward a positive future.

Each day be sure to check what you are giving first place in your life, and work to keep God at the top of the list.

God, please help me to recognize the potential idols in my life. Help me to keep You in first place every single day. Amen.

DAY 233

HE'S GOT YOUR BACK

"In the world you will have tribulation.
But take heart; I have overcome the world."
JOHN 16:33 ESV

Sometimes life can be scary. Almost every day you face tough decisions, encounter fears, or take on new challenges. Whether it's presenting a project in front of your class or standing up to a bully, life requires you to have courage to get through most days.

But you can't possibly face all of life's intimidating moments on your own. Being strong and fearless all the time will wring you as dry as a sponge. The good news is that God offers His strength if you will ask for it. He longs to lend a helping hand to His children. He will provide you with the strength and courage you need when you can no longer face life alone. If you wake up *every* morning knowing that God will take care of you in *every* circumstance, there will be nothing to fear. The meanest bully, the hardest test, the roughest day—none of it can separate you from His love and protection. He's got your back.

Father, thank You for watching over me and giving me strength when I ask for it. Help me not to be afraid or anxious when life throws new and difficult things my way. Amen.

DAY 234

ATTITUDE IS EVERYTHING

Not looking to your own interests, but each of you to the interests of the others. In your relationships with one another, have the same mindset as Christ Jesus.
PHILIPPIANS 2:4–5 NIV

Pastor and author Chuck Swindoll wrote a great article about our attitudes. He says: "Attitude. . .is more important than facts. It is more important than the past, than education, than money, than circumstances, than failures, than successes, than what other people think or say or do. It is more important than appearance, giftedness, or skill. . . . The remarkable thing is we have a choice every day regarding the attitude we will embrace for that day. I am convinced that life is 10 percent what happens to me and 90 percent how I react to it."

What a great reminder to all of us. Why not jump on the computer and Google that quote. There's a little more to it! Print it out and hang it on your wall or keep it someplace where you can see it often.

No matter what happens to you, you are always in charge of your attitude. The Bible wants our attitudes to be like Jesus. He was humble, He put others above Himself, and He was obedient to God (Philippians 2:7).

Dear God, please change my attitude to be more like Yours. Help me to be humble and be a servant to You and others. Amen.

DAY 235

DOES GOD GIVE HOMEWORK?

Such things were written in the Scriptures long ago to teach us. And the Scriptures give us hope and encouragement as we wait patiently for God's promises to be fulfilled.

Romans 15:4 NLT

Ever had a goldfish? At first it's the perfect pet. It swims happily around in its little bowl, not a care in the world. That is, until the water gets cloudy and the fish gets hungry. Hungry little fishies don't last very long, especially not in dirty water.

The same is true for your spiritual walk. The Word of God is like fish food for your soul, and your spirit cannot grow in relationship with God in cloudy water. Each day, you need to sprinkle fresh food into your life by reading the Bible and thinking about what it says. When you apply it, you'll get answers for your questions and help for your struggles.

And though the world may be cloudy and dirty, when you shine the light of Christ into the space around you, it will clear up just like fresh water for your fish.

Dear God, help me remember to study the Bible every day. And when I do, please help me understand what it says so I can apply it to my life. Amen.

DAY 236

TWO COMMANDS

Jesus said, " 'Love the Lord your God with all your passion and prayer and intelligence.' This is the most important, the first on any list. But there is a second to set alongside it: 'Love others as well as you love yourself.' These two commands are pegs; everything in God's Law and the Prophets hangs from them."

MATTHEW 22:37–40 MSG

Flip through the first five books of the Bible, and you'll find list after list of rules and regulations for God's chosen people, the tribe of Israel. The Ten Commandments are just the beginning. God's people received instructions on virtually every part of their lives, like how to settle disputes, offer sacrifices, farm the land, and how to prepare food. Most of the laws started with the words *do* or *do not*.

Jesus came to free God's people from the choke hold all of these rules had on their lives. His two-part message was simple to understand: Love God. Love others.

Christ came to earth to offer freedom through His sacrifice on the cross, but the biggest enemies of His message were the most religious people of His day. They wanted to hang on to the Old Testament laws and follow them to the letter. Such attention to detail left no room for the love Jesus preached about.

God, thank You for sending Your Son, Jesus, to set me free from lists and lists of rules. You ask for love above all. Please help me to love You and love others as well. Amen.

DAY 237

THE GOD OF HOPE

May the God of hope fill you with all joy and peace as you trust in him, so that you may overflow with hope by the power of the Holy Spirit.
ROMANS 15:13 NIV

Let's face it. Stuff happens. Life is full of surprises, and not all of them are pleasant. Things happen that you had nothing to do with, didn't cause, and certainly didn't plan on. And sometimes those things can make your life miserable. You're disappointed and confused and don't know what to do.

Being a Christian doesn't always shield you from bad situations. The difference between you and the nonbeliever is that when bad stuff happens, you have hope. Everything is possible with God. Nothing is too hard for Him. As you grab hold of that truth and learn to trust Him, you'll find yourself overflowing with hope, joy, and peace. The Bible says not to worry about anything, but pray about everything. Tell God what you need. He'll do the rest (Philippians 4:6–7).

Dear God, You are the God of the impossible. I put all my hope and trust in You. I know that You are the answer to any problem I have. Nothing is too difficult for You. Thank You for the peace and joy I have in You no matter what's going on in my life. Amen.

DAY 238

CHOOSE YOUR OWN ADVENTURE

I am offering you life or death, blessings or curses. Now, choose life! Then you and your children may live. To choose life is to love the Lord your God, obey him, and stay close to him.

Deuteronomy 30:19–20 NCV

You'll probably have to make at least ten choices before you leave the house tomorrow morning. What to wear, what to eat, how much to study, what to take for lunch. . . And then when you get to school, you'll have even more choices to make! All day long you are faced with choices. Some are easy to make and some much more difficult. But every choice you make has an effect on what happens next.

Have you ever read a "choose your own adventure" book? They give you the option to make choices throughout the book with an outcome of several different endings. Each choice affects the ending. The same is true for us.

God's will doesn't have to be very complicated. It's just making a series of right choices. If you decide to follow after God and you try to make choices that honor Him, you'll be seeking after God's will in Your life and headed down the right path. What a great adventure!

Dear God, please help me to make good choices. I want to live my life for You. Thanks for this great adventure! Amen.

DAY 239

WHAT'S YOUR ATTITUDE?

I pray that from his glorious, unlimited resources he will empower you with inner strength through his Spirit.
EPHESIANS 3:16 NLT

Isn't it strange how sometimes you feel strong and other times you feel weak? Some days you race through, getting everything done on your list—and you still have energy to spare. Then there are days when it's a struggle to finish even a few simple tasks.

Our level of strength is dependent on many things—including food, rest, water, exercise, and a positive attitude. That last one might throw you, but a positive attitude is important—especially for our inner strength. We can be physically fit and strong outside but weak and tired on the inside.

Negative attitudes will drain our inner strength because negative thinking blocks the wonderful things God wants to share with us. The power of His spirit can be a source of strength for you, but your attitudes and thoughts can put up a wall between you and that power.

Now for the good news! You can tear down that wall by opening your heart to positive attitudes, and God can then add strength, joy, and peace to your life. It takes practice to turn off the negative thinking, but you can do it with God's help. Just remember He is always there, waiting to give you the strength you need. Strong is good. God's strength is better.

Heavenly Father, forgive me for giving in to negative thoughts and attitudes. I know that You want me to be positive as well as a blessing to others. Amen.

DAY 240

GOD LISTENS

But God has surely listened and has heard my prayer.
PSALM 66:19 NIV

Sometimes when we pray, it feels like our words bounce off the ceiling and right back down into our hearts. We wonder if God is listening. We wonder if He can even hear us. But the Bible tells us that God does listen. He loves us, and He cares about what we have to say.

Psalm 66:18, though, tells us that if we have "cherished sin" in our hearts, God may not listen. That means that if we are doing something against God, and we're not sorry, and we plan to keep doing that particular sin, God may not listen to what we have to say until we get that issue right. We must constantly go to God and say, "God, I love You, and I want to please You. I'm sorry for the things I do that hurt You. Help me not to do those things anymore."

As long as God knows we're trying to please Him, He listens. He hears us. And He delights in giving us the desires of our hearts.

Dear Father, I'm sorry for the times I've sinned. I know You hear me. Thank You for always listening. Amen.

DAY 241

HE IS STRONG

"For the eyes of the Lord range throughout the earth to strengthen those whose hearts are fully committed to him."
2 Chronicles 16:9 niv

Jesus loves me!
This I know, for the Bible tells me so.
Little ones to Him belong.
They are weak, but He is strong.

You probably know the song well. But have you thought about the words? *"We are weak, but He is strong."*

At certain times in your life, you may feel particularly weak. You simply are not strong enough to do the task that is before you. Maybe you need to apologize to someone, but it's so hard to do. Perhaps you are experiencing some problems in your family that are just too big for you to handle. It could be that you know you should say no to something that's not good for you, but you just don't have the strength.

There is good news. You don't have to be the strong one. The Bible tells us in 2 Chronicles that God is *always* looking for His children in need of strength. He wants to be your strength. Call on Him. Tell God where you are weak, and ask Him to be strong in your place.

I am weak, Lord, but how wonderful to know that You are strong! Amen.

DAY 242

GOD'S GOT THIS!

Those who listen to instruction will prosper;
those who trust the LORD will be joyful.
PROVERBS 16:20 NLT

There are only twenty-four hours before the big day. Tomorrow maybe you'll be trying out for the team. . .or the votes will be counted for student council. . .or maybe you'll be standing up in front of everyone giving a presentation (when you're painfully shy). Right now, you're trying not to panic. Your brain is running down a mental checklist over and over and over. You've practiced and practiced. You've done all you know to do. Still, you can't help but wonder if it's possible to hitch a ride to the airport and hop a plane to a remote island. What were you thinking when you decided to do this?

It's time to trust the Lord! He knows how you feel! He planned your life journey to include experiences where you will do your best to prepare, without an immediate guarantee you'll get the results you want. In these moments, you need to force yourself to depend on Him to take you the rest of the way. Let go, then celebrate and say, "God's got this!"

God, I want to give You everything that is troubling me today. I want to smile with the satisfaction of knowing You've got this! Thanks for taking me the rest of the way. Amen.

DAY 243

JESUS KNOWS ME—I AM HIS!

"I am the good shepherd, and I know My own and My own know Me."
John 10:14 NASB

God gave man free will—the ability to choose right or wrong (Genesis 3). You can *choose* to follow His ways and standards, or you can *choose* to rebel against them (see 1 John 2:15–17).

He chose you (John 15:16), and if you accepted Jesus as your Savior, you answered His call. Does this mean you should continue with a life of sin? Should you live like the world lives? "How shall we who died to sin still live in it?" (Romans 6:2 NASB). You've been made new (2 Corinthians 5:17)! Jesus knows it all. . .He has you memorized! God knows who you are, what you want to do, how you spend your time. . .and everything else! He wants you to get to know Him as well. Just like best friends spend time together and get to know one another more and more, so is your relationship with God. You will grow in your knowledge of Him, His love, and His ways as you spend time with Him.

Lord, help me to appreciate Your calling more and more. I know I'm Yours—help me not to listen to the temptations of this world, but Your voice and Your voice alone. I love You, Lord. In Jesus' name I pray. Amen.

DAY 244

GIVE ME PEACE

I love the Lord, for he heard my voice; he heard my cry for mercy. Because he turned his ear to me, I will call on him as long as I live.

Psalm 116:1–2 NIV

This being sick thing is really getting old! You've been in bed for days. You haven't been able to sleep. Your body aches all over. You toss and turn. You finally give up all hope of sleep and turn on the bedside lamp and attempt to read a book. But then your mind begins to wander: you start thinking about the mountain of homework you'll have to make up once you return to school. . .all of the tests you've missed over the last few days. *Ugh!* You bury your head in your pillow, feeling completely defeated. But then you remember. . .

You get out of bed and fall to your knees to pray. You call out to God to give you the rest and peace that you really could use right about now. You then snuggle back under the covers, and it doesn't take long for you to doze off. Peace, peace, peace.

God, I know You hear my prayers. Help me not to forget You are always here for me. Amen.

DAY 245

SAYING GRACE

I will praise him among the multitude.
PSALM 109:30 KJV

Are you afraid to say a prayer of thanks for your food in public? Don't be embarrassed if you are. Sometimes it feels like the entire cafeteria stops mid-chew to watch the weirdo Christian say grace over his or her lunch tray. You might be tempted to disguise your prayer by rubbing your forehead. (Are you feeling okay? A little headache there?) Or maybe a good, hard, faux sneeze into your napkin will give you just enough time to bless your food. You could even bend over and tie your shoe while you thank God for the cafeteria pizza.

There! Food blessed, and no one the wiser!

It's always uncomfortable to feel like an oddball. Unless all of your friends are Christians who also pray for their food, you may feel a little uncomfortable doing so. But saying grace before meals is not just a family-around-the-dinner-table thing. And thanking God in public opens the door for you to witness to your unbelieving friends.

Don't be shy about asking God to bless your food. Depending on what they're serving in the lunch line that day, you just might need it!

Dear God, thank You for all my blessings, including the food that I eat. Give me courage to praise You publicly, even if others think I'm weird. Amen.

DAY 246

PROTECTION FROM DANGER

This I declare about the Lord: He alone is my refuge, my place of safety; he is my God, and I trust him.
Psalm 91:2 NLT

Danger is a topic taught from a young age. Moms advise their children, "Don't run with scissors!" And, "Don't stick anything into electrical outlets!" And, "If it starts to thunder, come inside immediately!"

Kids are taught to stay away from strangers because of "stranger danger." They are advised to choose the right friends because the wrong ones could influence them to make decisions that could lead them into danger.

God has offered Himself as a safe place in times of danger. He is like a place of safety in a storm. When His child looks for a place to run and hide, God opens His arms wide and provides a comfortable place to wait out the storm.

Dear Father, thank You for being a safe place for me. Help me to remember to come to You when I face a difficult situation, rather than trying to make it through on my own. You want to help me, and I trust You. In Jesus' name, amen.

DAY 247

ADORED

And I am convinced that nothing can ever separate us from God's love.
Romans 8:38 NLT

Have you ever received a birthday gift or Christmas present that you absolutely adored? Maybe you took it with you wherever you went, unwilling to let it out of your sight. Maybe you even slept with it. To "adore" something means you not only love it, but you can't bear the idea of being away from it! You're devoted to it. You can't give it up, no matter what!

Did you realize that God adores you? He's crazy about you, and nothing you do can change the way He feels! He won't give you up, no matter what! In fact, He cares so much about you that He doesn't like to be away from you, even for a few minutes. He hopes you feel the same way about Him.

The next time you start to wonder if anyone loves you, remember that God not only loves you. . .He adores you.

Lord, it's tough to admit this, but I don't always feel loved. Sometimes I wonder if people love me. But now I know that You adore me, even when I mess up. I'm so relieved! Thank You for that. Amen.

DAY 248

MY PROTECTOR

You protect me with salvation-armor; you hold me up with a firm hand, caress me with your gentle ways.
Psalm 18:35 MSG

On days when you are afraid and feel the need for protection—from the bully in class, from all the bad things you hear on the news, or horrible things that happen in your school or in your hometown—remember that you have a protector. Every day and always, you have God. He protects you from every kind of evil. And if you let Him, God will even protect you from yourself and the things you might do—the wrong choices you might make that would bring you harm. Remember, He is always there. Turn to Him instead of thinking you can protect yourself. With Him by your side, you have nothing to fear!

Dear God, thank You for always watching over me, always knowing what will happen even before I do. Please guide and direct me daily. Help me know what to do when I am afraid or when I am about to do the wrong thing. Help me to be quiet and listen for Your guidance and fully trust that You protect me from all things. Thank You for being my protector. Amen.

DAY 249

AN UNOPENED LOVE LETTER

Jesus answered, "It is written: 'Man shall not live on bread alone, but on every word that comes from the mouth of God.' "

MATTHEW 4:4 NIV

Beethoven was a famous musician who wrote beautiful music. He never got married but loved a woman, and a lot of smart people have spent years trying to figure out who she was. When Beethoven was forty-two years old, he wrote a love letter to this woman who no one knew. "Oh, why must one be separated from her who is so dear?" he wrote. "However much you love me—my love for you is even greater."

After he died, someone found the letter in Beethoven's desk. It wasn't stamped or addressed. Some people wonder if Beethoven's special lady ever knew how he felt because of this secret, unopened note.

I can't imagine not opening a love letter, can you? God has given you a love letter. It's called the Bible. It is God's story of longing for and desiring a relationship with the people He made. It's the main way you can hear Him speak to you. It's a light for you to know what to do in your life—and it's the most beautiful love letter ever written. Spend time reading it to get to know Jesus. You won't be sorry.

Lord, I want to know You better. Help me to spend time getting to know You through Your love letter to me. Amen.

DAY 250

THE BEST KIND OF FRIENDS

One who loves a pure heart and who speaks with grace will have the king for a friend.
PROVERBS 22:11 NIV

If you have a pure heart and your motives are good, you never have to watch your back. You don't have to worry about what other people may be saying about you or what they might think of you. The way you live your life is between you and God. If you are living a God-honoring life, you don't have to worry about the kind of friends you'll attract. Because the best kind of friends are those who want to honor God like that too.

But did you know that Jesus had people upset with Him all the time? That's a good reminder to us all that we can't please everybody. Even Jesus didn't do that. He doesn't want us to please everyone—just Him! God doesn't want you to be a people-pleaser; He wants you to be a Jesus-pleaser!

And as you seek Jesus, the purity and grace you develop will attract the best kind of friends, the kind of friendships that honor God.

God, help me to do my best to please You and not worry about what other people think or say about me. Help me to attract the best kind of friends. Amen.

DAY 251

BEAUTIFUL CREATION

Man is made in God's image and reflects God's glory.
1 CORINTHIANS 11:7 NLT

Have you ever wondered what God looks like? The Bible says that humans are created in His own image. Maybe that means He has characteristics like a body with arms to hold His children and legs to walk beside them. Maybe God has a face to show emotion, eyes to portray warmth, and a mouth to smile brightly.

God made us in His image because He wants us to identify closely to Him. Of all the living things He created in the beginning of time, He loved us the most and showed that love by placing a little bit of Himself in the way we look.

God looks at each of us and sees the beauty of His creation. No matter what you like or dislike about yourself, your heavenly Father sees the beauty of heaven in you.

God, it thrills my heart to know that You love us so much that you created us in Your perfect image! Amen.

DAY 252

LIFE'S NOT FAIR

". . .who shows no partiality to princes and does not favor the rich over the poor, for they are all the work of his hands?"

JOB 34:19 NIV

Is it fair that some kids grow up in wealthy areas with plenty of food and lots of entertainment, but others are born into poverty and starvation? Life isn't always fair; in fact, it seldom is. Yes, food, clothing, and shelter are important, but they don't sustain the spirit. Jesus teaches us to place little importance on worldly, material things and instead to set our eyes on the spiritual things that bring us eternal rewards.

There is no gain to feeding the flesh while the spirit starves. In other words, it doesn't help you at all if you take care of your body but let your heart go to waste.

God cares just as much for the starving child as He does for you. He weeps for those who hurt and aches for those who need. He created each of us, and He will provide according to our greatest needs. Today, ask God where He can use you to help those who are suffering. Perhaps letting you bless others was part of His plan all along.

Lord, it breaks my heart to know that some people have to suffer. Please help me see where You can use me to make a difference. Amen.

DAY 253

I AM NOT ALONE

The Lord is near to all who call upon Him.
Psalm 145:18 NASB

Sometimes when you have worked hard to do the right thing, everyone around abandons you and you find yourself very alone. It makes those choices even more difficult because nobody wants to be alone.

But the Lord understands those feelings all too well. One week, the crowds adored and praised Him. The next week, the crowds screamed for His death in hatred and ugliness.

Just remember that you are never, *never* alone. As a child of the King, He promises to never leave you. And the more you communicate with Him, the closer you will feel to Him.

So don't give up. Don't give in. Even if the world turns its back on you, remember that you have the God of the universe with you wherever you go.

Lord, it's hard when I feel alone, but I know that You understand better than anyone else. Help me continue to make the right decisions. Thank You for sticking with me through thick and thin. Amen.

DAY 254

ALWAYS THERE

Don't you know that you yourselves are God's temple and that God's Spirit dwells in your midst?
1 Corinthians 3:16 NIV

Many of us have been told that God is everywhere and that He's always with us. That sounds nice, but when we feel afraid or alone, it can be difficult to believe He's really right there. After all, we can't see Him. We can't touch Him. We can't hear Him speaking out loud to us.

Although we can't physically touch God, we can feel His presence. He loves us, and when we ask Him to live in us, He gladly accepts the invitation. He has promised never to leave us, never to turn His back on us. And though He doesn't talk out loud to us, if we listen, we can hear Him speaking to us in our thoughts. And we can always hear His words by reading the Bible.

And the great thing is, God *always* keeps His promises. That means that when we feel His presence, He's right there with us. And even when we don't feel His presence, even when we feel totally alone, He's still there. No matter what, He is always, *always* with us.

Dear Father, thank You for always being with me. Amen.

DAY 255

SIMPLE GOSSIP

It is foolish to belittle one's neighbor; a sensible person keeps quiet. A gossip goes around telling secrets, but those who are trustworthy can keep a confidence.
PROVERBS 11:12–13 NLT

We've all said something about somebody else that we wish we wouldn't have said. Gossip is a very common thing, and even church people don't see it as a very big deal sometimes. But it really is a big deal. Gossip hurts people!

It's been said that if you have to glance at the door to see if anyone is coming before saying something, you probably shouldn't be saying it! This is a hard lesson to learn and an even harder action to put into practice, especially if all your friends do it too.

Think about this:

- "Do not let any unwholesome talk come out of your mouths, but only what is helpful for building others up according to their needs, that it may benefit those who listen" (Ephesians 4:29 NIV).
- "Wrongdoers eagerly listen to gossip; liars pay close attention to slander" (Proverbs 17:4 NLT).

Simple gossip is simply sinful. It hurts others, it ruins friendships, and it is never harmless.

Dear God, please forgive me when I have gossiped. I know You want me to do—and say—the right thing. Amen.

DAY 256

FEAR NOT

"Be strong and courageous. Do not be afraid or terrified because of them, for the LORD your God goes with you; he will never leave you nor forsake you."
DEUTERONOMY 31:6 NIV

Not all fear is the same. Sometimes fear is healthy—like being afraid to break the law or fearing God. Those are the kinds of fears that keep you safe and help you lead a happy, productive life.

But sometimes fear can stop you from doing the things you need to do and can get in the way of the blessing God has for you. Being afraid to stand up for yourself, talk in front of a classroom full of people, defend your beliefs, or reveal that hidden talent are fears that can keep you from fulfilling your destiny.

The good news is you don't have to be afraid. God is with you. You are His child, and He will never leave you or forsake you. Just trust Him.

Dear God, Your Word says that You have not given me a spirit of fear. I choose to believe Your Word. I will not allow fear to keep me from doing the things that You want me to do and rob me of blessing. I will not fear. I will trust You to take care of me in every situation. Amen.

DAY 257

CONSTRUCTION, NOT DEMOLITION

Encourage each other and build each other up, just as you are already doing.
1 THESSALONIANS 5:11 NLT

Little kids love to build a tower of blocks or sculpt a sand castle only to gleefully stomp it to the ground. Destruction seems to be an instinct for humans.

God knows that our sinful nature gets pleasure out of seeing other people stomped to the ground. Even when we know what it's like to be on the receiving end of insults and mean words, sometimes we take pleasure in adding to the destruction of others by piling on words that are hurtful and mean-spirited.

The heavenly Father doesn't want to see His children destroy one another with words. His plan is encouragement. With every sincere, kind word, God adds another building block to the life of His child. And with every block of encouragement, we are made stronger to stand up to any destructive, stomping words that come our way.

Spend time today adding building blocks of encouragement to people around you. Soon you'll see that you'll be made stronger too.

Heavenly Father, help me to only speak encouraging words that build others up. Thank You. Amen.

DAY 258

WHAT SEASON IS IT?

There is a time for everything, and a season for every activity under the heavens.

ECCLESIASTES 3:1 NIV

The Bible tells us that everything has its season. Maybe you've been waiting for something to happen, but it's just not the right season yet. Hang on! Your day is coming!

Imagine you're in a "springtime" season. Everything in your life is blooming. You've got great new friendships, you're growing in the Lord. . .basically everything is going well. Then summer comes. Everything is now sunny and in full bloom. You're in a great relationship with your parents and getting along well with your brothers and sisters.

Next comes fall. Maybe you notice that some of your friendships are coming to an end, or perhaps there are other changes in your life. Maybe you used to take music lessons and now you don't; or maybe you were on a ball team and now you're not. Things are winding down. After fall comes winter. If you're in a winter season, maybe nothing seems to be working out. Perhaps you're lonely or disconnected—having a hard time with your prayer life.

No matter what season you're in, remember. . .that season will come to an end, and another will soon begin.

Dear heavenly Father, in winter, spring, summer, fall. . . I will trust You through all of life's seasons! Amen.

DAY 259

NO ONE UNDERSTANDS ME

For this reason he had to be made like them, fully human in every way, in order that he might become a merciful and faithful high priest in service to God, and that he might make atonement for the sins of the people.

Hebrews 2:17 NIV

Does it seem like no one understands you? Your parents, siblings, teachers, and friends may come close at times, but they're only human. People can never fill the Jesus-shaped spot in your heart. Only a personal relationship with Christ can meet the need every human being has to be known and understood.

Jesus left heaven for earth. While He was fully God, He was also fully human. He experienced emotions, such as disappointment and loss. Scripture tells us He wept. Yes, even Jesus cried. He felt angry. He was tempted. He was betrayed by those closest to Him. At times, Jesus was exhausted and needed rest.

You never need to wonder where that someone is who "gets" you. Jesus gets you. And He wants a close relationship with you. He longs to be the one you turn to when no one else understands. He will never leave you hanging or fall short of what you need. He understands!

Thank You, Lord Jesus, for understanding me when I am not even sure I understand myself sometimes! I love You. Amen.

DAY 260

I REALLY *NEED* THAT

Seek your happiness in the Lord,
and he will give you your heart's desire.
Psalm 37:4 GNT

"But I really need that!" How many times have you said those words?

Do we really *need* all the things we think we do? Or are they just *wants*?

When you think back to all the Christmas presents you received as a child—the ones you just couldn't live without—where have they gone? You were sure you needed those things. You didn't think your wants would change and never imagined you would desire something else after a short time.

There is a pretty big difference between needs and wants. And God is the only one who knows what you need. He longs to give you all your wants, but He also knows when and how you should get them. You may want the wrong things at the wrong time. He knows exactly what to give you and when.

If we give the desires of our hearts to the Lord, He can help us discover what is most important. He wants to be at the top of our wish list. We need Him first. And our relationship with Him is the key to happiness. After that, all the other things in our lives will come out in the right order of importance.

Dear Lord, I want to put You first on my list of wants. Help me to remember that You want to give me the desires of my heart. Thank You for providing for all my needs. Amen.

DAY 261

DREAM BIG!

Now all glory to God, who is able, through his mighty power at work within us, to accomplish infinitely more than we might ask or think.

Ephesians 3:20 NLT

How often do you daydream about what you're going to do with the rest of your life? Maybe you've thought about being a teacher. What about a doctor. . .or a scientist? . . . Perhaps even the president of the United States? Before you think none of those are possible for you, you need to understand that your dreams are no accident. God has placed them inside your heart as part of His plan for you. Furthermore, He has pre-arranged magnificent opportunities and customized connections specifically so you can fulfill the plan He created for your life. He has already coupled you to extraordinary blessings! That's why it is so important to consult the heavenly Father first before heading in any direction. With all He has in store for you, other options will never measure up. If things don't look so magnificent at the moment, you can rest assured that He is positioning you for bigger and better things to come.

God, I'm so excited that You have my customized future ready and waiting. Help me stay on the path to Your best for me. I know Your plans are the best plans. Amen.

DAY 262

GOD IS ALWAYS AWAKE

My help comes from the Lord, who made heaven and earth! He will not let you stumble; the one who watches over you will not slumber. Indeed, he who watches over Israel never slumbers or sleeps. The Lord himself watches over you!

Psalm 121:2–5 NLT

Stress and worry and fear are pretty common in kids your age. But it really doesn't have to be that way! God wants you to trust Him and leave your life and your worries in His mighty hands.

When you do have things that bother you, just talk to God about it. Anytime day or night. He is always awake! The Bible says that He never sleeps, He never takes a nap, and He's never looking the other way. He is always watching over you. He doesn't miss a thing!

And always remember, when you do talk to God about your worries and fears, a truly miraculous thing happens: He gives you His peace that will actually guard your heart and your mind (Philippians 4:6–7)! We can't even understand how that happens, but it really does. Give it a try, and give your worries to God. He's always awake.

God, thank You so much that You don't fall asleep while I'm talking to You. Thanks for not being bored by my problems. Show me Your peace. Amen.

DAY 263

JOY IN TRUSTING GOD

But let all those rejoice who put their trust in You;
let them ever shout for joy, because You defend them;
let those also who love Your name be joyful in You.
PSALM 5:11 NKJV

Do you ever find that you've put your trust in the wrong things? That you've trusted your friends more than God? That you look to your best friend to give you advice and even care more about what he or she might think than what your parents or even God thinks? Have you felt you've gone in the wrong direction because you aren't fully trusting God? You aren't very joyful on those days, are you? Remember that God made you and knows what is best for you *always*. Your friends don't always act in your best interest, but He does. Put your full trust in Him, and feel the joy!

Dear God, please help me to trust in You to guide me in the decisions I need to make each day. To look to You always, knowing that You are always there to defend me, to give me direction, to get me through each day so that I can be joyful again. Amen.

DAY 264

RESCUE SQUAD

The Lord says, "I will rescue those who love me. I will protect those who trust in my name."
Psalm 91:14 NLT

Believe it or not, physical danger is not the worst thing you can face. It's true that God protects you from many horrible dangers and catastrophes every day. In fact, we'll never know in this life just how many near misses we had when He spared us from injury. . .or worse. It's good to pray for and expect God's protection because He promised it to us.

But far better than saving us from a car accident or other painful experience is that He saves us from sin. Sin carries the promise of eternal devastation—far worse than anything we could experience here on this earth. God offers the blood of Jesus as our rescue from sin.

If you haven't already, ask Jesus to forgive you for your sins and cleanse you with His blood. Once you do that, it's a done deal—you're rescued—and you can trust that He is with you always.

Dear God, please forgive me for my sin and rescue me with the gift of eternal life. I want to walk with You. I'd love it if You'd protect me from danger in this life too. Amen.

DAY 265

WHEN THE GOING GETS TOUGH. . .

The LORD is my strength and my shield; my heart trusts in Him, and I am helped; therefore my heart exults, and with my song I shall thank Him.
PSALM 28:7 NASB

God was a shield to David and gave him strength. But first, David *trusted* Him.

What does it mean to trust God? You lay down your "own understanding" and "acknowledge" that He has always been, is, and always will be the supreme God of all creation (Proverbs 3:5–6 NASB).

When you rely on God's strength and not your own, God's able to take control. He says to you, "I will give you rest. Take My yoke upon you and learn from Me" (Matthew 11:28–29 NASB). He has offered to take our burdens. Why insist on keeping them when His arms are reaching down to lift your heavy load? He will give you the strength to persevere. Just trust Him. He's "a very present help in trouble" (Psalm 46:1 NASB).

Lord, I can't do this on my own. I surrender everything. I trust You, Lord God. Please give me the strength to "press on toward the goal for the prize" (Philippians 3:14 NASB). In Jesus' precious and holy name I pray. Amen.

DAY 266

TICK, TICK, TICK

Making the best use of the time, because the days are evil.
EPHESIANS 5:16 ESV

Have you ever noticed how quickly time slips by when you're online? Maybe you've just downloaded a popular new app and it's got you hooked. Or maybe you're checking out the hilarious video on YouTube that your friend mentioned. Techie gadgets are so cool! But they can also be dangerous. They're famous for sneaking off with the important hours that you should have spent doing something else. And once that time is gone, there is no way to get it back.

Popular apps come and go, but God's Word is forever. Set aside some time each day to read the Bible. It's not just a book full of big words in small print. It's God's love letter to you! And it's where you'll find answers to your questions and the keys to your future. Ask God to remind you when it's time to turn off your gadgets and do something more worthwhile. Remember that He has great plans for your life, and He wants you to get started on them!

Father in heaven, I don't want to neglect Your Word. Help me to be careful with the time I spend online, and tap on my shoulder if I start to get careless. Amen.

DAY 267

MARSUPIALS IN THE DARK

"Never will I leave you; never will I forsake you."
HEBREWS 13:5 NIV

I once owned two sugar gliders named Sassie and Stubbie. These cute, tiny, nocturnal marsupials looked like squirrels, weighed only four ounces, and spent their days sleeping in my pockets. At night, about the time I put on my pajamas, they woke up to have an evening party.

When I wanted to play with them at night, I had to quietly enter their dark playroom, close the door, then stand still and wait. If I moved, I could step on one of them. In less than fifteen seconds, they found me in the dark. Both of them always ran up my legs and sat on my shoulders. I was their human tree! Because they could see in the dark, we had a relationship.

Just like Sassie and Stubbie could see me in the dark, God can see you and me all the time too. When you feel like you are walking in the dark and like God isn't with you, remember He is always there.

Lord Jesus, thank You that You say You will never leave me or forsake me. And even though I don't always feel like You are with me, I trust that You are because You say You are. I lean on what You say, not on how I feel. Amen.

DAY 268

LET GO!

The other guests began to say among themselves, "Who is this who even forgives sins?"
LUKE 7:49 NIV

Have you ever picked up some candy at the store that you *just had to have* and not paid for it? Have you ever cheated on a test? What about taking money from your mom's purse without asking? You don't have to be told any one of these actions is wrong. You know it in your heart! But did you own up to your mistakes?

The good news is that God forgives you. He knows your heart. All you need to do is ask, and He will forgive any wrong that you've done. He forgives everything from the smallest mistakes to the biggest blunders.

Every day is a chance for a fresh, new start; another opportunity to do the right thing and make good choices. Now is the time to let go of the past and begin a new day full of God's wonderful blessings.

God, please help me to learn to forgive myself as You have forgiven me. Thank You for giving me free will—but help me to use my free will for Your glory. Amen.

DAY 269

THE GREAT BLUE OCEAN

Because of the LORD's great love we are not consumed,
for his compassions never fail. They are new
every morning; great is your faithfulness.
LAMENTATIONS 3:22–23 NIV

Have you ever wondered if God loves you? Everyone has asked that question at some point in their lives. Even your Sunday school teachers. . .even the writers of these devotions. That question is as common as ketchup on french fries and purrs from a kitten.

The nation of Israel had that same question too, and God's answer was simple: "I have loved you," says the Lord. And that is His answer to us today. His affection for us—for *you*—is as big and unfathomable as the great blue ocean. And yet His love is as tender and close as a mother's kiss on a baby's forehead.

God's kindness will never fail. It's new every morning like the dew on your lawn and the rising of the sun. God's love is sure, and His faithfulness is forever.

Even when I'm not very faithful to You, Lord,
and I sometimes forget to talk to You, I'm glad
You love me and watch over me. Thank You
for Your love and faithfulness. Amen.

DAY 270

PROMISES, PROMISES

"God is not human, that he should lie, not a human being, that he should change his mind. Does he speak and then not act? Does he promise and not fulfill?"
NUMBERS 23:19 NIV

Have you ever had someone promise you something and then break that promise?

That happens to everyone at some point in their lives. Sometimes promises get broken on purpose because the person just didn't want to keep it. Other times people want to keep their promises, but circumstances prevent them from fulfilling their word. Either way, it hurts.

God always, *always* keeps His promises. He's not like human beings, who forget or mess up or who can't control their circumstances. If God says He'll do something, He means it. And He'll do it!

We can't take advantage of God's promises, though, unless we know what they are. That's why it's important to read the Bible and learn what He has said. When we find ourselves in need of God's help, we can remind Him of His promises, and we can be certain He will keep them.

Dear Father, thank You for keeping Your promises. Help me to learn more about Your promises through Your Word. Amen.

DAY 271

HEARTBREAK HOTEL

The LORD is close to the brokenhearted and saves those who are crushed in spirit.
PSALM 34:18 NIV

At one time or another we all get our feelings hurt. But sometimes the hurt is so bad you think you just might die from it. It might be because of something a friend did or something your parents said. It could be a betrayal or worse. Whatever it is—it can leave you heartbroken.

In some people a broken heart can lead to bitterness, anger, and depression. But you don't have to go there. You're a child of God. He sees everything, and He knows just how you feel. You can choose to turn all that hurt over to Him. It might be hard at first. You might have to let it go again and again—especially in the beginning. But if you let Him, God will mend your heart and give you back your joy.

Dear God, You already know about every time I've ever been hurt. Because I don't want to get caught in a trap of anger and bitterness, I choose to let it all go. I ask You to heal my broken heart today. Help me release all my hurts to You so that I can live a life of joy and freedom. Amen.

DAY 272

FULLY UNDERSTOOD

This High Priest of ours understands our weaknesses, for he faced all of the same testings we do, yet he did not sin.
HEBREWS 4:15 NLT

Ever wonder if anybody understands you? Do they "get it"?

Sometimes others just don't understand. They won't get what makes you laugh hysterically. They can't understand what makes you cry until there are no more tears.

Jesus Christ understands everything about every one of His creations. He knows how you feel on the best of your best days and on the worst of your worst days. And usually it's hardest to find someone who understands us in the difficult times.

Jesus faced rough times on earth. His earthly parents didn't always understand His mission. His close friend betrayed Him. Another friend lied and said he never knew Jesus to keep himself out of trouble. And finally, society turned against Him and killed Him.

He knows what it's like to not be understood, but He truly understands all about us. Trust that He "gets it."

Dear Jesus, thank You for understanding everything about me and loving me anyway. Even on my worst of days, You are there, full of understanding. You are the greatest of friends! Amen.

DAY 273

MORE THAN ORDINARY

"And I tell you that you are Peter, and on this rock I will build my church, and the gates of Hades will not overcome it."

MATTHEW 16:18 NIV

Do you ever feel like you're too ordinary to do great things? You look at others and think, *If I were that talented, I could do great things too.* You don't feel very special. In fact, you feel very average. Cheer up! Ever see the movie *Rudy*? Talk about an ordinary guy doing extraordinary things. He didn't have a lot of talent, but he had a whole lot of heart. I've got news for you: God loves to use ordinary people to do extraordinary things.

Look at Peter. He was just a fisherman, but God called him "the Rock upon which I'll build My church." What about Mary? She was just a teenager, yet God chose her to give birth to Jesus. How about David? He was the little guy in the family. When his brothers went to war, he had to stay home and watch the sheep. Still, God called him to defeat the giant Goliath.

Know this: if you're feeling very ordinary, then you're the perfect person to do extraordinary things!

God, help me to see myself as You see me—capable of extraordinary things. Amen.

DAY 274

A CROWN FOR THE KING'S KID

Blessed is the one who perseveres under trial because, having stood the test, that person will receive the crown of life that the Lord has promised to those who love him.

JAMES 1:12 NIV

Choices, choices, choices. Not all of them are bad, but sometimes you are faced with really difficult ones. In your heart, you know what is right, but all your friends want you to go the wrong direction. Would it really be that bad. . .just this once?

Because we live in a sin-filled world, the choices we have to make get harder every day. The world around us doesn't care about God or His commandments. It wants to be free to do whatever it pleases. Because we're supposed to be happy and feel good, right?

The Bible reminds us that this life is going to be hard. We're going to have lots of temptations and lots of trials. But by making the right choices—following God's guidelines for our lives—the rewards will be immeasurable.

And as a child of the King, won't it be amazing to receive your crown from Him? How cool it will be to receive such a treasure and then get to lay it at His feet! Remember that next time you are tempted to go the wrong direction. Stay on track, dear one. Your crown awaits.

God, help me to guard my mind and my heart so that I can do the right thing today. Amen.

DAY 275

DON'T BE AFRAID

When I am afraid, I put my trust in you.
Psalm 56:3 NIV

Fear can creep up on any of us. Some of us (even adults!) are still afraid of the dark! But when we allow fear to have a firm grip on us, we aren't trusting God the way He wants us to.

In Luke 12:32 (NIV) after telling us how useless it is to worry, Jesus says, "Do not be afraid, little flock, for your Father has been pleased to give you the kingdom." Can't you hear and feel the love in God's heart for you? When you are afraid, give it to Jesus.

The next time you're really afraid of something, repeat these verses to yourself and let them sink into your heart:

- "I am leaving you with a gift—peace of mind and heart. And the peace I give is a gift the world cannot give. So don't be troubled or afraid" (John 14:27 NLT).
- "This is my command—be strong and courageous! Do not be afraid or discouraged. For the Lord your God is with you wherever you go" (Joshua 1:9 NLT).

Dear God, when I'm afraid, please help me to remember that You are always with me and that I can talk to You about it. Please give me Your peace. Amen.

DAY 276

A REAL HAPPILY-EVER-AFTER

"Whoever believes in him may have eternal life."
JOHN 3:15 NRSV

Have you ever read a story where the characters lived happily ever after? Maybe they rode off into the sunset together or shared a victory over evil, and you knew in your heart of hearts that all of their troubles were behind them.

Don't you just love a happy ending? God does! That's why He's got the perfect happily-ever-after planned out for you. It's all going to take place in a land far, far away. . .a place called heaven. In that regal place, you'll walk in streets of gold, live in a mansion, and dine with the King! It's true!

How do you get to this amazing place? It's really simple. Just place your trust in Jesus, God's Son. He gave His life for you so that you could one day spend eternity with Him. Talk about a happy ending!

God, I believe You sent Your Son, Jesus, to die for my sins. I ask Him to come into my heart and wash me clean. Because of what He did on the cross, I know that I can live forever with You in heaven. Thank You, Lord! Amen.

DAY 277

FRUITS OF THE SPIRIT

But the fruit of the Spirit is love, joy, peace, forbearance, kindness, goodness, faithfulness, gentleness and self-control. Against such things there is no law.

GALATIANS 5:22–23 NIV

What do your friends have to say about you? Would they be surprised if they learned that you are a Christian? The mark of a true Christian is that Jesus can be seen in every area of his or her life. There are certain traits that help identify a child of God. Love, joy, patience, and kindness are just a few. Do you believe that your friends would know by your love of others, your patience, and your kindness that you are a follower of Christ?

Take a look at your actions and your attitudes and make sure that they line up with the fruits of a true Christian. Jesus asks His children to be like Him in the way they deal with others. In fact, it's our treatment of others that sets us apart in the world. Jesus modeled perfect sacrifice and love for others. We need to share that love with those around us.

Dear heavenly Father, please help me take a good, honest look at myself as I consider whether I'm being a true representative of You. Help me to be a good example of Your love. Amen.

DAY 278

GOD IS IN CONTROL

In peace I will lie down and sleep, for you alone,
O Lord, will keep me safe.
Psalm 4:8 NLT

This world can be a scary place. Reports you see on the evening news or things you hear your parents discussing may sometimes frighten you. Indeed, life is not always as it should be. Ever since sin entered the world in the Garden of Eden, it has been less than ideal. That's a fact.

But the good news is that God is in control. What man means for evil, God is able to use for good. Even the worst or scariest circumstances are never too big for God. There is always hope with our heavenly Father.

The Bible promises that one day there will be no more tears and no more trials. In heaven, there will be no scary news reports and there will be no more pain. Until then, rest in the knowledge that God has commanded angels to watch over you. Lay your head on your pillow at night in peace. God is your safety. Nothing can reach you that hasn't first been filtered through His fingers.

God, sometimes I feel afraid. Thank You for Your promise that You will never leave me. I trust that You are in control. Amen.

DAY 279

I LOVE THAT!

But God, being rich in mercy, because of His great love with which He loved us, even when we were dead in our transgressions, made us alive together with Christ.

EPHESIANS 2:4–5 NASB

The word *love* is used for just about anything. We use it to describe all kinds of feelings or to express how much we enjoy something.

"I *love* this cake. I *loved* the movie. I *love* going to the park. I *love* to read."

But is *love* really the right word to use for everything? It could be we use it too much. If *love* really describes so many things, what word should we use for much deeper emotions and attachments? It's silly to use the same word for our affinity for cake as we do for the deep feelings we have for our parents. But it's the only word we know that fits. And Mom and Dad don't seem to mind, right?

That said, how can we even begin to understand the greatness of God's love? The only way is to know who lives behind the word: God IS love. It's more than just a feeling He has for us; it's a state of being. God loves us with something deeper than a word. He loves us with His entire being, as our Father and Creator. And it's a *big* love! Only when we know more of Him can we understand what His love really means.

Thank You, God, for Your great love for me. Help me to love others with a deeper love and to show them that You ARE love. Amen.

DAY 280

THE SPIRIT OF INTELLIGENCE

"I thought, 'Those who are older should speak, for wisdom comes with age.' But there is a spirit within people, the breath of the Almighty within them that makes them intelligent."

Job 32:7–8 NLT

Respect for your elders is a very important thing. But that doesn't mean that you have nothing to offer just because of your age. The Holy Spirit moves within each child of God and gives special understanding of spiritual things. Age is not a boundary or a limitation on God. So if He gives you something to say or gives you understanding, don't allow Satan to deceive you into feeling that you are too young to be taken seriously.

There are many areas of ministry that are great for young people to get involved in. Leading or mentoring those in younger grades, serving on planning committees for special events, or offering testimonies or prayers at youth events. The best thing you can do for the body of Christ though is to have a heart that desires to bring others to a saving knowledge of Jesus. Invite others to church and youth events, and learn enough about the gospel of Christ so that it becomes easy for you to share it with others.

God, thank You for choosing me to make a difference for You in the world. I love You. Amen.

DAY 281

BE CONTENT AND TRUST GOD

"I will make you strong if you quietly trust me."
Isaiah 30:15 CEV

People react to change in one of three ways. Some people are really nervous about every new situation, while others are too full of their own plans to accept what God has for them. And then there are some who are as happy to trust God in the difficult times as they are to rely on Him in the pleasant periods of life.

Has God given you something difficult to face such as a broken home, a new school, or a class you don't enjoy? Don't be nervous and jittery about your circumstances, waiting for a chance to go a different way. And don't be so full of your own plans that you can't trust God. Learn to be content with His plan. God loves you, and He knows best. Trust Him in all things and stand strong in the face of change or struggle. True trust reveals itself when things look the worst.

God, even though end results aren't always clear at the beginning of a trial I am facing, I will trust You. I will accept that You always know what's best. Amen.

DAY 282

THE HOPE OF HIS CALLING

I pray that the eyes of your heart may be enlightened, so that you will know what is the hope of His calling, what are the riches of the glory of His inheritance in the saints, and what is the surpassing greatness of His power toward us who believe.

EPHESIANS 1:18–19 NASB

You are a child of God. You are called (2 Timothy 1:9; John 10:3; 1 Thessalonians 4:7)—with hope!

What are you called to? You're called to prayer (Philippians 4:6–7). You're called to walk by faith (Galatians 2:20; 2 Corinthians 5:7). You're called to live with the fruit of the Spirit (Galatians 5:22–25). You're called to love the Lord with all your heart, mind, and strength (Matthew 22:37). And you're called to study His Word (Psalm 119:105; Matthew 7:24–25; 2 Timothy 2:15).

God's Word is our guidebook—our life manual. Everything we need to know about how God has called us to live is inside, waiting to be discovered! It is by *knowing* His hopeful calling and His Word that you will blossom into the young person He has called you to be.

Lord, thank You for calling me. Thank You for choosing me. I know that I am and always will be Yours—and for that I have eternal hope! Please help me to study Your Word diligently. In Jesus' name I pray. Amen.

DAY 283

HOPE: AN ANCHOR FOR THE SOUL

Be strong and take heart, all you who hope in the Lord.

Psalm 31:24 NIV

Have you ever heard someone say, "I hope I get a good grade," "I hope I get to go on vacation this summer," or "I hope that my birthday is awesome"?

For a lot of people, a hope is a wish. It's kind of like cotton candy; it's just a bunch of fluff. But the hope that God describes in the Bible is certain. . .it's a solid anchor for your soul.

Have you ever seen a boat with an anchor? When the waves start rolling, the fishermen throw the anchor over the edge into the water to steady the boat. That's what God's hope is. It's like an anchor to steady you when life is hard. Hebrews 6:19 (NIV) describes this hope: "We have this hope as an anchor for the soul, firm and secure."

Just like an anchor holds a boat steady when the waves are rolling, God's hope holds your thoughts and your emotions steady when life is difficult. All you have to do is believe and trust God. Then you can be steady even in a big storm of life.

Lord Jesus, I am so glad that hoping in You holds me steady when things get tough! I am glad that You are always my anchor and that You will never leave me. Amen.

DAY 284

WORRY DOESN'T HELP

Jesus said, "That is why I tell you not to worry about everyday life—whether you have enough food to eat or enough clothes to wear. For life is more than food, and your body more than clothing."

LUKE 12:22–23 NLT

Jesus talks a lot about the fact that we should never worry or be afraid. If we do worry and fear a lot, it means we're not really putting our trust in Him very much, right? Here are some more verses to think about the next time you start to worry:

> "Look at the ravens. They don't plant or harvest or store food in barns, for God feeds them. And you are far more valuable to him than any birds! Can all your worries add a single moment to your life? And if worry can't accomplish a little thing like that, what's the use of worrying over bigger things?"
> Luke 12:24–26 NLT

He doesn't want you to worry about having the best clothes or the most expensive phone. You don't have to be afraid of what's going to happen to you this summer or who your friends will be next year. Worry won't change a thing, so trust God instead.

Dear God, forgive me for all the times I worry. I want to trust that You're in control. Please give me Your peace. Amen.

DAY 285

OOPS!

Pride ends in humiliation, while humility brings honor.
PROVERBS 29:23 NLT

Do you ever wish you had a time machine? A sleek little gadget that could transport you back in time? Back to that moment when you said the wrong thing and hurt a friend's feelings? Back to that day when you really goofed up and upset your parents? To that instant when you made a bad decision and knew that your heavenly Father was less than pleased?

Life is full of mistakes. It's part of being human! But being a child of God means fixing those mistakes as soon as possible. How? Not through time travel, but by being humble. By telling the person you hurt or upset that you're sorry.

God may be disappointed in your bad decision, but He loves it when you humble yourself in prayer and ask for His forgiveness. Your parents may be upset by your goof, but they'll appreciate your apology. Your hurt friend will feel a lot better when they hear you say you're sorry.

Don't putter around in the garage, trying to figure out how to build a time machine. Take the humble route. It works every time.

God, when I do something wrong, I feel so terrible about it. Please help me to always make things right. . .as soon as possible. Thank You. Amen.

DAY 286

A PLAN FOR ME?

"I know what I'm doing. I have it all planned out—
plans to take care of you, not abandon you,
plans to give you the future you hope for."
JEREMIAH 29:11 MSG

Are you a planner who likes to be in control of what happens? Are you one of those people who doesn't even like to participate in something unless it was your idea in the first place? Or do you prefer to let other people do the planning? However you approach the future, know that God has a plan for you.

If you're a planner and like to be in control, do you realize that someone bigger than you and wiser than you might direct you off your planned path? As a Christ-follower, that has to be okay with you. Remember that no matter how independent and confident you are that your way is the right way, you can't see the future.

Trust in God's wisdom, and know that He really does care for you and wants the very best for you. Knowing that's true and knowing that He sees all things, does that make it easier for you to let go of your own will and trust Him fully?

Father, I give up my own will and surrender control to You. I trust that You will direct me to what's best for me. Thank You for loving me enough to have a plan for me. Amen.

DAY 287

PRETTY SPECIAL

"Fear not, for I have redeemed you.
I have called you by name, you are mine."
Isaiah 43:1 ESV

Do you ever wonder how God keeps all his children straight? How can He possibly remember all our names? How can He remember details about our personalities, or what we need, or what makes us laugh or cry?

But the truth is, God does remember all those things. While we humans may forget a name or forget someone's birthday, God *never* forgets. He loves us. We belong to Him, and because of that, He takes a deep interest in everything about our lives.

The reason He loves us so much is because we are important to Him. And if the God of the universe says we're important, we can believe it's true. Next time you feel forgotten or like you don't matter, remind yourself of this one truth: *The God of the universe, the King of kings and Lord of lords, calls me by name. That makes me pretty special!*

Dear Father, thank You for knowing me, for calling me by name, and for thinking I'm special. Help me to remember who I am in You. Help me make others feel special too. Amen.

DAY 288

D-I-S-C-I-P-L-I-N-E

The Lord disciplines those he loves,
as a father the son he delights in.
Proverbs 3:12 NIV

How many times have you heard those words from one of your parents? "I'm doing this for your own good." They usually follow them with other words you don't like to hear: "No, you can't spend the night with your friend" or "You have to clean up that messy room!"

Discipline—how we dislike the word. When your parents discipline you, they are taking the time to correct your behavior. Maybe you were supposed to clean up your room days ago but didn't. Now it's time to pay the piper. You can't spend the night with your best friend, and you've got to stay in there all day, doing what you neglected earlier. Maybe you were rude (or mean) to your little brother, and now you have to do extra chores (fold the clothes or wash the dishes).

Here's the truth: If your parents didn't love you, they wouldn't discipline you. If they didn't give you boundaries, you wouldn't know the difference between right and wrong. And believe it or not, when they use those words—"I'm doing this for your own good!"—they really are!

God, thank You for loving me enough to discipline me when I need it. Amen.

DAY 289

RAINBOW HUES

O Lord, thou hast searched me, and known me.

Psalm 139:1 KJV

Rainbows wouldn't be very impressive if they were only one color. The seamless layers of red, orange, yellow, green, blue, indigo, and violet are what make them beautiful. And it's the myriad layers of human emotions that make you who you are! Cheery yellow, daring orange, fiery red, sensible brown. . .hue after hue of personality make up the person that is uniquely you.

Ever had a blue day or felt a twinge of envious green? No human would be complete without them. The trick is keeping all of those emotions—good and bad—in check. Have fiery red and melancholy blue mixed to create a gloomy purplish mood? Or maybe that twinge of green has blossomed into full-blown emerald jealousy. Tell your Creator! He understands you like no one else can and knows exactly how to brighten a dark, unbecoming mood.

Pray about your feelings. Remember that as God's child, you have the power to rule over them instead of letting them rule you!

Dear God, my Creator, You know how I feel and why. Teach me to control my feelings before they cause me to act in an unbecoming way. Amen.

DAY 290

IT'S TOUGH TO LOSE SOMEONE YOU LOVE

Brothers and sisters, we do not want you to be uninformed about those who sleep in death, so that you do not grieve like the rest of mankind, who have no hope. For we believe that Jesus died and rose again, and so we believe that God will bring with Jesus those who have fallen asleep in him.

1 Thessalonians 4:13–14 NIV

When someone you love dies, it hurts—a lot. Death can separate you from people you care about. You can't touch them or hear their voice. You can't call them on the phone or make plans to meet next weekend. All you have left are memories.

Because you are a believer, death has no hold on you (1 Corinthians 15:55). When Jesus died and rose again, He defeated death once and for all. The Bible says that when a believer leaves this life, they go to be with the Lord (2 Corinthians 5:8). Even though you may be separated from someone you love, it won't be forever. You'll see them again in heaven. Now that's a comforting thought!

Dear God, my heart hurts when I think of people I love who have died. It hurts to know I can't reach out to them anytime I want. I'm SO glad I have hope in You. I'm thankful I will see them again because of what Jesus did on the cross. Thank You for defeating death for me and those I love. Amen.

DAY 291

CHOOSING THE RIGHT THING

And whatever you do [no matter what it is] in word or deed, do everything in the name of the Lord Jesus and in [dependence upon] His Person, giving praise to God the Father through Him.

COLOSSIANS 3:17 AMPC

Choices. . . Which one? Where? When? So many questions await decisions.

Some decisions are simple and can be made rather quickly. Others take some time to pray and think through. It's during those times that we need to seek the Lord, making choices that aren't determined by our own wants. At times our first thought is, *What should I do?* But making decisions in light of what Christ wants for us can be more difficult. It may mean sacrificing something or dying to our own desires. It's no longer *What should I do?* but, *Lord, what do You want me to do?*

All decisions—large or small—should be made in order to bring our heavenly Father the praise He deserves.

Dear Father, help me to seek Your guidance as I make decisions. Please make me willing to do whatever I need to so that Your name is praised as a result of my choices. In Jesus' name, amen.

DAY 292

THE KING, MY PROTECTOR

Neither death nor life, neither angels nor demons, neither the present nor the future, nor any powers, neither height nor depth, nor anything else in all creation, will be able to separate us from the love of God that is in Christ Jesus our Lord.

ROMANS 8:38–39 NIV

When bad things happen to good people, it's hard to understand. But as a child of God, you are sealed in Him. That doesn't mean that nothing bad will ever happen to you, but it does mean that your King—the Lord God—loves you so much that you can never be snatched out of His hand.

You can have confidence that nothing in this world can keep you from God. Nothing in this world can separate you from God. And nothing—absolutely *nothing*—can take away your eternal life in Him. Your future—your eternity—is protected.

God, thank You that nothing can separate me from Your love. Help me not to be afraid even when things are really bad, but to trust in You. . .no matter the circumstances. You are my King, you are my protector. Amen.

DAY 293

SECRET SERVICE MAN

Deliver me from my enemies, O my God;
protect me from those who rise up against me.
Psalm 59:1 NRSV

If you ever watch the president of the United States on TV, you've probably noticed the men in the background dressed in black. These are his bodyguards, and they're called the secret service. They always travel with the president and stick very, very close in case anyone tries to harm him in any way. If that happens, these trained protectors jump into action to make sure the president stays safe!

Did you know that God is the ultimate secret service man? He's always on your side, protecting you from the enemy. You don't always see how He protects you, but He does! He keeps you safe as you go back and forth to school. He protects you from harm as you sleep at night. He sends His angels to watch over you and guards your steps everywhere you go. Why? Because He loves you. You're His kid, after all!

The next time you're afraid, just remember that God is your ultimate protector. He's watching over you to make sure you're safe and sound.

Thank You, Lord, for protecting me! I feel like I have my very own personal bodyguard, always looking out for me to keep me from harm. Amen!

DAY 294

YOU'VE GOT TALENT!

Just think—you don't need a thing, you've got it all! All God's gifts are right in front of you as you wait expectantly for our Master Jesus to arrive on the scene for the Finale. And not only that, but God himself is right alongside to keep you steady and on track until things are all wrapped up by Jesus. God, who got you started in this spiritual adventure, shares with us the life of his Son and our Master Jesus. He will never give up on you. Never forget that.

1 Corinthians 1:7–9 MSG

Do you know you have special talents that are unique to only you? It's true! Do you remember the Parable of the Talents in Matthew 25? A man was going on a long journey, so he called his servants together. To one he gave five talents; to another he gave two; and to another he gave one. Then he left. The man with the five talents gained five more. The man with two talents gained two more. But the man with one talent dug a hole and buried it. When the master returned, he was pleased with the men who had doubled his money. But he was upset with the man who had hidden his talent. The master took the one talent from him and gave it to the servant who had the most talents.

You see, if we hide our talents, we're no better than the servant who buried his talent. (And God called him wicked!) Don't let fear or laziness keep you from shining for God. Remember, God gave you those talents, and He will gladly help you develop them and use them for His purposes.

Thank You, God, for giving me special talents unique to only me. Amen.

DAY 295

A GRAND ADVENTURE

"For I know the plans I have for you," declares the Lord, "plans to prosper you and not to harm you, plans to give you hope and a future."

Jeremiah 29:11 NIV

Making plans can be a lot of fun. Like calling up your friends to meet you at Starbucks, or getting a group together to go to a basketball game at school, or organizing a sleepover, or just creating some fun time to hang out and chat. God likes to be in the midst of all your dreaming and planning for the future.

In fact, God has a design for your whole life, just like a beautiful picture. He wants the best for you—a one-of-a-kind, grand adventure—better than you could ever imagine for yourself. He wants to help you make the most of your talents and keep you close to Him.

Right now, as you read these words, He's here with you. The God of the universe wants to talk to you. He's whispering thoughts of hope, and He's asking to guide you in the wonderful adventure He has planned for your life. All you have to do is listen to that still, small voice.

Thank You, Jesus, that You have a perfect design for my life. Help me to see it clearly so my steps will always be in the right direction. Amen.

DAY 296

PROMISE KEEPER

"I have set my rainbow in the clouds, and it will be the sign of the covenant between me and the earth."
GENESIS 9:13 NIV

Do you know the story of Noah and his great ark? It's probably one of the first Bible stories you heard as a little child. Remember all the animals loading onto the great ship, two by two? Remember the flood? And then. . .the rainbow! God put it in the sky as a reminder to Himself and to all humankind. He will never again flood the earth to destroy all of life.

When you see a rainbow in the sky, think about God's promise. His brushstrokes of color are like whispers from heaven.

God keeps His promises. You can rest assured He will never again flood the whole earth as He did in Noah's day. And if He keeps that promise, wouldn't it make sense that our God would keep all of His promises?

Your heavenly Father promises to never leave you. He promises that He has great plans for you—plans for a future, for hope, and never to harm you. Trust Him. He's a promise keeper!

Heavenly Father, thank You for the rainbow in the sky that reminds me I serve a promise-keeping God! Amen.

DAY 297

THE FORCE OF THE FLOW

"Be strong and courageous. Do not be afraid or terrified because of them, for the Lord your God goes with you; he will never leave you nor forsake you."

Deuteronomy 31:6 NIV

Courage can be like the faucet you use when you wash your face in the morning. The more you turn the valve, the more forceful the water flows; and in the case of courage, the knob needs three turns for maximum flow. Turn one is a willingness to stand up to any negative self-talk going on in your mind. Don't let your inner conversations tell you your situation is hopeless. Turn your courage up another notch by recognizing God will never leave you alone in any situation. He is a big God who is standing beside you! He doesn't believe in hopelessness! Turn three on your valve of courage is believing God has a specific plan for your life, no matter what is happening today. He wants you to succeed!

By eliminating fear within, knowing you are not alone, and recognizing He is there to show you the way to success, you cause your courage level to hit maximum flow!

God, help me to be brave and strong. I know You are with me through everything. Amen.

DAY 298

CHRIST'S AMBASSADORS

For God was in Christ, reconciling the world to himself, no longer counting people's sins against them. And he gave us this wonderful message of reconciliation. So we are Christ's ambassadors; God is making his appeal through us. We speak for Christ when we plead, "Come back to God!"

2 Corinthians 5:19–20 NLT

Do you know what an ambassador is? In this instance, Dictionary.com defines it as "an authorized messenger or representative." When we accept Jesus as our Savior, we become one of God's messengers—an ambassador for Christ!

It's a very important job to tell—and show—others about what God has done in our lives. Because of the great love that Jesus showed for us on the cross, God is not counting our sins against us! We're free from guilt! Free from shame! And free to live a life of joy for all eternity!

That's worth telling the whole world about, right? That's our main purpose here on earth: to be Christ's ambassador!

Dear Jesus, thank You for not counting my sins against me. Thank You for Your great love. I want to be an ambassador for You. Give me the courage to share this message with the people in my world. Amen.

DAY 299

HOW CAN I MAKE SOMEONE LOVE ME?

We love because he first loved us.

1 John 4:19 NIV

Have you ever asked, "How can I make someone love me?" The movies say you have to be good looking to get love. Maybe your friends say you have to be popular, or the kids at your school might say you have to be rich. The problem is that none of these things will earn you true love. Here's why: true love starts in the heart of the one who loves; not in the heart of the one who receives the love. This means true love is not earned. It's freely given, like a gift.

This is wonderful because it means that you don't have to be perfect or beautiful, rich or smart to get true love. This is how God loves. He loves us even though we aren't perfect. Even if you are stubborn, mean, impatient, or unkind, God will never stop loving you.

What a relief, huh? You can't earn God's love, and He will never stop loving you. He chose to love you not because of who you are, but because of who He is.

Lord, I am so thankful that there is nothing I can do to earn Your love. I am so grateful that You will never stop loving me. Help me to love You the way I am loved by You. Amen.

DAY 300

MY TESTIMONY

Always be prepared to give an answer to everyone who asks you to give the reason for the hope that you have.

1 PETER 3:15 NIV

The world wants to know why you are a Christian. Maybe you've been asked about your faith before. Did you know what to say? God tells His followers to be prepared to answer anyone who asks us why we believe what we believe.

It's not as scary as it sounds, and it's important to think about your answer before you're asked the question. When someone opens the door for you to share your testimony, talk about your faith in three minutes:

Minute one: Talk about what your life was like and what struggles you had before you accepted Christ.

Minute two: Share your story of how you became a Christian and what steps you took to come to that point.

Minute three: Tell about how your life has changed since beginning a relationship with Jesus and the hope you have in spending eternity with Him in heaven.

Your testimony is a special story that is unique to you. It doesn't have to be earth-shattering or tragic to show others the power of Jesus in your life. Your testimony is an amazing recollection of a miracle God performed in you, His child.

Dear heavenly Father, please help me to know just what to say when someone asks me about my faith. Thank You! Amen.

DAY 301

THE SEEDLING PRINCIPLE

"Truly, truly, I say to you, unless a grain of wheat falls into the earth and dies, it remains alone; but if it dies, it bears much fruit."
JOHN 12:24 NASB

Our Father's the master gardener of all Creation. He loves everything He's made. Have you ever watched a flower grow? What must a seedling do in order to spring forth its beautiful flower?

Jesus said that unless a seed dies, it remains alone. But if it dies, it bears much fruit (see also Romans 5:3–4).

"Walk in a manner worthy of the Lord, to please Him in all respects, bearing fruit in every good work and increasing in the knowledge of God" (Colossians 1:10 NASB).

We must die to our selfish desires if we want to bear fruit for Christ. God's asking you to surrender *everything* so He may give you *opportunities* to grow.

For instance, how can we learn patience if we never have to wait? How can we learn to trust Him if we never surrender?

Just remember, God's given you everything you need: His everlasting love.

Lord, help me to die to myself and grow in You. The desire of my heart is to follow You no matter what. In Jesus' name I pray. Amen.

DAY 302

WHAT A GLORIOUS DAY!

"And everyone who has left houses or brothers or sisters or father or mother or wife or children or fields for my sake will receive a hundred times as much and will inherit eternal life."

MATTHEW 19:29 NIV

You miss your grandmother. She was so special to you. Now she's in heaven—and it's affecting everyone in the family. You tiptoe around your mom. You allow your sister to sleep in your room. You even give her your favorite stuffed animal.

You walk around remembering the good times you shared with your grandmother. There were so many! But then you think about all the things she will miss—your sporting events, your school plays, your high school graduation—and your heart feels crushed, like you'll never feel joy again.

But then God reminds you that He offers the gift of eternal life—and you've already accepted that wonderful gift. And someday your grandma will greet you in heaven. What a glorious day that will be!

God, thank You for offering me eternal life. Take care of my loved one until I get to heaven. Amen.

DAY 303

I CAN DO IT!

"This is my command—be strong and courageous! Do not be afraid or discouraged. For the LORD your God is with you wherever you go."

JOSHUA 1:9 NLT

You may be wondering how you will ever accomplish the things God has for you to do. It's tempting to give in to the fears that hold you back and prevent you from soaring. Even when you know that you must do what God asks of you, it's easy to be intimidated by how big the job appears to be.

The Bible tells a story about Moses sending spies into the Promised Land. The chosen men came back with reports of giants living in the land. They were afraid that the giants would kill everyone if they tried to take the land God had promised them. They said they felt like grasshoppers next to the giant inhabitants. If only they had compared the giants to God instead, they could have seen how easy it would have been to win—God was on their side, after all!

God is on your side too; and He will provide all the courage you need if only you will believe. He will go with you into every scary situation. When you feel discouraged, remember how big God is compared to whatever it is you have to accomplish. With God, you can do anything—even slay giants!

Heavenly Father, help me to know I can have courage because You are beside me in everything I do. Help me to see that nothing—not even a giant—is too big for You. Amen.

DAY 304

ON MY SIDE

The Lord is on my side; I will not fear. What can man do to me?
Psalm 118:6 ESV

Did you ever sing that song "Nobody loves me, everybody hates me, I'm gonna eat a worm?" That's a silly song, indeed. After all, even if nobody loved us, how could eating a worm possibly make things better?

But that song isn't just silly. It's untrue. It doesn't matter who we are or what we've done, we can never claim nobody loves us. Because God loves each of us deeply, and He's always on our side. Even when it feels like the world is against us, God is always, *always* for us.

When friends are mean, we can remind ourselves of these words: *the Lord is on my side.*

When we get in trouble for something we didn't do, we can remember: *the Lord is on my side.*

When we fail a test or spill lunch in our laps or get chosen last for the kickball team, we need to tell ourselves: *the Lord is on my side.* No matter what happens, we can always be assured that God loves us *with all His heart*, and He will never leave us. He's rooting for us. He's on our side.

Dear Father, thank You for loving me.
Thank You for always being on my side. Amen.

DAY 305

OH, HAPPY DAY!

"Until now you have asked nothing in my name. Ask, and you will receive, that your joy may be full."
JOHN 16:24 ESV

What makes you happy? New clothes, shoes, video games? Some people treasure time with friends or going somewhere special. Do those things really make you happy or are they simply things you enjoy?

Everything mentioned in that list is temporary. It will pass away. If your happiness is dependent on any of those things or anything else that's temporary, it too will pass away. True happiness means being joyful and satisfied with whatever your circumstances are. It means that no matter what you have or what you get to do, you still have a smile on your face because your happiness comes from something permanent.

God wants to be the source of your joy. In Him you can find fullness and everything you could need to make you happy. When you love God, your life is filled with so much joy that you don't even chase after those things you once did.

Lord, sometimes I'm not happy unless I have things. I want to change that about myself. Will You help me find my joy in You? Thank You for providing everything I need to be truly happy. Amen.

DAY 306

A TICKET TO HEAVEN

"God loved the world so much that he gave his one and only Son so that whoever believes in him may not be lost, but have eternal life."

JOHN 3:16 NCV

Getting in to see a movie is pretty easy. You just buy a ticket, show it to the ticket taker, select a seat, and enjoy. Without that ticket though, the ticket taker would have to turn you away from the movie. That ticket proves that you are worthy to enter the movie because you have paid the price for admission.

So it is with heaven. We need a ticket to enter heaven, and the price for that ticket must be paid. At the gates of heaven, we must present our ticket and show that we are worthy to enter. Is it our good works that will make us worthy to enter heaven? No! Can we somehow earn or purchase a ticket to enter heaven? No! There is only one way into heaven, one ticket, and that is through Jesus Christ. He has already bought your ticket and has freely offered it to you. You only need to receive it.

Dear heavenly Father, thank You for sending Jesus to provide a way for my entrance into heaven. Amen.

DAY 307

THE SECURITY OF GOD'S LOVE

For I am convinced that neither death nor life, neither angels nor demons, neither the present nor the future, nor any powers, neither height nor depth, nor anything else in all creation, will be able to separate us from the love of God that is in Christ Jesus our Lord.

Romans 8:38–39 NIV

When you were very young, perhaps you had a special stuffed animal or blanket that you just had to carry with you wherever you went. Many children are attached to something soft and cuddly that brings them a feeling of security. How many parents have spent hours searching for "blanky" so their child would go to sleep!

Now that you are growing older, you realize that while a stuffed animal is a cute "friend," it really doesn't provide security. True security only comes through a personal relationship with Jesus. God's Word promises that He will never leave you. Check out the list in Romans 8! Nothing today or in your future, no distance, no power, nothing heavenly or demonic, nothing in the world can separate you from the love of God!

When you feel alone, remember that you always have God. He loves you with an everlasting love.

Lord, I am so thankful that nothing can come between us. Remind me on my darkest days that You are always with me. Amen.

DAY 308

THE RIGHT FRIENDS

Don't befriend angry people or associate with hot-tempered people, or you will learn to be like them and endanger your soul.
Proverbs 22:24–25 NLT

Sometimes it's hard to find good friends. But remember that God is always with you, and He gives you clear direction so that you can pick the right friends to hang out with.

This proverb tells us not to be friends with angry people or those with a hot temper. That doesn't mean that you should be rude to people like that and start ignoring them. It just means you shouldn't spend a lot of time with angry people or friends who have a really short temper. If you do, it can start to rub off on you and soon you're more angry and short-tempered too!

You can tell a lot about a person by how they treat other people and how they talk about them behind their back. Pay close attention to how your friends talk about other people when they aren't around. They probably will do the same thing to you when you're not there too.

God, thank You that You are always with me to help me make wise decisions about my friends. Please provide me with friends who want to honor You. Amen.

DAY 309

WHAT'S LOVE GOT TO DO WITH IT?

Love is patient, love is kind. It does not envy, it does not boast, it is not proud. It does not dishonor others, it is not self-seeking, it is not easily angered, it keeps no record of wrongs.

1 Corinthians 13:4–5 NIV

Okay, so what does it really mean to love others? Does it mean feeling all warm and fuzzy about people you don't even like? The truth is, you can treat someone kindly, refuse to get angry and bitter, and treat someone with respect even if you don't like them very much. By doing this, you show the love of God. The world has a different view of love, but God's definition is the one that counts.

The world says you only have to love those who love you back. God says there is a more excellent way. God says love everyone. It's not always easy, but how else will the world know that we are His? What's love got to do with it? Just everything.

Dear God, thank You for Your love for me. Help me to love others in a way that shows them who You are. Sometimes it's hard to love people who hurt me or make me angry. Help me to love even those I don't like so that I can be the kind of example You want me to be. Amen.

DAY 310

PRAY ANYWAY

Now when Daniel knew that the writing was signed,
he went into his house; and his windows being open. . .
he kneeled upon his knees three times a day, and prayed,
and gave thanks before his God, as he did aforetime.

Daniel 6:10 KJV

Think about Daniel for just a minute. He was a man with a lot of great stories to tell. It all started when he was a boy—maybe not a lot older than you. The powerful Babylonians captured Jerusalem, and Daniel was taken captive, but he certainly wasn't treated poorly. The king could tell Daniel was wise, so Daniel received an excellent education and royal treatment.

From the start though, Daniel determined to stay true to God, and he continued to remain faithful throughout his life. He knew that he would face the lions if he bowed to any but proud King Darius. But even in the face of that threat, Daniel openly prayed to God.

When you face taunting or rules saying you can't pray, be like Daniel and pray anyway. Stay true to God. Prayer is a gift from Him. Use it daily—no matter what.

Father God, may I always have the courage to stay true to You. No matter what, I will pray anyway! Amen.

DAY 311

THE PATH TO TAKE

In all your ways acknowledge Him,
and He shall direct your paths.
PROVERBS 3:6 NKJV

With so many choices and directions you could take in your life, it's hard to always know which path to choose.

That's why it's so important to go to the Lord for direction. Not only in prayer, but by reading your Bible.

We have the awesome privilege today to have God's Word so handy. We can read it in book form, on our computers, even on our iPads or phones! It's truly our guidebook. Filled with stories of triumphs and failures, God's Word is exactly what we need to help us through each day. No matter the obstacle.

Why not make a commitment to read more of the Bible—it will guide you and show you the path to take.

Father, I want to know You better, and I need help in choosing the correct path. Please give me the yearning to study Your Word more, and show me exactly what I need each day. I want to grow and learn in You. Amen.

DAY 312

LETTING IT GO

If we confess our sins, he is faithful and just and will forgive us our sins and purify us from all unrighteousness.

1 John 1:9 NIV

God knew we would sin from time to time. In fact, He even has a system in place to help us. It's pretty easy to think you don't need help when you get caught "borrowing" your sister's iPad without asking. She'll get over it, right? But when we really mess up, the consequences can be severe. Our trust and respect meters hit zero with family and friends. We begin to have feelings of guilt and shame associated with our misdeed. We need to remember what God told us to do in these moments.

He wants us to honestly admit our sins to Him. He won't erase the consequences because they usually help us remember not to make the same poor decision again; but He also doesn't want us to walk around forever feeling guilty or ashamed. Confess to Him, and let it go. We can't go back in time, but we can *always* have a fresh start with God.

Dear God, thank You for understanding that I will mess up from time to time. I'm sorry for my sins, and I choose to do my best today. Thank You for Your forgiveness. Amen.

DAY 313

STRESSFUL THOUGHTS

Don't worry about anything; instead, pray about everything. Tell God what you need, and thank him for all he has done. Then you will experience God's peace, which exceeds anything we can understand. His peace will guard your hearts and minds as you live in Christ Jesus.

PHILIPPIANS 4:6–7 NLT

Your life can feel pretty stressful at times, right? Right now you can probably think of at least a handful of things that are causing you stress and making you feel uncomfortable. What can you do about all that stress? These verses in Philippians have an answer.

First, you pray! Tell God how you feel and what you need. Then thank Him for how He has always been there for you! The Bible says that doing that will give you a peace in your heart that you can't possibly understand.

Next, you change the way you think! Listen to the rest of the paragraph: "Fix your thoughts on what is true, and honorable, and right, and pure, and lovely, and admirable. Think about things that are excellent and worthy of praise" (Philippians 4:8 NLT).

Whenever stress starts to bother you, pray! And then fill your mind with good things instead!

Dear God, thank You for giving me answers for all of my problems. When I'm stressed, I will talk to You about it! Amen.

DAY 314

MAKING TIME FOR GOD'S WORD

All Scripture is inspired by God and is useful to teach us what is true and to make us realize what is wrong in our lives. It corrects us when we are wrong and teaches us to do what is right.

2 Timothy 3:16 NLT

There are many demands on your time. Homework. Chores. Sports or musical instrument practice. Time with friends. And the list goes on and on. . .

Trying to juggle all of these activities can be frustrating. And if you don't currently read the Bible daily, adding one more thing to your routine may seem nearly impossible.

But what better practice for a child of God than to read His letter? He tells His followers that His Word can teach us to do what is right simply by reading the Bible! That makes it sound so easy.

And it is. The more time we spend with God in His Word, the more we will become like Him. And that is the Christian's goal—to become more like their heavenly Daddy.

Start small. Read five minutes a day and then increase your time as you can. You'll benefit by growing closer to Jesus.

Dear Lord, help me to take time to read the Bible daily because I want to know You better and learn to do what is right. Amen.

DAY 315

THE PRAYING STANCE

"And when you stand praying, if you hold anything against anyone, forgive them, so that your Father in heaven may forgive you your sins."
MARK 11:25 NIV

Sometimes when we start to pray, we find we have bad feelings about someone. When this happens, we need to think about it. Because to be forgiven by God, we need to forgive others. Whether or not others know they've harmed us, whether or not the hurt was intentional, we need to bring our anger and resentment before God and forgive them.

So if you are carrying a grudge against someone because you think he treated you badly, forgive him and then let it go. If you are angry at a friend because she didn't do what you wanted her to or even because she's mad at you, forgive her and then let it go. If you resent someone because she got a better grade than you did or the teacher was nicer to her today, forgive her and let it go. If you don't like someone because she doesn't like you, ask God to forgive you, to help you love her anyway, and then let it go.

If you want God to forgive you, you need to forgive others. So when you pray, forgive and then let it go. You'll feel better about things, and so will God!

Dear God, please help me to forgive others who have hurt me. . .and then help me to let it go! Amen.

DAY 316

20/20 VISION

Fixing our eyes on Jesus, the pioneer and perfecter of faith.
HEBREWS 12:2 NIV

Have you had your eyesight tested this year? Do you have perfect vision or are your eyes a little fuzzy and in need of some help from your glasses? Glasses or no glasses, God's Word tells us to fix our eyes on Jesus. That's the only way we are clearly able see how to live a godly life every day.

When our eyes are fixed on Jesus, we are able to see the good in every situation. We are able to see what needs fixing in our own life. We are able to see the truth. . .clearly! Where are your eyes fixed? Do you often see the negative side of things? Are you looking at the waves instead of the one who calms the storms? Fix your eyes on Jesus and ask Him to give you "heavenly vision"!

Jesus, please help me to see things clearly—as You would have me see them. I want to keep my eyes on You! Amen.

DAY 317

YOUR INNER UMPIRE

Let the peace of Christ rule in your hearts.
COLOSSIANS 3:15 NIV

When I was in high school, I played basketball. At every game, we had a referee. This man in the black-and-white-striped shirt stopped the game when the ball went out of bounds and blew the whistle when a player broke a rule.

The Bible says that peace from God is like an umpire in your heart. If you listen to this peace that comes from God, it will show you the way to go.

For example, if a friend says, "Come on, take these drugs with me," and you feel uneasy and your peace is gone, you know you are headed down the wrong road. This is God's "inner umpire" for you. It's God's gift to help guide you.

Colossians 3:15 says to let peace rule in your heart just like a referee rules a basketball game. Let peace have its way. When peace shows you the way to go, don't ignore it. You'll never be sorry—and you'll stay out of trouble.

Dear Jesus, sometimes it's hard to know what is right and what is wrong. Help me to know Your Word and listen to my inner umpire of peace so that I can be kept from harm. Amen.

DAY 318

OUTRUN YOUR SHADOW

But as he who called you is holy,
you also be holy in all your conduct.
1 Peter 1:15 ESV

Have you ever tried to outrun your shadow? It would obviously be an impossible thing to do. The influence you have on others is much like that shadow. No matter how you try, it doesn't go away. You are accountable for what your words and actions lead others to think about Jesus. Your behavior has a direct impact on the thoughts and the salvation of the people around you.

What kind of influence do you have? Are you kind, honest, and faithful? Do you live in a way that would cause unsaved people to want to know Jesus?

Kids of the kingdom should influence other kingdom dwellers to live for Jesus too. Do you have that kind of influence?

Being out under the bright sun gives you a good, sharp shadow. Living close to the Son of God helps you build a good, strong Christian influence.

God, I know the influence I have on others cannot be avoided any more than I can remove a shadow on a sunny day. Please help me to impact others to live for You. Amen.

DAY 319

SOMETHING SPECIAL

And we know that in all things God works for the good of those who love him, who have been called according to his purpose.
ROMANS 8:28 NIV

When I was about twelve years old, I was convinced that I had been born with no talent. I thought perhaps God had forgotten to add that special something into my DNA when He was creating me. All of my friends had passions and pursuits: sports, art, dance. I didn't feel like there was anything special about me. I wasn't even sure what my dreams were. I felt like a dull weed in a garden full of colorful flowers.

If you feel this way, rest assured that God has not forgotten you. Your future may seem cloudy and unpromising now, but God has handcrafted a specific and wonderful plan just for you. He doesn't want you to compare yourself to anyone else, because He created you to be a unique individual. He gave you a special set of talents that you can use for His glory. You have a future full of hope and promise!

God, please help me not to compare myself to others. When I'm feeling plain or ordinary, help me to remember that You created me for a purpose, and You are in control. Amen.

DAY 320

BREAKFAST OF CHAMPIONS

Man doth not live by bread only, but by every word that proceedeth out of the mouth of the Lord.
Deuteronomy 8:3 KJV

What do you usually eat for breakfast? A bowl of cereal? Pancakes with syrup? Eggs and toast? Whatever it is, chances are you don't start your day without putting something in your stomach. But how many times have you headed off to school without feeding your soul?

As a child of God, you face a lot of challenges. Choosing between right and wrong, fighting temptation, and dealing with difficult people all take spiritual muscles. The best way to build those muscles is with a steady diet of God's Word. Reading the Bible is like giving your soul a big stack of pancakes. It provides the spiritual energy you need to make it through the day.

Start your morning with God. Instead of reading the back of the cereal box, read a few passages from the Bible. Then take a moment to pray and ask God to help you with whatever you might face. That's the breakfast of a champion! And what an amazing difference a well-fed soul can make.

God, remind me to begin each day feeding my soul with Your Word. Amen.

DAY 321

NEW THINGS!

Joshua said to them, "Do not be afraid; do not be discouraged. Be strong and courageous. This is what the LORD *will do to all the enemies you are going to fight."*

JOSHUA 10:25 NIV

Next week is your first day at a new school. Terrifying, right? The school has lockers that look way too complicated, a brand-new teacher for each class (as if one new teacher wasn't bad enough), and hundreds of students (and you don't even know one of them!). You feel like running away—going back to the old school and old friends you knew so well. Your stomach is full of butterflies.

God will give you courage to look forward! Face the day with Him by your side. Before you leave the house, read a Bible verse and say a prayer to calm your worries and fears. Then keep the peace God provides with you throughout the day.

New experiences will bring new friends, brand-new adventures, and many blessings. Reach for the door of opportunity God has provided. You just never know where it might lead.

Lord, give me courage in all of my activities. Allow the butterflies in my stomach to settle. Amen.

DAY 322

HIDDEN TREASURES

"The kingdom of heaven is like treasure hidden in a field. When a man found it, he hid it again, and then in his joy went and sold all he had and bought that field."
MATTHEW 13:44 NIV

Imagine a map of a deserted island, one that would lead you to the greatest buried treasure ever found. You follow the map until you come across a chest filled with priceless gold coins. What would you do with all that money? Splurge on something nice for yourself? Spread the joy by taking your friends out for ice cream? Help your parents pay the bills?

The Bible says that the kingdom of heaven is like a treasure hidden in a field. It is a thing of great value. When you come into a relationship with Jesus, you've discovered the greatest treasure of all—one that will lead you all the way to heaven one day. The Christian life is a priceless gift, one you can't take for granted.

And guess what! God wants you to share that gift with others. Leave clear directions for others to follow so that they too will one day discover this awesome treasure!

Dear heavenly Father, help me to stay on course on the path You have for me. I want to share the treasure of heaven with others! Amen.

DAY 323

I HAVE OVERCOME

"These things I have spoken to you, so that in Me you may have peace. In the world you have tribulation, but take courage; I have overcome the world."

JOHN 16:33 NASB

God has provided many ways to help us overcome our fears. Here are a few helpful "Courage Boosters" He has supplied:

One: Remember He promises to be with you—no matter what (Matthew 28:20; Psalm 23:4)!

Two: Pray. God's always ready to hear your voice. He *encourages* us to speak to Him! "Be anxious for nothing, but in everything by prayer. . .let your requests be made known to God. And the peace of God, which surpasses all comprehension, will guard your hearts and your minds in Christ Jesus" (Philippians 4:6–7 NASB; see also Matthew 11:28 and 1 Thessalonians 5:17).

Three: "Take. . .the sword of the Spirit, which is the word of God" (Ephesians 6:17 NASB). We can memorize and study God's Word. That's what He's given it for! He wants you to meditate on it, beloved. It's your life manual. It shows you who God is, what He likes, how He acts. . . (See Psalm 119. David knew the importance of God's Word!)

Lord, I need Your strength and courage to overcome these fears. Help me to take up the sword of the Spirit and wield it unceasingly. Thank You for giving me strength to resist the devil. In Jesus' name I pray. Amen.

DAY 324

MAKE A WISH

For in this hope we were saved. Now hope that is seen is not hope. For who hopes for what he sees? But if we hope for what we do not see, we wait for it with patience.
ROMANS 8:24–25 ESV

Make a wish when you blow out the candles. Wish upon a falling star. Wish when you throw a coin into the fountain. Make a wish with a wishbone. Do you see a pattern here? A wish requires an object attached to it. If we pray to God, is it okay to make a wish. . .or is that the same thing as a prayer?

A wish is like tossing a need out into the universe, expecting some angelic force will grab it and do something about it. Prayer is speaking directly to God and asking Him to meet a need or provide a desire. There's no point in talking into a vacuum when the counsel of your best friend is a heartbeat away.

When we trust that God will do good for us and we surrender our needs to Him, we are trusting in His promises.

Dear Lord, I trust in Your unfailing Word and surrender my needs to You. I don't want to wish into an empty vacuum hoping that someone hears me, when I have You, my best friend, a heartbeat away. Thank You for hearing me. Amen.

DAY 325

YOU WANT ME TO LOVE WHO?

"As the Father has loved me, so have I loved you. . . . If you keep my commands, you will remain in my love. . . . I have told you this so that my joy may be in you and that your joy may be complete. My command is this: Love each other as I have loved you."

John 15:9–12 NIV

Love each other. It doesn't sound so hard. Love your family, love your friends, love that nice lady at church who gives out peppermints. . . that's pretty easy. But what about that guy in math class who keeps cheating off your papers even though you've asked him to stop? And what about the girl in gym class who makes catty remarks about everyone—including you? Do you have to love those people too?

Yep. Jesus makes it pretty clear that loving others isn't an option. He has commanded us to love everyone, even our enemies. By loving this way, the world will know that we belong to Him. Love makes all the difference.

Dear God, thank You for Your love for me. You loved me even when I was still a sinner. Because I love You, I want to be obedient to Your commands. Please let Your love work in me so that even the people I don't like will see You in me. Amen.

DAY 326

MY ETERNAL SHEPHERD

"My sheep hear My voice, and I know them, and they follow Me. And I give them eternal life, and they shall never perish; neither shall anyone snatch them out of My hand."

JOHN 10:27–28 NKJV

Sheep can be ornery creatures. They stink. They bite. They like to wander off. Just like human beings. And humans need a shepherd just as much as those wooly beasts do. One of the definitions of *shepherd* is: a person who protects, guides, or watches over a person or group of people.

Isn't it amazing that you have a Shepherd? He's always there to guide, direct, discipline, and protect you.

What's more—He's offered you eternal life. The price? Free. He paid it by dying on the cross for your sins. He sacrificed Himself to the "wolves" so that you could have the chance to spend eternity with Him.

Once you've made that heart decision, you're eternally part of His family. Isn't that wonderful? Is there someone you could share that with today—someone else who needs the Shepherd? Someone who needs the gift of eternal life?

God, thank You so much for giving me eternal life. Thank You that You know me, You love me, and nothing can take me from You. Please help me to share my faith with someone else today so that they might have a chance to spend eternity with You too. Amen.

DAY 327

KEEP GOING

Always be joyful. Never stop praying.
Be thankful in all circumstances, for this is God's
will for you who belong to Christ Jesus.
1 THESSALONIANS 5:16–18 NLT

Everyone struggles with having a bad attitude sometimes. Maybe it only takes one bad thing to spoil your mood for a whole day. It may seem impossible to improve your attitude once you start feeling upset, but God says there's another way.

Pray. Choose to be joyful. Find ways to be thankful for what's happening in your life. This is what God wants His children to do every day, no matter how difficult life is. Sound challenging?

You may have to start out small. When you feel like your attitude is slipping, take a moment to pray and ask God to help change your outlook. Thank Him for something that is important to you. Then practice joy. Take these God-directed steps, and He'll help pull your attitude out of the dumps.

God doesn't want you to go through life with a sour attitude. Choose today to live with the outlook of Christ, and He'll give you the strength to make it through.

Father God, when life is tough, it's hard for me to have a good attitude. Please give me guidance to get through it: to be joyful, to keep praying, to give thanks. Amen.

DAY 328

KINDNESS MATTERS

Get rid of all bitterness, rage, anger, harsh words, and slander, as well as all types of evil behavior. Instead, be kind to each other, tenderhearted, forgiving one another, just as God through Christ has forgiven you.
EPHESIANS 4:31–32 NLT

Nobel Peace Prize recipient Mother Teresa said: "Kind words can be short and easy to speak, but their echoes are truly endless." That just means that when you say something nice to another person, you have no idea how God will use that to brighten their life! So use your words for good and not harm. Here are some other verses to remember about kindness:

- "Therefore, as God's chosen people, holy and dearly loved, clothe yourselves with compassion, kindness, humility, gentleness and patience" (Colossians 3:12 NIV).
- "Love is patient, love is kind. It does not envy, it does not boast, it is not proud. It does not dishonor others, it is not self-seeking, it is not easily angered, it keeps no record of wrongs" (1 Corinthians 13:4–5 NIV).
- "Your kindness will reward you, but your cruelty will destroy you" (Proverbs 11:17 NLT).

Dear God, I see how important kindness is to You. Please forgive me for the times when I've acted on my anger instead of being kind. Amen.

DAY 329

UNDERSTAND. . . OR MISUNDERSTAND?

O Lord, You have looked through me and have known me. You know when I sit down and when I get up. You understand my thoughts from far away.
PSALM 139:1–2 NLV

Have you ever had a misunderstanding with a friend? Maybe you said something and she took it the wrong way? Or maybe you tried to be helpful, but she didn't like what you had to say? Having someone misunderstand your words is tough! Lots of friendships end because one person gets upset over something the other one said. Sad, right?

Thankfully, God never misunderstands you. He never takes your words the wrong way or makes a big deal out of things that aren't a big deal. In fact, He knows what you're really thinking, even before you say a word! God also knows what you're going to say. . .and why. That's because He can see inside your heart and knows why you're feeling the way you do about things. He not only sees, but He truly understands.

So, no misunderstandings with Him. No sir!

Lord, I'm so glad You understand what I think and say. I don't always say all the right things, but You know my heart. Thank You for taking the time to really get to know me and to care about what I'm thinking and feeling. I'm so grateful! Amen.

DAY 330

LEADER OF THE PACK

Dear brothers and sisters, honor those who are your leaders in the Lord's work. They work hard among you and give you spiritual guidance.

1 Thessalonians 5:12 NLT

Have you ever thought about the word *respect*? Do you know what it means to respect your elders (those who are older than you)? Think about the adults you know—your parents, grandparents, and church leaders. Did you realize God has placed them in your life for a reason? And He's watching you closely to make sure you treat them with the respect they deserve.

Imagine this. . . A leader at your church (maybe your Sunday school teacher or kid's church pastor) isn't getting a lot of respect from the kids in the class. Maybe some of your friends are talking when they should be listening, or interrupting when the teacher is speaking. What can you do to help? By far the best thing you can do is treat the teacher with respect. Then encourage others to do the same. Don't be part of the problem—be part of the solution. The teacher will be so grateful, and pretty soon all of the kids will follow your lead.

So, why treat your leaders with respect? Because it's the right thing to do!

Father God, help me to always show proper respect to others. I know it's the right thing to do, and I want to please You. Amen.

DAY 331

BEHAVING WISELY

I will behave myself wisely in a perfect way. O when wilt thou come unto me? I will walk within my house with a perfect heart.
PSALM 101:2 KJV

You know the story of young David. He had proven he was responsible enough to care for his father's sheep. When wild beasts attacked, he showed wisdom in the way he protected the sheep. When he was given the task of carrying food to his soldier brothers, he probably didn't anticipate that God would use him to win an important victory, but he was prepared when it happened. While he was still young, God called upon David, who had already served as King Saul's musician, to be the next king of Israel.

Why was God able to use David this way? It's simple, really. David had determined to live wisely and maturely. He chose this path when he was a child, and you can choose it too. You can decide that with God's strength you will walk perfectly. Then others will trust you, and God will use you in a special way!

Father God, I am determined to walk wisely. I want others to see You through my words and actions. Amen.

DAY 332

WHITE NOISE

"For God so loved the world, that he gave his only Son, that whoever believes in him should not perish but have eternal life."
JOHN 3:16 ESV

Some people can only sleep with those white-noise machines that fill their quiet bedroom with the sounds of the ocean, birds chirping, or even street clamor. Silence is just too loud. There is a lot of clatter going on around us, especially when we look for answers about faith, religion, and God. Everyone has a different opinion. And everyone thinks theirs is the right one.

Where can you go to get good advice and answers about the things of God? Your parents would be able to answer that question for you by pointing you in the direction of the people you can trust who will give you godly counsel and advice found in scripture. Make sure that, even in the midst of all the noise around you, you're listening carefully for God's voice through the chaos. He will make Himself known to you if you listen closely.

Dear God, please help me hear You through all the noise in my life. Help me know Your voice even as others shout at me and try to turn me away from You. Amen.

DAY 333

LOVE LETTER

"So have I loved you."
John 15:9 KJV

My darling,

You don't know Me well, but I have been watching you for a long time.

Do you know how much I love you? No, of course you don't. How could you? My love is so deep, so vast, that it cannot be expressed in this simple letter. It would take many letters—volumes of them! Indeed, they are written. Will you read them if I give them to you? Will you cherish My words, savor them, reflect upon them until they are written on your very heart?

I want you to trust Me. To believe in Me. Oh, if you will only love Me as I love you, then you can ask Me for anything and I will give it to you. I will stay by your side always and protect you as fiercely as a lion! For you are My dear one, and My most precious gift is yours.

Will you accept My love?

I shall wait for your answer.

Eternally yours,
God

Dear God, I want to know more about You. As I read Your Word, the Bible, teach me how to love You as You love me. Amen.

DAY 334

THE GREEN-EYED MONSTER

Love is patient and kind, never jealous, boastful, proud, or rude.
1 Corinthians 13:4–5 CEV

Face it—there are others who are better than you. He jumps higher. She gets all A's. She runs faster. He seems to have it all together—all the time. It's tough to admit, isn't it? This is usually when the green-eyed monster shows up.

Jealousy. Yep, it's a hard emotion to control. No matter what sport or activity you participate in, there will always be someone better than you. That's just life. In addition, there will also always be someone better looking, smarter, richer, taller, thinner. . .the list goes on. But don't let that drive you crazy with jealousy. Just accept the fact. . .forget about those who are better. . .and set your sights on becoming the best version of you! You don't ever need to worry about anyone else.

Instead of flaws, focus on your positive traits. You are unique! God made you special. You have wonderful talents and strengths. So the next time that green-eyed monster rears his ugly head, turn your head upward and thank God for making you—you!

God, I admit that I am jealous sometimes. Please help me to stop feeling jealous and just focus on being the best version of me. Amen.

DAY 335

LIVING FOREVER

I write these things to you who believe in the name of the Son of God so that you may know that you have eternal life.

1 John 5:13 NIV

I remember when my grandfather died. I was twelve years old. I'd been away at a slumber party, and when I came home, my mother told me Granddaddy had gone to see Jesus. That sounded nice; everyone knows heaven is a great place. But I was still heartbroken to know I'd never see him again here on earth.

But I know I'll see him again in heaven. The reason I know that is because Granddaddy believed that Jesus was God's Son. He believed Jesus died on the cross to take the punishment for our sins so we could spend eternity in heaven. And I believe that too. God's Word tells us that if we believe in Jesus and what He did for us on the cross, we won't ever really die. Our bodies will die, but our spirits—the part of us that makes us who we are—will live forever in heaven with Jesus and with all those who also believe in Him.

Dear Father, I believe Jesus is Your Son and that He died in my place as punishment for my sins. Thank You for sending Him, and thank You for eternal life. Amen.

DAY 336

THE BEST SECRET KEEPER

Blessed be the God and Father of our Lord Jesus Christ,
the Father of mercies and God of all comfort.
2 Corinthians 1:3 NKJV

It doesn't matter what you are upset, hurt, angry, or sad about. God wants to hear what you have to say. He is the God of *all* comfort, which means He is interested in the little details as well as the humongous ones. If your friend embarrassed you at lunch or you're having parent drama, tell God all of your troubles. Don't be afraid to tell Him any mean or unkind thoughts you may be having too. He can take it. He understands what you're going through.

Find a quiet, private place where you can tell Him what's going on. Hold nothing back. Share it all. He's the best secret keeper there is! Soon you'll experience a release from your burdens as you give them away to Him. He'll show you how to move forward and will comfort you as you go.

Dear God, please give me Your comfort as I share what hurts me or makes me sad. I know I can depend on You to keep my secrets and trust You to help me find my way. Amen.

DAY 337

LIAR, LIAR

The Lord detests lying lips, but he delights in those who tell the truth.
Proverbs 12:22 NLT

You've heard the little taunt "Liar, liar, pants on fire." You may have even said it a time or two. Does it apply to you? Are you in the habit of telling lies? Not HUGE lies. . .but those little white lies that don't seem to make much of a difference? You know. . .telling Mom you finished all of your homework when you really have two more problems to solve or telling your best friend that a certain boy likes her just to make her feel good when you don't know that for sure? You get the idea.

The Bible is crystal clear on lying: God hates it! Even the little white lies that are meant to make others feel good. If you are really curious, look up Revelation 21:8. It describes what happens to people who make a lifelong habit of lying. Yikes! Ask God to help you be truthful in everything you say and do.

Dear heavenly Father, please help me to avoid lies at all times. . .even lies that don't seem that big of a deal are a very big deal to You. I want to walk in truth. Amen.

DAY 338

OBEY. . .IT'S THE SAFEST WAY

Children, as Christians, obey your parents. This is the right thing to do. Respect your father and mother. This is the first Law given that had a promise. The promise is this: If you respect your father and mother, you will live a long time and your life will be full of many good things.

EPHESIANS 6:1–3 NLV

It's not always easy to obey, is it? So many times we want to have our own way, to do our own thing. As you read today's scripture, you can see that God makes a promise to us when we obey our parents. Our lives will be filled with many good things if we just follow the proper direction.

Imagine you're crossing the street on your way to school. The crossing guard blows her whistle, letting you know that traffic is coming. If you disobeyed her warning and stepped out into the street, what would happen? You could get badly injured! The same is true with God's directions. We must obey for our own safety. If we do, He promises us a long life filled with great things! So stay safe. Obey!

God, it's not always easy to obey! Sometimes I just want to have my own way, to do what I want to do. Thank You for showing me how to obey, even when I don't feel like it. Amen.

DAY 339

SEND YOUR GORILLAS RUNNING

Finally brothers and sisters, whatever is true, whatever is noble, whatever is right, whatever is pure, whatever is lovely, whatever is admirable—if anything is excellent or praiseworthy—think about such things.

PHILIPPIANS 4:8 NIV

When I was seven years old, my sister and I went to a circus. I don't remember anything about it—except for one scary thing.

Halfway through the show, two men rolled out a male gorilla in a cage. One of the men opened the cage to let the black beast out. Suddenly, the gorilla jumped over the chain-link fence and ran up the bleachers. All the kids sitting in front of me screamed and darted away. I did too. In fact, I ran all the way home.

When I got older, I figured something out. . . . The gorilla wasn't a gorilla at all. It was just a man in a gorilla suit!

I learned something important from this funny event: what you think and believe will affect how you act. So if you let your mind be filled with bad thoughts, then you'll behave badly. If you let your mind be filled with fearful thoughts, you'll act afraid.

So if you want to be strong to live the way God wants, focus your mind on true thoughts from the Bible such as Philippians 4:13 (NIV), which says, "I can do all this through him who gives me strength."

Lord, always help me to fill my mind with Your thoughts. Amen.

DAY 340

THE WHOLE PUZZLE

And we know that in all things God works for the good of those who love him, who have been called according to his purpose.
ROMANS 8:28 NIV

Have you ever tried to assemble a jigsaw puzzle without having the picture on the front of the box? It's not easy. You may have a thousand pieces that somehow fit together to make a beautiful portrait, but without the whole picture, they look like nothing more than a mess of colors.

Our lives on earth are something like that. We cry out to God, asking for His help to make sense of the jumble of problem pieces we have that we can't sort out. God is the only one who owns the finished picture. He sees how the happiness and trouble in our lives fit together in the end.

He answers our prayers, telling us to give our burdens to Him. He helps us work them out, arranging the pieces of our puzzles in a way that will make the picture full and complete in the end. We won't always understand why He's doing what He's doing, so He asks us to follow Him in faith.

What trouble pieces do you have in your life? Ask God to take care of those problems by placing them in the right spot so they will ultimately work together for good.

God, I am so thankful that You see the picture of my life as it's meant to be. I trust You to help me put the pieces together according to Your will. Amen.

DAY 341

NO REVENGE

"But I say to you, love your enemies, bless those who curse you, do good to those who hate you, and pray for those who spitefully use you and persecute you."
MATTHEW 5:44 NKJV

Did you ever have someone you thought you could trust give away a secret? You may have wanted to teach her a lesson by doing the same to her. Or how about when someone pushed you? Did you ever feel like pushing him right back?

It's not hard to want to treat others the same way they treat you. But God wants you to love them even when they don't seem lovable.

But here's what's so cool. When you treat others the way God wants you to—by loving them, doing good to them, and praying for them no matter what—you will be so much happier with yourself. And you may be very surprised by the change of heart they might have by your kindness toward them.

Father, when someone treats me badly, I am so tempted to get even—but I know that's not what You want me to do. Help me to do the right thing, God. Amen.

DAY 342

GO. AND SIN NO MORE!

And Jesus said, "I do not condemn you, either.
Go. From now on sin no more."
JOHN 8:11 NASB

We're humans. . .born sinners. Nothing we ever do can erase that (Romans 3:23). But there's good news! God forgives us (Colossians 2:13)! He sent Jesus—the pure, sin-*less* Son of God—to die as a living sacrifice for *our* sins. That means we're forgiven. . .we've been set free (Galatians 5:1)!

That freedom isn't something we should take advantage of or take for granted. Some Christians continue in sin because "they're forgiven no matter what." But God says that's wrong (Galatians 5:13, 24–25). "Are we to continue in sin so that grace may increase? May it never be! How shall we who died to sin still live in it?" (Romans 6:1–2 NASB).

We've died to the world. . .we're alive in Christ (1 John 2:15–17; Philippians 1:21; 1 Corinthians 15:22; Ephesians 2:4–6). As Christians, Jesus calls us to show others the light of salvation and His perfect, everlasting love (Matthew 5:13–16).

Christ *died* for us so we can *live.*

Live for *Him*!

Lord, I know that I'm a sinner. I can't fathom why You've forgiven me. . .why You've cleansed me. But Your Word says You have. So I believe it. Help me to walk in Your Spirit and not in sin. In Jesus' precious name. Amen.

DAY 343

HOW MANY TIMES?

Then Peter came up to Him and said, Lord, how many times may my brother sin against me and I forgive him and let it go? [As many as] up to seven times? Jesus answered him, I tell you, not up to seven times, but seventy times seven!

MATTHEW 18:21–22 AMPC

Sometimes people are unkind. Even your best friends can seem more like enemies when they gossip about you. It's painful to be rejected or to discover a friend has said something horrible about you. You might be tempted to turn against those who have hurt you—and decide to *never* forgive them. *Never ever!*

The funny thing is, some people who have hurt you may not even care that you won't forgive them; or maybe they simply made a mistake and are truly sorry. Holding a grudge, even if you think it's deserved, creates a dark sore in your heart. And maybe, if you wait too long to forgive someone, you just might ruin the chance for a lifetime friendship.

Think how wonderful it will be if you choose to forgive. Your offender may not come around right away, but you'll experience the joy of living without that ugly grudge in your heart. And who knows what other amazing things might happen because you chose to say, "I forgive you"?

Dear Lord, I don't want to hang on to my bad feelings because I have been hurt by others. Please help me learn to forgive, and teach me how to be a good example. And thank You for forgiving me first! Amen.

DAY 344

THE CRY OF YOUR HEART

Search me, O God, and know my heart; test me and know my anxious thoughts. Point out anything in me that offends you, and lead me along the path of everlasting life.

Psalm 139:23–24 NLT

Have you ever been afraid you might not be doing this "Christian thing" right? Maybe you're worried that you aren't good enough or that you'll somehow mess it up.

The truth is you're probably NOT going to get it right all the time. None of us do. The thing to remember is: God's grace is bigger than your sin. And if you really have a desire in your heart to make Him proud, you can pray Psalm 139:23–24. God will always honor that prayer. He'll send the Holy Spirit to nudge you and let you know when something isn't right. He'll make sure you stay on the path of everlasting life because He wants the best for you.

Dear God, although I want to please You all the time, I know there are times when I don't. I'm glad that You love me no matter what. Please help me to be a reflection of You. Know my heart and guide me in the way that I should go. Keep my feet on the path of everlasting life, and help me to honor You with my life daily. Amen.

DAY 345

FINISH STRONG!

Let us run with perseverance the race marked out for us, fixing our eyes on Jesus, the pioneer and perfecter of faith.
HEBREWS 12:1–2 NIV

If you've ever run track at school or competed in any kind of race, you might have heard your coach yell, "Finish strong!" as you headed toward the finish line. Coaches often urge their runners to sprint the last part of the race—even during practice runs. The desire to finish strong pushes runners farther than they knew they could go and faster than they thought they could run.

Well, I've got news for you. We have a coach up in heaven giving us the same direction to "finish strong!" No matter how hard life gets, God wants us to keep going. Maybe you're having a tough time right now. Maybe you're wondering if you'll ever achieve your goals. Maybe you feel like nobody cares about you. No matter how you're feeling, God wants you to know that He is on your side. He is cheering you on to victory. He has already given you everything you'll ever need to run your race. Just keep your eyes on Him and finish strong.

God, help me to keep my eyes on You and run the race You have set before me. Help me to finish strong. Amen.

DAY 346

WITH OPEN ARMS

Even though I walk through the darkest valley, I will fear no evil, for you are with me; your rod and your staff, they comfort me.
PSALM 23:4 NIV

A few months ago, a friend lost her father. Everyone tried to comfort her. They made sure she ate, got dressed, and talked about her feelings. All of the friends cried together. But even the comfort of her friends couldn't completely heal the wound on her heart.

God comforts you—just like a warm blanket wrapped around your shoulders on a cold day. Open His Word and discover the healing you can find in scripture. God is always there, offering His warmth and His love to your broken heart.

When you suffer a loss isn't the only time the heavenly Father will wrap you in His loving embrace. He's there to hold your hand when you don't get the spot on the team you wanted so badly. He's there when you get sick on the night you had special plans. He's there. . .with open arms to comfort you—*always*.

God, thank You for Your comforting arms. Please let me experience Your unconditional love. Amen.

DAY 347

WOW—HE LOVES ME!

But God demonstrates His own love toward us,
in that while we were still sinners, Christ died for us.
ROMANS 5:8 NKJV

Have you ever had someone in your life who really got on your nerves? Maybe they played pranks on you and your friends. Maybe they even bullied you or stole from you. In general this person annoyed everyone around them and made life difficult.

Even though you probably really disliked—possibly even hated—this person, did you know that God loves them just as much as He loves you?

It's a hard pill to swallow. But think about it this way: God made the world. He made all the rules. And then all of humankind disobeyed. We sinned. We lied and murdered and cheated. Bullied, stole, annoyed others. But guess what? God showed us He loved us by sending His Son to pay the price—even though we were sinners! (And obnoxious and annoying!)

Today, take some time to remember how much He loves you—even though you're a sinner. . .and share that love with someone who may even get on your nerves. You'll be glad you did.

God, help me share Your love with someone else today. And when someone is mean to me or annoying to me, please remind me that You love them just as much as You love me and that I'm supposed to love them too. Amen.

DAY 348

HIDING PLACE

You are my hiding place; you will protect me from trouble and surround me with songs of deliverance.

PSALM 32:7 NIV

A few years ago, we had a pet fish. He lived in a bowl in our living room among strands of ivy, some blue rocks, a small plastic castle, and a bridge. Whenever we stood near the bowl and looked at him, he would hide among the ivy. We must have looked pretty scary to him; enormous pairs of eyes peering through the bowl!

Sometimes life can be scary. Whether we're frightened of bullies or a hard test or a new school, God says we can hide in Him. He'll comfort us and keep us safe. He'll protect us from trouble and help calm us down so we're not afraid anymore. He sings peaceful lullabies into our spirits and lets us know everything will be okay.

The next time you see trouble headed your way, run to God. He'll wrap you in His comforting arms and let you bury your face in His neck. You can know that everything will be okay as long as you use God as your hiding place.

Dear Father, thank You for letting me hide in You and for delivering me from all kinds of trouble. Amen.

DAY 349

ALL THE WAY TO YOUR TOES

Finally, be strong in the Lord and in his mighty power.
EPHESIANS 6:10 NIV

What do you do when you hear some interesting gossip? Do you lean in so you can hear it a little better? Do you nod and grin, hoping you'll hear more? Do you chime in with more gossip to make the story more shocking?

What if those hurtful lies are about your best friend? Do you stand up for him or her, or do you say nothing? Maybe you're scared the gossiping group will laugh at you if you frown on their bad behavior. It takes courage to stand up for what's right. Being courageous isn't a lot of fun, and it isn't easy.

But God will give you the strength to stand strong. To be able to walk away when you need to. Or to be able to speak up in love when you know you should. It'll make you feel good inside—not only all the way to your toes, but all the way to your heart!

Lord, help me to always know what is right, and then give me the courage to do it. Amen.

DAY 350

PRECIOUS GOODS

Children, obey your parents in all things:
for this is well pleasing unto the Lord.
Colossians 3:20 KJV

Obey my parents? But they're so unfair! They don't understand me, and they never let me do what my friends get to do!

Almost every kid on the planet has felt that way at least once in his or her life, so you shouldn't feel bad if you do too. If you were to ask your parents, they would probably admit that sometimes they *are* unfair. Sometimes they really don't understand, and sometimes they won't let you do what your friends get to do.

Why?

Because they love you.

God has tasked your mom and dad with a very serious responsibility: taking care of precious, irreplaceable you! So make it easy for them. Your parents aren't perfect. They *do* make mistakes, but their decisions—especially if they are Christians—are meant to help you be the best that you can be. Respect and obey your mom and dad even when you don't agree with them. Remember that doing so is well pleasing unto the Lord.

Dear God, sometimes it's hard to submit to my parents. Remind me that when I obey them, I'm really obeying You. Amen.

DAY 351

BAD NEWS

Be of good courage, and He shall strengthen your heart, all you who hope in the Lord.
Psalm 31:24 NKJV

Have you had your television on lately? Do you watch the news? It seems like a new tragedy strikes somewhere every single day. From school shootings, to attacks on public figures, to shootings in places like malls and movie theaters. People get hurt, and natural disasters destroy homes and even entire towns. Sadly, it's the bad news that gets our attention in the headlines. It's what people notice. There's always something, and it's always scary.

Yes, God does allow for things to happen; and yes, it can be scary. But the blessing is that He has called us to be a light for His truth in this dark world, and He will give us the strength we need to carry out that mission. Be thankful for His presence in your life, and be willing to follow the call He has for you no matter what's happening around you. Rest in Him and trust in the protection of His mighty hand.

Lord, please help me to be strong and courageous as I face this world of trial and tragedy. Help me to be a voice that spreads the truth of Your Word to hurting people. Please give me strength and courage. Amen.

DAY 352

SALTY CHRISTIANS

"You are the salt of the earth. But if the salt loses its saltiness, how can it be made salty again? It is no longer good for anything, except to be thrown out and trampled underfoot."
MATTHEW 5:13 NIV

Imagine you're at a fast-food place and have just ordered a cheeseburger and french fries. You taste the fries, only to discover there's no salt on them. In fact, you can't find salt anywhere in the restaurant. Sure, you go ahead and eat the fries, but they're not very tasty, are they? And it's not like you need a lot of salt to fix the problem. Just a little bit would be enough.

That's how it is when you share your faith with people who don't know the Lord. Just a pinch here and there goes a long, long way. They don't need you to preach to them. (Talk about overloading the salt!) They just need little sprinkles, enough to make them thirsty for the gospel.

That's our job, after all—to make people thirsty for the Lord. He calls us to reach others for Him. What an adventure! So, grab that saltshaker! God's got work for you to do!

Heavenly Father, help me to spread pinches of salt everywhere I go! Amen.

DAY 353

DIG IN!

Your word is a lamp to my feet and a light to my path.
PSALM 119:105 ESV

If you've ever used a shovel or a hoe, you know what it's like to dig, dig, dig! It's tough work, but so worth it when you're done, especially if you're doing something fun, like planting a garden. The deeper the roots, the stronger the plants will grow!

The same is true with reading God's Word. It's not enough to just quickly read a verse or two. God longs for you to dig, dig, dig! Use your spiritual shovel and really dig deep. Ask Him to "uncover" some new truths so that you can learn more every time you read. Sure, reading can feel like work at times, but the payoff is great! While digging through the stories in His Word, you will learn so much! You'll be like those plants, deeply rooted and ready to grow strong and beautiful. So grab your spiritual shovels, and let's start digging!

Lord, thank You for giving me the Bible. It's more than just a book of stories. It's a lamp to light my way. Help me to dig deep so that I can grow strong in You. Amen!

DAY 354

A BLOB OF GOO

But when they measure themselves by one another and compare themselves with one another, they are without understanding.
2 CORINTHIANS 10:12 ESV

The Bible tells us that it's not wise to compare ourselves with other people. God created us to be unique. No matter how hard you tried, you could never look exactly like another person or think exactly like another person. And you will make yourself miserable trying to do either of those things.

The twenty-sixth president of the United States, Theodore Roosevelt, said: "Comparison is the thief of joy." You will lose all joy in your life if you keep comparing yourself to others and trying to fit into a mold that God did not intend for you to fit in.

Have you ever poured Jell-O into a mold? It flows right into the mold, and when it sets, it comes out looking exactly like the original mold. Now imagine putting peanut butter into that same mold. It would be sticky and messy and never set up right—coming out looking like a big blob of brown goo.

Comparing yourself to someone else is kind of like putting peanut butter into a Jell-O mold. You'll always come out looking like a blob of goo!

God, please help me not to compare myself to others. Help me to just be me and to be happy about that! Amen.

DAY 355

THE FINISH LINE

Do you not know that in a race all the runners run, but only one gets the prize? Run in such a way as to get the prize.
1 Corinthians 9:24 niv

Have you ever run a race? If you show up on race day wearing a sweatshirt, boots, and a heavy coat and carrying a big jug of water, you can be sure you'll be at the back of the pack. All those things will slow you down as you head toward the finish line.

A runner must wear light clothes that add as little extra weight as possible. In fact, good clothes for runners are designed to help with speed and agility, wick away sweat, and let the air flow freely to cool the body.

Christians are running a big race. We must plan ahead like a marathoner and choose carefully what we're going to carry with us on the journey. If we run our race bogged down with sin, temptation, and fear, our race will be slow. But if we allow Jesus to carry those burdens for us, we can run free.

Dear Jesus, please carry my burdens for me so I can run the race free from the weight of this world. I want to cross the finish line and celebrate as I claim my prize. Amen.

DAY 356

A FREE DO-OVER

But God shows his love for us in that while we were still sinners, Christ died for us.
Romans 5:8 esv

Have you ever done something you really regretted? Like telling your mom a little lie to get out of trouble? Or maybe giving an unpopular kid at school the cold shoulder? Afterward the guilt can be overwhelming. You may feel like you've turned down a dark path and you can't retrace your footsteps.

But you aren't stranded! Jesus died on the cross for you so that you wouldn't have to be burdened by guilt. No matter how far you've wandered, Jesus can rescue you. If you ask for forgiveness, He will erase your sins—big and small. His grace never runs out; it's like a river that never runs dry. Just as parents delight in giving their child a gift, so does Jesus delight in giving you a free do-over. And whenever the urge to lie or exclude someone tempts you again, remember that Jesus can give you the strength to avoid the temptation and do the right thing.

Jesus, thank You for loving me enough to die for me. Please forgive me for anything I've done that has hurt You and others. Thank You for giving me unlimited do-overs whenever I ask for them. Amen.

DAY 357

GOD WANTS ME TO DO RIGHT

For it is better, if it is the will of God,
to suffer for doing good than for doing evil.
1 Peter 3:17 NKJV

Sometimes it's hard to do the right thing—especially when friends are telling you it's okay to do what you know is wrong. They say it's not really *that* bad, and "everyone else is doing it." It's hard to stand up for what God wants you to do when you're worried that your friends will make fun of you or leave you out of their future plans and activities. But remember you will never completely be able to enjoy doing something that you know is wrong anyhow. You'll feel guilty for saying yes when you should have said no. You know what God wants you to do. Ask Him to give you the courage, and then do it.

Dear God, I have to admit that sometimes I want to go along with my friends, even when I know I shouldn't. Please help me to be strong and to do what I know I should. Please help me to stand up for what's right and encourage my friends to do the right thing too. We can find something better to do with our time—something pleasing to You. Please give me the desire in my heart to always do what's right. Amen.

DAY 358

AN INVITATION TO REST

Then Jesus said, "Come to me, all of you who are weary and carry heavy burdens, and I will give you rest."
MATTHEW 11:28 NLT

There are times things just don't go according to plan. A friend can break a confidence. The test that took so much time to prepare for can still be failed. A relative might be struggling with an illness. The burdens can add up, making it feel like there's a heavy weight on your shoulders.

But Jesus offers an invitation to all of His children to come to Him. He isn't looking for the "perfect" ones—the ones who look like they have everything all together. Because really, no one does. Everyone has weariness and heavy burdens at times.

So take Him up on His offer. Go to Him and give Him the hard things you're going through. He wants to listen. But it doesn't stop there. He also wants to give you rest. He may not take away the tough times, but He will comfort you as you go through them.

Dear Lord, thank You for caring about the times that I struggle. Thank You for wanting to hear from me and for promising to give me rest even while I'm going through hard times. Amen.

DAY 359

DO YOU FEEL LIKE YOU DON'T FIT IN?

Now you are the body of Christ,
and each one of you is a part of it.
1 CORINTHIANS 12:27 NIV

When Jennifer started junior high, she felt like she didn't fit in. All the other kids had cool new shoes; she had the same pair from last year. They seemed happy; she felt insecure.

Maybe there are times when you feel like you don't fit in either. It might seem like the kids around you are standing *in* a circle together, and you are standing *outside* the circle—alone.

God has a very special plan for you. This is why there will be times when you can't—and shouldn't—do what everyone else is doing. You won't look like them, wear the same clothes, or have the same interests because God has something special for you to do that they can't do. God made you different on purpose for a purpose.

Remember: sometimes being great for God means you need to be different.

Lord Jesus, thank You for making me special. In the same way that You made the animals different, the planets different, and the stars different, You made me different. I am Your amazing creation. Help me to remember this when I feel like I don't fit in. Amen.

DAY 360

FIGHTING THE LIES

"Do not let your heart be troubled;
believe in God, believe also in Me."
JOHN 14:1 NASB

Life can be really hard. . .and the devil's lies don't help one bit!

Just as your ears hear different voices, your heart can hear different voices too. They usually come from your mind. They're lies that you've heard—lies the devil plants.

But take courage! There's truth throughout the Bible that contradicts Satan's lies. God knows when you're struggling. And He supplied a way to help you in the hard times (1 Corinthians 10:13). His comfort is within reach. . .right at your door.

God gave you an amazing gift for the rough times: prayer. He's always here to listen. And He asks you to call out to Him (Matthew 7:7–8). Even if you don't know what to say, His Spirit "intercedes for us with groanings too deep for words" (Romans 8:26 NASB). God knows your tender heart, and He will help you along every step of the way.

Father, I don't know why I'm going through this or exactly how to handle it. I feel __________. Help me to trust You, Lord. Thank You for Your everlasting love, Your always-within-reach comfort, and the wonderful gift of prayer. In Jesus' holy name I pray. Amen.

DAY 361

ENCOURAGE YOURSELF!

But David encouraged himself in the Lord his God.
1 Samuel 30:6 KJV

Discouragement. Everybody deals with discouragement once in a while—even mighty men and women of God. Remember David in the Bible? He was called a man after God's own heart, yet he battled discouragement too.

Especially on one particular day. . . David was doing exactly what God had told him to do—fighting battles for God—but when he and his men returned from war, they found their city had been burned and all of their wives and children had been taken. You talk about a reason to be discouraged! And, to make matters worse, all of David's men got mad at him and wanted to kill him! Things looked pretty bad, but David didn't give up. Instead, the Bible says David encouraged himself in the Lord. And it wasn't long before the entire situation turned around in David's favor. In fact, seventy-two hours later, they had all of their possessions and their families back, and David was made king!

No matter how many times you feel like giving up, *don't*! Just follow David's example. Encourage yourself in the Lord, and watch your situation turn around!

God, help me to be quick to encourage myself by thinking about You and Your goodness to me. Amen.

DAY 362

YOU ARE ALWAYS ON HIS MIND

How precious are your thoughts about me,
O God. They cannot be numbered!
Psalm 139:17 NLT

No matter who you are, no matter how popular, no matter how shy, no matter how smart—there are probably days when you feel invisible. You wonder if anybody notices you at all. Maybe your teachers seem to overlook you. Maybe your parents seem more concerned about their own problems than you. Or you feel like the odd one out even when you're with your friends.

But you never have to worry about being invisible to God. He thinks about you all the time. His love for you will last forever. You are His "handiwork, created in Christ Jesus to do good works" (Ephesians 2:10 NIV). No matter what happens, God will fulfill His purpose for you. He will not abandon the works of His hands. (That's you!)

Dear God, thank You that I am important to You. I'm thankful that You are always thinking of me. I'm grateful that You love me and created me for a special purpose. Help me to always walk close to You so that I can be all You created me to be. Amen.

DAY 363

HIDDEN IN MY HEART

Your commands are always with me and
make me wiser than my enemies.
PSALM 119:98 NIV

It's been a long six weeks. You've been memorizing dozens of scriptures from the Old and New Testaments. You want so badly to earn a new Bible that your Sunday school teacher has promised as a reward—if, and only if, you pass her test on Sunday.

You've studied hard. Mom has quizzed you on the Ten Commandments and listened to you recite Bible verses over and over and over again. You've spent hours in your room thumbing through your Bible and repeating scriptures in your head.

Then Sunday comes, and the nerves hit! Your teacher takes each member from your class one by one and gives an oral test. Everyone is doing last-minute reviews of the scriptures. Before it's your turn, you say a quick prayer for God to calm your pounding heart.

At the end of class, the teacher announces that everyone passed. Next Sunday, everyone will receive a new Bible—including you! And best of all, you have hidden God's Word in your heart for today and always.

Thank You, God for Your Word. Your Word encourages and gives me commands that will live within me forever and ever. Amen.

DAY 364

TUTTI-FRUTTI

"Make a tree good and its fruit will be good, or make a tree bad and its fruit will be bad, for a tree is recognized by its fruit."

MATTHEW 12:33 NIV

Did you know that people recognize you by your fruit? No, we're not talking about apples and oranges here. We're talking about the fruits of the spirit: love, joy, peace, patience, kindness, and so on. If you stick close to Jesus (like vines clinging to the branch of a tree), you will bear good fruit, but if you wander far away, you will bear bad fruit.

There's nothing more disgusting than rotten old fruit. Ever eat a brown, squishy banana? How about a dried-up orange? Ever had a mushy strawberry or a squishy peach? Gross, right?

Here's the thing. . . When people look at you, they either see good fruit or bad fruit. They either see love, joy, and patience, or they see someone who's grumpy, hard to get along with, and impatient! They either see someone who has a helpful attitude, or someone who always wants to get their own way.

So, which is it? Good fruit? Bad fruit? Happy fruit? Or sad fruit? The decision is up to you.

Heavenly Father, I want to be recognized by my good fruit. I praise You today! Amen.

DAY 365

BRIGHT FUTURE

Take therefore no thought for the morrow: for the morrow shall take thought for the things of itself.
MATTHEW 6:34 KJV

Come closer, child, and look into my crystal ball. See how the colors swirl about! They are the clouds that obscure your future. Now I will part them and reveal. . .

What?

Your high school graduation? Your future spouse? (Okay, that might be *too* scary!) But it couldn't hurt to take a little glimpse into the years to come. Or could it?

Even if you could get your hands on a crystal ball, knowing the future wouldn't prepare you for it. That's why God has chosen not to show you what lies ahead. He wants you to live moment by moment, *trusting Him*! Every step that you take on the winding path of life's journey has been specially designed for you by your heavenly Father. He has everything planned for your good—even the scary parts! Don't fret about what's lurking around the next corner. God has promised that He will walk each mile with you. Leave the future in His great big hands and concentrate on making this moment your best ever!

Dear Father, remind me that no matter what the future holds, You've got everything under control. Amen.

CONTRIBUTORS

Michelle Medlock Adams: Days 1, 22, 60, 81, 96, 114, 136, 151, 168, 188, 211, 273, 294, 334, 345, 361

Michelle Medlock Adams is an award-winning journalist and best-selling author. Michelle has written more than 1,000 articles for newspapers and magazines and published dozens of books since graduating with a journalism degree from Indiana University. Michelle is married to her high school sweetheart, Jeff, and they have two daughters, Abby and Allyson.

Janet Lee Barton: Days 9, 12, 27, 44, 61, 80, 93, 106, 120, 147, 169, 180, 190, 213, 223, 248, 263, 315, 341, 357

Janet Lee Barton was born in New Mexico and has lived in Arkansas, Florida, Louisiana, Mississippi, Oklahoma, and Texas. She and her husband now live in Oklahoma, where they feel blessed to live near one daughter and her family. Janet loves researching and writing Christian fiction.

Emily Biggers: Days 5, 17, 31, 49, 68, 84, 101, 117, 130, 149, 167, 182, 195, 210, 228, 241, 259, 278, 296, 307

Emily Biggers is a Tennessee native living in Arlington, Texas. She teaches gifted and talented students in first through fifth grades. She loves to travel, write, spend time with family and friends, and decorate.

Deborah Bates Cavitt: Days 64, 85, 109, 128, 146, 165, 186, 219, 244, 268, 302, 321, 346, 363

Deborah Bates Cavitt lives with her husband near Dallas, Texas. She has contributed to *Hello Future*, *Angel Digest*, and *Heavenly Humor for the Teacher's Soul*. She has also written lesson plans and articles for *Library Media Connection* and published a children's book, *Amber's Fair-y Tale*, in 2011. Deborah enjoys reading and writing devotions.

Cheryl Cecil: Day 12

Cheryl Cecil lives in Fort Wayne, Indiana. Two married daughters and three granddaughters inspire her to write for girls of all ages. She loves finding any reason to celebrate life.

Jan Cline: Days 3, 18, 35, 58, 73, 90, 111, 124, 137, 156, 175, 209, 225, 239, 260, 279, 303, 343

Jan Cline is an author, freelance writer, and speaker from the Northwest. She also directs a Christian writers' conference and leads a writers' group in her area. Jan has seven grandchildren and loves to travel and play golf.

Debora M. Coty: Day 320

Debora M. Coty is a popular humorist, speaker, and award-winning author of numerous inspirational books, including the bestselling Too Blessed to Be Stressed line. Deb considers herself a tennis junkie and choco-athlete (meaning she exercises just so she can eat more chocolate). A retired piano teacher and orthopedic occupational therapist, Debora currently lives, loves, and laughs in central Florida with her husband, Chuck, and three grandbuddies and one grandprincess.

Rebecca Germany: Days 230, 232

Rebecca Germany works full-time as a fiction editor and has written and compiled several novellas and gift books. She lives in Ohio, where she enjoys country life.

Renae Brumbaugh Green: Days 7, 23, 38, 50, 77, 134, 153, 176, 192, 207, 222, 240, 254, 270, 287, 304, 335, 348

Renae Brumbaugh Green lives in Texas with her handsome country-boy husband, her noisy children, a rowdy dog, and a bunch of chickens and ducks. She's published more than twenty-five books and a whole bunch of articles. Her favorite color is blue, unless you're talking about nail polish, in which case her favorite color is bubblegum pink.

Jennifer Hahn: Days 24, 41, 55, 63, 78, 98, 113, 132, 157, 174, 179, 193, 208, 229, 246, 272, 291, 314, 358

Jennifer Hahn resides in Lancaster County, Pennsylvania, with her husband and three children. She loves homeschooling her kids and is also active in her church, working with the youth, and assisting with editorial and proofreading tasks. Her desire is that, through her writing, readers will strengthen their relationship with Christ.

Anita Higman: Days 2, 52, 100, 141, 183, 224, 269, 295, 349

Bestselling and award-winning author, **Anita Higman**, has dozens of books published (several coauthored) for adults and children. She's been a Barnes & Noble "Author of the Month" for Houston and has a BA degree, combining speech communication, psychology, and art. Anita loves good movies, exotic teas, and brunch with her friends.

Gale Hyatt: Days 15, 30, 46, 72, 97, 119, 138, 154, 173, 214, 220, 245, 266, 285, 289, 333, 350, 365

Gale Hyatt discovered her passion for writing in the third grade. Since then, she has written numerous songs, poems, articles, short stories and devotionals. She continues to write while home educating her three children in beautiful Lithia, Florida.

Wendy Lanier: Days 8, 28, 42, 66, 87, 102, 121, 140, 161, 184, 200, 216, 237, 256, 271, 290, 309, 325, 344, 362

Wendy Lanier is an author, teacher, and speaker who writes for children and adults. She has written books for Lerner Books, KidHaven Press, Lucent, and Capstone Press as well as articles in online and print publications, such as *Highlights for Children* and *Clubhouse Magazine*.

Kelly McIntosh: Days 29, 171, 185, 194, 199, 201, 203

Kelly McIntosh is a wife, mother of twins, and editor from Ohio. She loves books, the beach, and everything about autumn (but mostly pumpkin spice lattes).

Hillary McMullen: Days 16, 36, 75, 123, 142, 233, 319, 356

Hillary McMullen received a BA degree in English from Sam Houston State University, and she has had a short story published in the *SHSU Review*. After graduating, Hillary gained editorial experience by critiquing Christian fiction and nonfiction. Writing, music, and youth ministry are a few of her passions. Hillary currently lives in Houston, Texas, with her husband.

Brigitta Nortker: Days 48, 91

Brigitta Nortker lives and works in Nashville but takes every opportunity to travel that she can. In her free time she enjoys an excellent book, a cup of coffee, and spending time with friends and family.

Nicole O'Dell: Days 34, 54, 62, 83, 95, 112, 129, 148, 163, 205, 217, 235, 252, 264, 277, 280, 281, 286, 305, 306, 318, 324, 332, 351, 355

Youth-culture expert **Nicole O'Dell** resides in Paxton, Illinois, with her husband and six children—the youngest of which are toddler triplets. She writes and speaks to preteens, teenagers, and parents about how to prepare for life's tough choices.

MariLee Parrish: Days 4, 11, 13, 32, 47, 53, 59, 70, 86, 99, 107, 110, 118, 126, 135, 144, 152, 158, 162, 164, 177, 191, 204, 212, 215, 226, 234, 238, 250, 255, 262, 275, 284, 298, 308, 313, 316, 328, 337, 354

MariLee Parrish lives in Colorado with her husband, Eric, and children. She's a freelance musician and writer who desires to paint a picture of God with her life, talents, and ministries.

Rachel Quillin: Days 25, 39, 150, 310, 331

Rachel Quillin is the author of several gift books and coauthor of the devotional prayer book *Prayers & Promises for Mothers*. She makes her home on a dairy farm in Ohio with her husband and children.

Shana Schutte: Days 14, 43, 57, 65, 89, 115, 131, 198, 231, 249, 267, 283, 299, 317, 339, 359

Shana Schutte is an author and speaker. She is a former editor for *Focus on the Family*, has authored more than 300 articles, and hosts a nationwide radio program called *Beyond Imagination* that airs daily on more than 400 Christian stations. Shana also leads seminars across the country.

Melanie Stiles: Days 6, 37, 79, 108, 125, 143, 159, 172, 189, 206, 227, 242, 261, 297, 312, 336

Melanie Stiles has won numerous writing awards and accumulated hundreds of bylines in various publications. Her recent book, *The Heart of a Ready Scribe*, continues to be well received. She is a Christian Life Coach specializing in author services and personal one-on-one sessions.

Janice Thompson: Days 40, 56, 71, 76, 92, 104, 116, 133, 160, 178, 247, 258, 276, 288, 293, 322, 329, 330, 338, 352, 353, 364

Janice Thompson hails from south Texas. She is a Christian author and mother of four grown daughters. Janice has written over forty books.

Annie Tipton: Days 74, 94, 236, 251, 257, 300, 327, 340

Annie Tipton made up her first story at the ripe old age of two when she asked her mom to write it down for her. (Hey, she was just two—she didn't know how to make letters yet!) Since then she has read and written many words as a student, newspaper reporter, author, and editor. Annie loves snow (which is a good thing because she lives in Ohio), wearing scarves, sushi, Scrabble, and spending time with friends and family.

Kayla Woodhouse: Days 20, 21, 26, 45, 67, 82, 103, 122, 145, 166, 181, 196, 197, 221, 243, 265, 282, 301, 323, 342, 360

Kayla Woodhouse loves the Lord and wants to share His Word with others—especially teens. Living with a rare nerve disorder, Kayla has been featured all over national television and in hundreds of magazines and newspapers.

Kimberley Woodhouse: Days 10, 33, 51, 69, 88, 105, 127, 139, 155, 170, 187, 202, 218, 253, 274, 292, 311, 326, 347

Kimberley Woodhouse is a multi-published author of fiction and nonfiction. A popular speaker/teacher, she's shared her theme of Joy through Trials with more than 150,000 people at more than 1,000 venues across the country. She lives, writes, and homeschools in beautiful Colorado with her husband of twenty-plus years and their two awesome teens.

SCRIPTURE INDEX

OLD TESTAMENT

Proverbs

Ecclesiastes

Isaiah

Jeremiah

Lamentations

Daniel

Amos

Micah

Zephaniah

Zechariah

NEW TESTAMENT

Matthew

Mark

Luke

John

Acts

Romans

1 Corinthians

2 Corinthians

Galatians

Ephesians

Philippians

Colossians

1 Thessalonians

2 Thessalonians

2 Timothy

Titus

Hebrews

James

1 Peter

2 Peter

1 John

Revelation